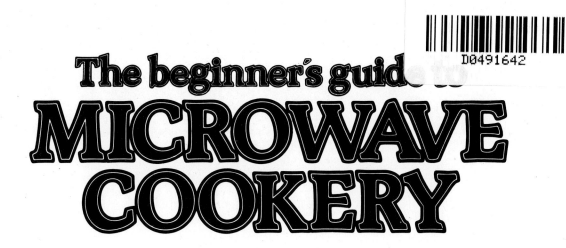

The beginner's guide to MICROWAVE COOKERY

Val Collins

DAVID & CHARLES
Newton Abbot   London   North Pomfret (Vt)

D0491642

To Eleanor and Madeleine

Acknowledgements

I should like to thank Cathy Morton-Lloyd, Kate Pike and Anne Ross for their assistance in testing the recipes and preparing the food for the photographs. To Thorn EMI Major Domestic Appliances Ltd I offer my grateful thanks for supplying Tricity microwave cookers and assisting with the photography and line drawings. Colour photography by John Plimmer, RPM Photographic, Havant. Line illustrations by KPA Advertising Ltd, Kettering, Northants.

British Library Cataloguing in Publication Data
Collins, Val
    The beginner's guide to microwave cookery.——
2nd ed.
    1. Microwave cookery
    I. Title
    641.5'882   TX832
ISBN 0–7153–8790–1

© Text Val Collins 1982, 1986
© Colour illustrations Thorn EMI Major Domestic Appliances Ltd 1982, 1986

All rights reserved. No part of this
publication may be reproduced, stored
in a retrieval system, or transmitted,
in any form or by any means, electronic,
mechanical, photocopying, recording or
otherwise, without the prior permission
of David & Charles Publishers plc

Photosetting by ABM Typographics Ltd., Hull
Printed in The Netherlands
by Smeets Offset BV, Weert
for David & Charles Publishers plc
Brunel House   Newton Abbot   Devon

Published in the United States of America
by David & Charles Inc
North Pomfret   Vermont 05053   USA

Contents

Introduction

I have been using microwave cookers now for so many years that I think I take all the advantages they offer me for granted. Rather like the freezer, a microwave cooker is now so much a part of my kitchen and daily life that it is difficult for me to remember how I ever coped without it.

On thinking back to the early days when first introduced to the idea of 'cooking by microwave', I too had all the doubts and questions that I'm sure you have considered – 'Is it safe? Will it cook a jacket potato, or a cake, defrost and cook a chicken, reheat a sausage roll?' The answer to all these is 'yes'. And because a microwave cooker is so adaptable, it will cook many other dishes that you not even have thought of, from something as simple as scrambled eggs in two to three minutes, to a chocolate pudding in six.

Prime cooking operations – thawing, melting, poaching, boiling, simmering, roasting and baking – can be carried out in seconds and minutes rather than minutes and hours, with no more effort than it takes to place the food in the oven and operate the controls. Because food is cooked so quickly, fewer valuable nutrients are lost and as all the heat is produced in the food itself and is not wasted elsewhere, this means that the microwave cooker is also very economical to use. On average, up to 75 per cent can be saved on normal cooking times and up to 50 per cent of your cooking fuel bill. Food can be cooked and served in one dish, so saving on the washing up; also, as little heat is produced in the oven, the kitchen will remain cooler and cleaner too.

In a nutshell, a microwave cooker gives you a more nutritious meal, cooked more quickly thus using less electricity, and after the meal there are fewer dishes to wash up and a cool oven which cleans with a wipe.

The microwave cooker is easy to install – you just plug it into a 13 amp or 15 amp socket outlet which means that it can be situated in the kitchen, in the dining room, or on a trolley so it may be wheeled from room to room, or even out on to the patio to assist with the barbecue. With power levels to set and timer controls to adjust, the microwave cooker is so simple to operate that any

member of the family can reheat cooked meals or snacks left for them, in the refrigerator or freezer, when they arrive home late.

As you use the microwave cooker more and more you will find that you use your conventional cooker less often, although you will still need it for some foods that the microwave cooker just cannot cope with – yorkshire puddings, pancakes, roast potatoes, some pastries and foods that are deep fat fried, for example. But as a complement to the conventional cooker, refrigerator and freezer, a microwave cooker will make life easier for all those of you involved in the preparation and cooking of food.

I have written this book as a guide for those of you taking your first steps in microwave cookery. You will find the section 'Simple Beginnings' particularly useful and helpful in getting to know your microwave cooker. Whichever model you have chosen, this book gives all the basic information and will enable you and your family to benefit and enjoy all your favourite dishes – as well as some new ones – cooked in a fraction of the time normally spent in meal preparation.

Your questions answered

Here are fifty of the most common questions asked. Further information is given throughout the introductory and recipe sections of the book.

Q How does the microwave cooker work?
A Electricity is converted into microwaves which are similar to radio waves by the magnetron in the cooker. Microwaves agitate the water molecules in the food causing friction which produces heat, so the food cooks. Microwaves are reflected from the metal construction of the oven cavity but pass to the food through non-metallic containers without heating them.

Q Is is easy to use?
A Very easy, but start off slowly, learn the basic skills first and refer to the manufacturer's operating literature. This book will help too!

Q How much does it cost to run?

A Depending on what you cook, the shorter cooking times and lower loading means you can save to up 50% of your cooking bills. Even if you used it for 1 hour continuously on 100% (full), it would only cost about 1½ units of electricity.

Q It is safe?

A The absence of radiant heat and the in-built automatic cut-out switches makes it one of the safest known cooking methods even for young children or elderly people.

Q Does it replace my conventional cooker?

A Not really, but as you use your microwave more and more, you will find that you use your conventional cooker less, though there are some foods a microwave cannot cook. You may find that there are certain dishes you prefer to cook conventionally anyway.

Q Should I buy a combination model?

A If you intend keeping your conventional cooker (which I would recommend), you will have the traditional oven and grill which can be used at the same time as the microwave. If you feel that microwave and a browning facility in one compartment is an advantage, then it is worth considering paying the extra cost to have just one cooker. It is usually a larger unit, so it also depends on how much room you have available.

Q Is touch control worth the extra money?

A Touch control models usually incorporate electronic programming which offers more features such as temperature probes, automatic programming and memory. Timings can be set with great accuracy and the control panels are very easy to wipe clean too!

Q Is it worth buying a microwave with a shelf?

A It means you can pack more into the cavity but as the amount of microwaves remains the same, the extra volume in the oven will take longer to cook.

Q I have the offer of a second-hand cooker. Should I buy it?

A Have it checked by a qualified microwave engineer first; contact the manufacturer for names and addresses.

Q What can go wrong with a microwave cooker?

A Usually very little as they are subjected to many checks and tests during development and production. The most expensive items to replace are the transformer and the magnetron. Your manufacturer can advise on costs.

Q Are regular service calls necessary?

A Not usually, as reliability is extremely high. Most reputable manufacturers provide an extended low cost scheme or will come out on request.

Q Will microwaves affect a heart pacemaker?

A Modern pacemakers are fitted with a shield to protect them from interference of any kind and there is normally no problem with BEAB approved domestic appliances tested to BS 800. Do check with your doctor for reassurance though.

Q Is a microwave cooker easy to keep clean?

A Usually just a wipe is all that is necessary. As the walls of the oven do not get hot, splashes do not bake on. Microwave/convection models may require more vigorous rubbing as the presence of heat can bake soilage onto the oven walls. More information is given in 'Cleaning and Care' on page 28.

Q What metals cause arcing? Will arcing damage the magnetron?

A Precious metals such as gold or silver trims on china or the manufacturer's mark on the base of a dish will cause arcing – blue flashes of light. Most other metals can cause arcing particularly if they come into contact with the interior metal walls of the oven cavity. Arcing will only cause damage to the magnetron in certain conditions.

Q What about using aluminium foil when the general rule is not to use metal?

A Providing the metal is solid and small in proportion to the mass of food – as when small, smooth pieces of foil are wrapped round chicken wing-tips, drumsticks etc – no harm should result. Do not use double thickness of foil or allow it to touch the interior walls of the oven cavity, but if arcing does occur, switch off and rearrange or remove the foil.

Q Can I use a temperature probe for sugar boiling in the microwave?

A Most temperature probes are not calibrated to the high temperatures required for sugar boiling and preserve making. Conventional sugar (or meat) thermometers should not be left in the oven during cooking unless specially designed for use in the microwave.

Q Can I use metal skewers in the microwave?

A Yes, providing that the mass of the food is greater than the mass of the metal skewers and they are not allowed to touch each other or the interior walls of the oven cavity. Alternatively, use wooden ones.

Q Do I have to stir, even with a turntable?

A Yes, occasionally during heating and cooking. Stirring ensures that food is brought from the outside edges of the dishes to the centre and vice versa for even cooking.

Q I thought dishes remained cool. Why don't mine?

A Some dishes are less efficient and absorb microwave energy, making them hot. If in doubt, it may be worth carrying out a simple test to ensure the dish is suitable (page 11). In addition, glass, pottery and china dishes may get comparatively hot during cooking from the transfer of heat from the food to the dish.

Q What dishes increase cooking times?

A Dishes which absorb microwaves (see above). There are other factors which affect cooking times such as quantity of food, the temperature of the food at the start of cooking, the shape and size of the container and the output of the oven.

Q What should I look for when buying microwave dishes?

A Make sure they are efficient in use, ie the material allows microwaves to pass through. Check their suitability for heating fats, jams and syrups and any temperature limitations for conventional oven use should this be a requirement. Moulded handles on the sides of the dishes usually remain cooler in use than those which are formed on the top of the lid.

Q Are browning dishes worth their cost?

A They are useful to have for browning some foods (see page 14) but not essential. Get to know your microwave cooker first to see if you find the results of cooking chops, chicken portions etc acceptable without using a browning dish, or you may prefer to cook those food items conventionally. Browning dishes require preheating which to a degree negates the advantage of quick cooking in the microwave.

Q Is there special clingfilm for microwave use?

A Heavy duty clingfilm is easier to handle and withstands higher temperatures but is not essential.

Q Is standing time always necessary?

A Standing time is an advantage when cooking some foods (page 18), but if the food is cooked satisfactorily when it is removed from the oven at the end of the cooking time, it is not necessary to let it stand.

Q Why should I leave a glass of water in the oven when it is not in use?

A Only in case the cooker is switched on accidentally by meddling fingers! You should not operate the oven empty so the glass of water provides a load, just in case.

Q Is it possible to cook a complete meal in a microwave with a turntable?

A Yes but not all the dishes at once! With a little experience and using standing times to advantage, complete meals can quickly and easily be prepared.

Q What about timings for cookers with different outputs?

A The recipes in this book were tested in a microwave oven with 650 watt output. A guide to timings for cookers with different outputs is given on page 16.

Q Why do some foods cook quicker than others?

A Because foods have different densities, shapes and starting temperatures. The type, size and shape of the cooking container will also affect cooking times.

Q Why does food cook more around the edges than in the centre?

A Because microwaves penetrate the surface of the food to the depth of about 2·5cm (1in) and the rest of the cooking takes place by conduction, just like conventional cooking but quicker. Therefore the centre is slower to heat or cook. That's why stirring is recommended when possible and why standing times and/or a lower power level help some foods to cook.

Q Are there any general rules for covering food?

A The majority of foods benefit from being covered to avoid splashing, to retain moisture or to ensure more even cooking. The exceptions are baked items – cakes, breads and pastries – or any foods which are required to remain crisp and dry. Kitchen paper towels can be used to absorb moisture (see page 12 and below).

Q How can I prevent sausage rolls and pastry dishes from becoming soft when reheated?

A Place them on, or cover them with, kitchen paper towel to absorb moisture; but ensure that it is plain white and not coloured or patterned as the colour can transfer onto the food.

Q Why does an egg yolk cook quicker than the white?

A Because the high fat and protein of the yolk absorb microwaves more readily so it cooks faster.

Q Can meringues be cooked in the microwave?

A Not the traditional home-baked meringues which have a slightly soft centre. But fondant meringues made with icing sugar, similar in texture to shop-bought ones, can be cooked. There is a recipe on page 125 but you must be prepared to experiment a little at first as timings can be critical.

Q Can I shallow fry or deep fry in the microwave?

A No, because the temperature of the fat or oil cannot be controlled.

Q What about browning?

A The microwave cooker does not brown food in the traditional way due to the speed of cooking. Larger joints and poultry will brown to a degree due to their longer cooking times and a browning dish or the use of microwave seasonings will help some foods. Otherwise your conventional oven or grill can be used after microwave cooking to finish and brown dishes.

Q Is it true that I shouldn't add salt to food?

A No, but you will need less of it. Do not sprinkle salt directly onto the food as it can draw moisture and toughen the surface – add to the liquid or, if in doubt, adjust after cooking. Using less salt in fact brings out the real flavours.

Q What about recipes for combination cookers?

A Different models vary so much in their operation that it is best to be guided by the manufacturer's cookbook. After a little experience you should have no problem in converting other recipes. Refer to the guidelines on p25.

Q What causes microwave-cooked cakes to go stale quickly?

A Usually because they have been slightly overcooked or insufficient liquid was added so that the mixture was too dry. Take the cake out of the oven when it is still moist on top. To prevent it drying out, wrap or ice the cake as soon as it has cooled sufficiently.

Q Does cooking in the microwave affect the taste of food?

A It can improve the taste of most foods because the retention of moisture, vitamins, nutrients, colour and texture is better and, as less seasoning is necessary, the real taste comes through.

Q Are there any guidelines for arranging foods, for plate meals for example?

A Try to keep an even density of food across the dish. When cooking foods of uneven shape, such as broccoli spears, place the tender curds towards the centre of the dish with the stems towards the outside. For plate meals, place thin items such as sliced meat in the middle of the plate and arrange the vegetables evenly around.

Q What foods are best cooked conventionally?

A Other than shortcrust for a prebaked flan case, most other pastries and pies are best cooked in the conventional oven although precooked pastry dishes can be reheated successfully. Large soufflés, batters for pancakes and yorkshire puddings etc are not successful, nor are roast potatoes. It makes sense therefore to cook Sunday lunch in the conventional oven, leaving the microwave free for the vegetables, gravies, sauces and puddings. Boiled eggs should not be attempted unless using the method on page 41.

Q Can I convert my favourite recipes for cooking in the microwave?

A Yes, most adapt very well but experience will help. Follow a microwave recipe closest to the one you wish to convert and be guided by the information it gives. Refer to the guidelines on page 24.

Q Is there a formula for reduced quantities?

A As with conventional cooking and recipes, there is no formula because a lot depends on the type of dish; but refer to the guidelines given on page 25.

Q Can I cook soya beans in the microwave?

A Yes, no problem. Details of soaking and cooking pulses are given on page 102.

Q Are there any rules for defrosting and cooking convenience foods?

A Take them out of any metal or foil container and place on a suitable microwave dish for best results. The convenience food charts on page 32 will be a useful guide to defrosting, heating or cooking a selection of foods.

Q Are there any precautions to prevent foods boiling over?

A Ensure that the container is large enough for the food to be defrosted, heated or cooked and allow room for stirring. Make sure steam can escape by piercing clingfilm or ensuring the lid does not fit too tightly. Turn to a lower power level if simmering is required rather than allow the food to boil vigorously on 100% (full). Light cakes and puddings rise well, so do not fill the container more than half full before cooking. Take care when boiling liquids, particularly milk; you will need about double the space in the container.

Q How can I improve the appearance of microwave cakes?

A Have a selection of toppings and icings readily to hand for decoration, to help disguise the paler result.

Q What about cooking for one or two people?

A You will find a selection of dishes for smaller quantities in the recipe section Simple Beginnings on page 35.

Q Can I cook offal in the microwave?

A Yes, but hearts and tongues require low power settings for best results. Further information is given on page 82.

Q Why do foods sometimes 'pop'?

A It can be an indication of foods overcooking, but usually is caused by a build up of steam inside vessels and membranes within the food – offal, egg yolks and fish are particularly susceptible. Ensure skins of fish are slit, egg yolks are pricked and any cores and pipes are removed from offal. Turn to a lower power setting should 'popping' occur, but otherwise it cannot be avoided.

The microwave cooker

While a microwave cooker is basically very simple to use, it would take many pages of text to cover the full details of the intricate operation of this revolutionary appliance. The basic facts which need to be known by the cook, however, are reasonably easy to explain. All reputable manufacturers give detailed information on the installation, operation and care of each particular model while ensuring that it is electrically safe, complying with the British Electrotechnical Approvals Board requirements, and that it will be functional and give satisfactory service to the user. Before first using your microwave cooker, it is important to know how it operates and to understand all the facts given in the manufacturer's handbook.

What is microwave energy?

Microwaves – or microwave energy – are electromagnetic, non-ionising high-frequency radio waves, close to but not as powerful as infra-red rays. They must NOT be confused with X-rays, gamma rays, or ultra-violet rays, which are ionising and are known to cause irreversible chemical and cellular changes to take place with little or no temperature change. Of equal importance, microwaves are non-cumulative.

Microwaves vibrate millions of times per second; that is, they have a very high frequency and very short wavelength – hence the term 'microwave'. At a frequency of 2·450MHz or megahertz ('hertz' after the German scientist Heinrich Hertz who first detected electromagnetic energy), microwave energy is absorbed by materials with a high water content – like most foods – and the effect is a rise in temperature. The molecules contained within the food tend to align themselves with the energy and move rapidly back and forth. This causes high-speed friction between the molecules, converting microwave energy into heat. A similar experience can be felt when rubbing your hands together; feel them become warm, and the faster you rub, the warmer they become.

Some materials such as metal and foil – and thus the metal construction of the microwave oven cavity – reflect microwave energy. Other materials such as glass, china, pottery, paper and some plastics allow microwaves to pass through – thus making suitable microwave cooking containers. The effect is, therefore, that microwave energy is only absorbed by the food in the oven making the microwave cooker a very effective and efficient cooking medium. An example of this is solar energy; or imagine standing in front of a window on a cold, sunny day. The sun's energy in the form of heat passes through the window without heating it and it feels cold to the touch; but the molecules in our body behave like tiny magnets, converting the energy from the sun into heat and we feel warm.

Is it safe?

Cooking by microwave is safe – frequently safer than cooking conventionally when you take into consideration the relative lack of heat and, therefore, practically no risk of conventional accidental skin burns.

To try to put the safety aspect into perspective, compare the chance of being physically damaged by microwave energy from a microwave cooker to the possibility of obtaining a skin tan from moonlight. The worst thing that could happen if you were exposed to microwave energy would be a nasty burn – and you would feel it just as if you had placed a hand or finger into a naked flame. It is far more dangerous to sunbathe in the direct glare of the sun for hours on end or subject oneself to a sunlamp. Protection from unnecessary exposure to microwave energy is a requirement in all microwave cookers.

Modern technology and statutory electrical safety standards have ensured that cut-out microswitches are built in and operate as soon as the door is opened, so that the microwave energy switches off immediately. It will not start again until the door is securely shut and the start or 'cook' button operated. The microwave cooker door is built to precise specifications to ensure that, when shut, the oven cavity is effectively sealed against energy leakage.

How does it work?
This diagram shows the main components of the microwave cooker although designs may vary between the various manufacturers' models.

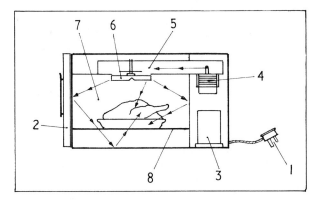

1 *The plug top*
When the plug top is inserted into the socket outlet and switched on, it enables the microwave cooker to be operated.
2 *The oven door*
As soon as the oven door is closed and the controls set, the 'cook' button or switch is operated and the energy begins to flow.
3 *The transformer*
The main function of the transformer is to convert the low voltage of the domestic electrical supply to the high voltages required by the magnetron.
4 *The magnetron*
This is the microwave energy generator. The magnetron receives the high voltage electrical

supply and produces and transmits microwave energy.
5 *The waveguide*
The waveguide directs the microwave energy from the magnetron into the oven cavity.
6 *The stirrer blade*
The microwaves enter the oven cavity via the stirrer blade which ensures that the energy is evenly distributed throughout the oven cavity. Some models do not have a stirrer blade but rely on a turntable shelf to turn the food through the microwave energy (see page 10).
7 *The oven cavity*
The metal construction of the oven cavity directs the microwave energy through suitable cooking containers (see page 11) onto the food.
8 *The oven shelf*
All food for cooking is placed on the shelf which is so positioned within the oven cavity to gain maximum energy distribution and coverage. In some models, the oven shelf is in the form of a revolving turntable (see page 10).

The microwave cooker should never be operated when the oven is empty. If there is nothing to absorb the microwaves they will bounce off the oven cavity walls and reflect back onto the magnetron. This has the effect of shortening its life. A

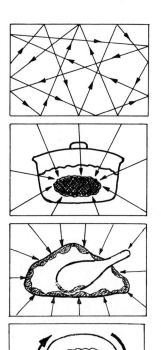

Microwave energy bouncing off the metal interior of the oven cavity

Microwaves passing through suitable cooking containers onto the food

The penetration of microwaves to a depth of about 2·5cm (1in)

The turning of dishes during the cooking cycle for even results cup of water left in the oven when it is not in use just in case the cooker is accidentally switched on would be a wise precaution.

A characteristic of microwave energy is its ability to penetrate food materials to a depth of approximately 2·5cm (1in) and produce heat instantaneously; consequently the outer surface of the food may receive more heat than the centre. This is why some recipes will recommend the stirring or turning of foods during cooking and a heat 'equalising' or 'standing' time is suggested on the completion of some microwave cooking to allow heat to be conducted from the outside of the food through to the centre.

Microwave cooker features

Timer controls
As most microwave cooking operations are gauged by time instead of time and temperature, the timer control is one of the most important features and is marked so that shorter heating or cooking periods can be set with a degree of accuracy.

Stirrer blade
The stirrer blade is usually situated in the top of the oven cavity ensuring an even distribution of microwave energy throughout the oven and, therefore, around the food to be cooked. Different manufacturers may refer to stirrer blades by other terminology but they all work on the same basic principle.

Turntable
Some microwave cookers do not incorporate a stirrer blade but include a revolving turntable which also serves as the oven shelf. The turntable rotates the food in the oven through the microwave energy, making sure that an even result is obtained.

Stirrer blade and turntable
Both these features are incorporated in some microwave cookers which in theory must be the ultimate combination for even distribution of the microwave energy for cooking, although in practice either one of the methods ensures that the microwave energy is evenly distributed around the food item being defrosted, reheated or cooked.

Variable power and defrost control
These controls allow a greater flexibility of the cooking speed by varying the energy or power level into the oven cavity – equivalent to conventional oven settings. With many food items it is not necessary to vary the power level, but it can be invaluable for those recipes or dishes which may benefit from a longer, slower cooking time.

Browning element
A browning element is positioned in the top of the oven cavity to enable food to be browned on the surface before or after microwave cooking. This can be a convenient way of giving a microwave-cooked dish a traditional browned appearance and can be an advantage if your conventional cooker does not incorporate a grill element or burner.

Two level cooking
Some models contain a shelf allowing more food to be cooked at one time. However, the increased volume of food will take longer to cook as the amount of microwave energy available remains the same.

Combination cookers
These are microwave cookers with the addition of a conventional convection oven – usually forced air circulation via a fan – in the same compartment, giving you the choice of either or both modes of cooking. Usually the change from convection to microwave can be carried out independently or in automatic sequence. This type of microwave gives the best of both worlds in one compartment, enabling food to be browned conventionally and/or cooked quickly by microwave energy. It would be ideal for those who may have insufficient space for separate units in the kitchen. Further information is given in 'Combination Cooking' on page 25.

Electronic programming
Electronic programming relies on a microprocessor which enables multiple-sequence cooking to be carried out. By setting the program at the beginning of food preparation, the microwave cooker will automatically switch on, defrost, rest, cook – at different power levels if required – and finally switch off. Very often, it is also possible to program in certain cooking sequences which are then retained in a memory bank. This can be used most effectively for repeat food items such as proving bread doughs, or pre-programming a cycle for a dish which can then be effortlessly cooked by a member of the family while you are out. Sometimes the electronic programming is in the form of a computer system.

Temperature probe
A temperature probe allows you to set the oven to cook by temperature instead of, or in addition to, cooking solely by time. The probe is positioned

into the food and the plug is inserted into the receptable situated in the oven roof or wall. Once programmed, the probe will automatically switch off the microwave cooker as soon as the food has reached the pre-set temperature. Alternatively, it is possible to cook by time and temperature and check the exact temperature the food has reached when required. The temperature probe is usually a feature of microwave cookers with electronic programming and offers the advantage of leaving the food to cook in the microwave unattended. Further information is given in the section 'Cooking by Temperature' on page 19.

Touch controls

Touch controls are usually featured on the more sophisticated models with electronic programming. Without any control knobs, dials or switches, the microwave cooker is operated simply by touching the appropriate section of the control panel, and has the advantage of your being able to set times and power levels with great accuracy.

Sensor controls

Sensor controls are normally only featured on microwave cookers with electronic programming. The sensory processor control detects the vapour (aroma, moisture or humidity) emitted from the food as it cooks and automatically adjusts the cooking times and power level for various food items and quantities. Some sensor controls work in conjunction with a weighing device. Food is placed on to the cooking shelf in the microwave oven and the weight of the food is automatically calculated before cooking takes place in the microwave cooker by sensor control.

Utensils

One of the advantages of microwave cooking is that foods may be cooked and served in the same dish. Also, owing to the fact that heat is produced within the food itself, nothing burns on, so containers are generally easier to clean and food tends not to stick.

Microwave energy is reflected from metal, which means that aluminium, aluminium foil, tin, copper or stainless steel containers should *not* be used as the cooking results will be impaired and arcing (blue flashes of light) can occur which may damage the magnetron. However, microwave energy passes through glass, pottery and china and so, provided they have no metal trim, they all make excellent containers when cooking in the microwave oven.

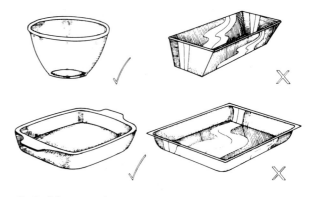

Suitable containers

Most cupboards have an assortment of glass or pottery bowls and pie dishes suitable for microwave cooking. A large shallow casserole dish with an upturned plate or saucer in the base makes an ideal roasting dish with trivet. Ovenproof glass and pottery flan dishes can be used equally well in the conventional oven or the microwave cooker for tarts or quiches; also oven-to-table casserole dishes are excellent for microwave cooking. Roasting and boiling bags are ideal for cooking some foods as they can be easily shaken or turned over to stir the contents during the cooking process, and clingfilm is an effective covering for puddings, casseroles and plate meals.

Container test

Some pottery and china absorb more microwave energy which makes them less efficient. If in doubt, it is worth checking a container by carrying out a simple test. Place the dish in question into the microwave together with a glass of water. After 1½ minutes cooking time the water should be hot and the dish cool. If the reverse is found then the dish must not be used. On the other hand, if the dish and the water are both warm, then the dish could be used, but as it is absorbing some microwave energy it is less efficient and cooking times would be longer. Most dishes remain cool as microwave energy passes through them to be absorbed by the food, but during cooking there may be some heat transfer from the food to the dish so be careful when handling them.

Shapes and sizes
Generally, the more regular the shape of the container the better it is for even heating or cooking. A round dish is preferable to an oval one and a straight-sided dish better than one which is curved. A container which is slightly rounded at the corners rather than one with square corners will help to prevent food from overcooking at these sharper edges. Larger, shallow dishes are preferable to smaller, deep ones as the greater surface area allows more penetration of the microwave energy. It is important to ensure that the container is large enough to hold the food to be heated or cooked. Light cake and pudding mixtures in particular rise extremely well – to almost double their volume – so remember to only half fill the container with the uncooked mixture.

Tall, narrow containers such as jugs rather than shallow wide ones – soup plates for example – are best for heating liquids. Again, make sure the container is large enough for the boiling liquid, such as milk, where you will probably need double the capacity. Do not use a dish which is too large when defrosting some foods – a casserole for example – otherwise the juices will spread over the base of the dish and overheat before the rest of the food is defrosted.

Specially designed microwave containers
A good choice of disposable and durable special microwave cooking containers and dishes is now widely available on the market. Make sure that they are efficient in use, ie the material allows microwave energy to pass through. Check their suitability for heating fats, jams and syrups and any temperature limitations for conventional oven use should this be a requirement.

Moulded handles on the sides of the dishes usually remain cooler in use than those formed on the top of the lid. Decide on your particular needs and requirements before making a selection. Some of these utensils are intended for conventional as well as microwave cooking, while others are suitable for both microwave and the freezer, which are added advantages. Disposable plates, dishes and containers are ideal for heating snacks or shorter-term cooking operations.

Plate covers, plate stacking rings, roasting dishes with trivets and microwave thermometers are just a few of the specialist microwave cookware utensils available from your local stockist or by mail order.

Glass
Any type of glass utensil may be used providing there is no metal trim. Thus glass ovenware – eg Pyrex dishes, jugs, casseroles, plates, tumblers and bowls – can be used. Ceramic glass dishes also function extremely well in microwave cooking and make attractive serving dishes. *Do not* use thick or cut glass as heat from the food may cause them to crack. Crystal glass contains lead so should *not* be used in the microwave.

China and pottery
These can be used in the same way as oven glassware *providing there is no metal trim or manufacturer's mark or design in gold or silver.* This can cause arcing – blue flashes of light – when the metal trim or pattern will discolour and peel. Some types of pottery absorb more microwave energy than others, which slows down the cooking thus making these containers less efficient. They also may become fairly hot to the touch and the use of oven gloves is advisable.

Paper
Many individual servings of food may be heated on serviettes or paper plates. Frozen gâteau, pastries, sandwiches, etc may be placed on paper doyleys before defrosting in the microwave oven. Lightly greased greaseproof paper or baking parchment can be used most effectively for lining containers when cooking cakes and bread etc.

Wax-coated paper cups, plates and paper may be used for short periods only, as prolonged heating may cause the wax to melt.

Do not use paper and metal twist ties as they can burn very quickly. Make sure they are removed from plastic freezer bags before placing in the microwave oven to loosen.

Kitchen paper towels
Kitchen paper towels can be used to absorb moisture. Greaseproof paper can be used to cover food to prevent splashing in the oven, but kitchen paper towels are just as good and normally less expensive. *Do not*, however, place coloured or patterned kitchen paper towels close to food items as the colour may transfer onto the food.

Plastic
Specially designed plastic microwave cookware is ideal, being transparent to microwave energy. Rigid plastic or heat-resistant plastic dinnerware can be used but may absorb some microwave energy and will be hotter to the touch than other

dishes. Freezer containers or lightweight plastic containers can be used for short periods but the heat from the food they contain can cause them to melt during prolonged exposure to microwaves.

Do not use cream cartons, yoghurt pots, ice cream containers or plastic bags as they will melt, but the 'boil-in' type bags are excellent although you must remember to prick them to allow steam to escape.

Do not use plastic freezer bags in the microwave cooker although frozen food wrapped in plastic bags may be placed into the oven for a short period in order to loosen the package before transferring its contents to another more suitable container.

Cotton/linen
As these are natural fibres they can be used to wrap bread or rolls. Stale bread can be refreshed by wrapping in a damp serviette or tea towel. Do not use material containing synthetic fibre.

Clingfilm
This is excellent for covering dishes and plate meals; however, as it is inclined to stretch and dilate during cooking due to the steam trapped underneath, it is advisable to pierce or slit the clingfilm with a knife or scissors before placing the dish in the microwave cooker. This is not necessary though when proving dough in the microwave oven. Heavy duty microwave clingfilm is usually easier to handle and withstands higher temperatures, although it is not essential.

Linings
The use of clingfilm to line dishes has the advantage of enabling delicate cakes and puddings to be removed more easily from the container (especially when still warm) and placed the right way up on the cooling rack. Also it practically eliminates the need to wash the dish afterwards. The one disadvantage of using clingfilm as a lining is that it is sometimes difficult to obtain neat corners and edges which may be important to the shape of the cooked result. In this case, it is preferable to line the base of the greased dish with greaseproof paper or baking parchment. It is better not to dust with flour, as this is inclined to result in a doughy crust forming on the outside of the baked product.

Roasting bags and boiling bags
These are extremely convenient for cooking a variety of foods ensuring excellent results. Roasting bags are inclined to enhance the browning of joints and poultry and enable vegetables and fruits to be cooked with very little if any additional liquid.

Do not use the metal ties provided with the bags; elastic bands or string ties can be used instead.

Wicker and straw baskets
These may be used in the microwave for short-term heating only as long exposure to microwave energy may cause them to dry out and crack. However, they are absolutely ideal when thawing or reheating bread or rolls before a meal or dinner party.

Heatproof spatulas and wooden spoons
Plastic spatulas and wooden spoons may be used in the microwave cooker for stirring and mixing. If wooden spoons have absorbed grease or moisture they will become hot.

Metal
Metal pots and pans and other utensils with a high proportion of metal must not be used in the microwave oven. This includes tin, aluminium, copper and stainless steel cooking utensils. The reason for their non-use is that microwave energy is reflected from metal, thus preventing the food within the metal container from cooking, while the reflected microwave energy may cause damage to the magnetron.

Commercially frozen food in aluminium foil containers should be removed and placed in another dish (see aluminium foil below). Never put an unopened can into the oven – always remove the contents and place in a suitable container.

Aluminium foil
Small smooth pieces may be used to cover bones or narrower ends of poultry, meat or fish for part of the heating or cooking time to prevent overcooking. Care should be taken to ensure the foil is smoothed tightly around the ends and, if necessary, secured into position with wooden cocktail sticks. By using aluminium foil in this way you are in fact preventing the microwaves from reach-

ing that area of the food as they are reflected from metal, thus slowing down the cooking time. *Do not* use a double thickness of foil or allow it to touch the sides, back, roof or door of the oven cavity. If arcing (blue flashes of light) does occur, switch off and rearrange or remove the foil. Shallow aluminium foil containers can be used providing they are less than 2.5cm (1in) deep. This is because they are shallow enough to allow penetration of microwave energy from the top of the dish, although cooking times will be longer.

Always check with your manufacturer's instructions with reference to the use of aluminium foil in your particular model.

Metal skewers
These may be used if they are placed carefully in large joints. The skewers must not touch one another or the metal sides, rear, top or door of the cooker. Providing these rules are followed kebab skewers may be used in the microwave oven, but if sparking or arcing occurs rearrange or remove the skewers. An ideal alternative is to use wooden skewers.

Thermometers
Thermometers which are specially designed for use in the microwave cooker are now available and should be used according to the manufacturer's instructions. Unless specially designed, other meat or sugar thermometers must not be used. Foods can of course be removed from the cooker and checked with a conventional cooking thermometer.

Browning dishes
colour page 19
With a microwave browning dish, it is possible to prepare an entirely new range of dishes in the microwave cooker as it enables some cooked foods to attain the traditional golden-brown appearance normally associated with conventionally cooked foods. The browning dish functions in a similar way to a frying pan or griddle and is capable of browning or searing food items

such as beefburgers, steaks, chops and chicken joints; larger joints of meat and poultry brown anyway during their longer cooking time.

Whether the browning dish is used as a skillet or griddle, it functions in the same way. Unlike the remaining surface of the dish which allows microwaves to pass through, the underside of the browning dish absorbs microwaves when preheated. This makes the bottom surface of the preheated empty browning dish very hot. When foods are placed on to the hot surface they brown in the same way as other foods do when added to a hot frying pan.

The temperature of the food, however, cools the browning dish, so the dish will therefore need reheating (for about half the original preheat time) before placing the next batch of food in. Food initially placed on the hot surface browns most attractively. When the dish, containing the food, is placed back in the oven, microwave energy cooks the food while the base of the dish continues to brown the underside.

Preheating
Preheat times vary with the size and shape of the browning dish, the output of the microwave cooker, the type and quantity of the food being cooked and the degree of browning required. Larger browning surfaces require up to 2 min longer preheat time than the smaller ones.

It is important to experiment a little when first using the browning dish so as to determine your personal preference. Try the minimum preheat time initially, but if you prefer browner meats then increase the time – to 6 min for smaller dishes and up to 8 min for the larger ones. Preheat time for vegetables is about 3–5 min, for breads about 2–4 min and eggs 1–2 min.

Placing a little oil or butter in the preheated dish immediately before adding the food improves the browning of many items, but in this case preheat the browning dish for 1 minute less than the normal time, then add the oil or butter.

Points to note
1 Do check with the instruction leaflet for your microwave cooker and be guided by the manufacturer's recommendations regarding the use of browning dishes in your particular model, and with its use in conventional ovens.
2 Any feet on the base of a browning dish prevent it coming into direct contact with the oven shelf or a kitchen work surface and care should be taken when it is hot to ensure that the dish is not placed on a surface which could be damaged by the heat emanating from the underside, including the oven shelf.

3 The base of the browning dish becomes very hot so the use of oven gloves is advisable when handling the dish.

4 Browning dishes should not normally be preheated for longer than 6–8 min; but do check with the manufacturer's instructions.

5 The dish will require preheating again when cooking a second batch of food. Remove all excess food and drippings and preheat the dish for about half the original preheat time.

6 Turn the food over while there is still sufficient heat in the surface for browning the second side, but serve the food with the browned-first side face up.

7 To increase browning of the underside, flatten or press the food with a spatula to gain more contact with the base of the dish before placing it back in the microwave cooker.

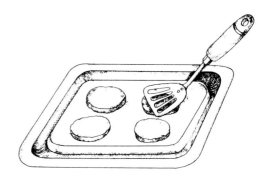

8 Foods should be thawed before placing on the hot surface as any ice crystals present may prevent browning, although thinner foods – such as beefburgers or fish fingers – thaw out quickly during the cooking period.

Browning dish chart
POWER LEVEL 100% (FULL)

The preheat and cooking times are intended only as a guide, as times vary depending on the size and shape of the dish, the output of the microwave cooker, the quantity of food being cooked and the degree of browning required.

Food	Preheat	Butter or Oil	First Side	Second Side
1 Steak, 175g (6oz)	6–7 min	15g (½oz) butter or 1 × 15ml tbsp (1tbsp) oil	1½–2 min	1½–2 min
2 Pork chops, each 225g (8oz)	5–6 min	15g (½oz) butter or 1 × 15ml tbsp (1tbsp) oil	3 min	8–10 min
4 Beefburgers from frozen	6–7 min	15g (½oz) butter or 1 × 15ml tbsp (1tbsp) oil	1½–2 min	2–3 min
4 Bacon rashers	5–6 min	15g (½oz) butter or 1 × 15ml tbsp (1tbsp) oil if required	1 min	30–45 sec
2 Chicken pieces 225g (8oz) each	5–6 min	15g (½oz) butter or 1 × 15ml tbsp (1tbsp) oil	5 min	3–5 min
4 Sausages, large	5–6 min	15g (½oz) butter or 1 × 15ml tbsp (1tbsp) oil	6–8 min	turning 3–4 times
4 Cod portions in breadcrumbs	4–5 min	1 × 15ml tbsp (1tbsp) oil	2–3 min	3–4 min
6 Fish fingers from frozen	5–6 min	Brush food with oil or melted butter	2 min	1–2 min
2 Slices french toast	4–5 min	1 × 15ml tbsp (1tbsp) oil	45 sec	45–60 sec
1 Pizza 17.5cm (7in), whole	3–4 min	15g (½oz) butter or 1 × 15ml tbsp (1tbsp) oil	3–4 min	—
Oven chips 225g (8oz)	3½–4 min	—	2½–3 min	2½–3 min
2 Eggs	2–3 min	15g (½oz) butter or margarine (prick yolks)	1½–1¾ min —	

Microwave cooking techniques

Do not think that cooking by microwave means that you must learn completely new cooking techniques. Indeed, most of the basic rules still apply. It is just a case of adapting those rules and yourself to this new method of cooking food. Special points to watch for are given in the recipes but it important to be aware of the factors which govern successful results.

Power of the oven and cooking times
Most microwave cookers have total power inputs of up to 1,600 watts with outputs of up to 700 watts. The difference between the input and output power is used by the magnetron, stirrer blade, cooling fan, power converter and the interior and indicator lights.

It is the output power from the magnetron which controls the amount of microwave energy used in the oven cavity. The instruction leaflet provided with your particular model should give details of the input and output power of the cooker, and timings on recipes should be adjusted accordingly. Cookers with lower outputs will require longer cooking times while higher outputs will need slightly shorter times.

When in doubt about cooking times, always *underestimate*. Food can easily be cooked for a little longer if necessary and it is preferable to over cooking.

Recipes in this book have been tested in microwave cookers with outputs of 650 watts. Here is a guide to cooking times in ovens of different outputs:

600–700W	500–600W	400–500W
30 sec	35 sec	40 sec
1 min	1 min 10 sec	1 min 20 sec
5 min	5 min 45 sec	6 min 45 sec
10 min	11 min 30 sec	13 min 30 sec
20 min	23 min	27 min
30 min	34 min 30 sec	40 min 30 sec
1 hr	1 hr 10 min	1 hr 20 min

Density and texture
Because microwave cooking is so fast, differences in densities and textures will show up much more quickly in the end result. You will soon find out that a slice of light-textured french or vienna bread will thaw and heat much more quickly than the sliced, prepacked variety and that a sponge cake will heat through faster than a meat pudding. This is because the lightness in the texture of the food allows the microwave energy to penetrate more easily.

Moisture
Moisture too can affect times as microwave energy reacts mainly on water molecules. Some of the recipes in this book have been adjusted to use more or less liquid than you are perhaps used to, in order to ensure successful results; for example, many vegetables can be cooked with very little water ensuring maximum flavour retention, but most cake mixtures have to be wetter than normal for a good even rise and a moist result.

Starting temperature
Differences in the temperature of the food when placed in the microwave cooker will affect the length of cooking time required. The colder the food, the longer the heating time, so allowances must be made when using directly from the refrigerator or freezer.

Quantity
As the quantity of food placed into the oven is increased, the length of cooking time needs also to be increased proportionately. For example, one jacket potato weighing 100–150g (4–5oz) will take 5–6 min, two will take 7–9 min and three will take 10–11 min, and so on. A rough guide would be to allow approximately between one-third and one-half extra time when doubling the quantity of food to be heated. Similarly, if you use less than the quantities given in the recipes in this book, then the cooking times must be reduced accordingly. (See Adjusting quantities page 25).

Shape
The shape of the food should be as uniform as possible to obtain the best results, but of course this will not always be possible. To protect legs and wings of poultry or the thin ends of fish or a joint, such as a leg of lamb, from overheating, it is quite in order to wrap them with a small smooth piece of aluminium foil, which will slow down the cooking of these sections of the food (see page 13). Generally, foods which have an overall longer, flatter surface area will heat more quickly than foods which are densely packed into a small dish.

Seasonings
Salt can have a toughening effect, especially on meat and poultry, so use minimal seasoning during the cooking process and, if in doubt, adjust the seasoning at the finish.

Utensils
The shape of the dish will affect timings in the microwave; also some utensils will absorb more microwave energy than others. In the latter situation, the cooking times will be affected. This is explained more fully under the section 'Utensils' (page 11).

Covering the food
The majority of foods cooked in the microwave benefit from being covered, either to retain moisture, to ensure more even heating or to avoid splashing onto the oven cavity. As, when cooking conventionally, lids on dishes or saucepans speed up the food heating process, so it is when cooking in the microwave. Whether a lid is placed on the casserole dish or the food is covered with clingfilm, steam is trapped inside and this will enable even and slightly faster results to be obtained. Covering food also allows minimal liquid to be used and ensures no flavour loss.

However, when heating through some items, for example crusty rolls or pastry dishes, it would be undesirable to trap the steam as this would prevent a crisp result. In these cases it would be preferable to cover the dish with a piece of kitchen paper towel, which would assist in absorbing the moisture given off from the food.

Arrangement of food
When defrosting, heating or cooking a number of foods of the same type – rolls, buns, cakes, biscuits, jacket potatoes – they should be arranged in a circle on a plate or directly on the oven shelf and be of equal size and shape. If this is not possible, it may be necessary to rearrange the foods halfway through the heating process – outside ones to the inside and vice versa – to ensure that an even result is obtained. Uneven portions of food such

as chops or cutlets of fish should be arranged with the thinner ends towards the centre of the dish to avoid overcooking.

There may be occasions when you require to heat foods of varying type at the same time, for example vegetables with a jug of sauce, or a sponge pudding with a bowl of custard. If different heating times are required, ensure that each item is removed from the oven as soon as it has heated sufficiently.

Stirring and turning

As with conventional cooking, soups, sauces, casseroles and stews require stirring occasionally to bring the food from the outside of the dish to the centre and vice versa. Foods which cannot be stirred – cakes and bread for example – may need turning round to assist the heating process. Meat, poultry and whole fish should generally be turned over once during cooking.

When food is placed into the oven cavity for heating, defrosting or cooking, microwave energy is directed into it from all directions including the base of the cavity beneath the glass shelf. Microwaves penetrate the food only to a depth of 2.5cm (1in) so the outside surfaces of the food will heat through while the very centre remains relatively cool. The heating of the centre of the food relies on the conduction of heat through to this point, therefore the turning of the dishes or the stirring of some foods will be necessary. The turning around of dishes means simply giving the dish a quarter turn (90°) or half a turn (180°) on the oven shelf. Turning dishes is not always necessary if you have a microwave cooker with a turntable, but stirring is still advisable.

Standing time

Foods continue to cook by the heat retained after their removal from the oven and some food items will require this standing, resting or 'heat equalisation' period to assist with the general defrosting, heating or cooking process. However, if the food is cooked to the desired degree on removal from the oven, it is not necessary to let it stand.

When defrosting a joint, for example, it may begin to cook around the edges before thawing completely in the centre, thus a period of standing time in between periods of exposure to microwave energy is required to allow more even defrosting. Due to the continuation of the heating or cooking process during the standing time, it is possible to keep foods quite hot while further dishes are being cooked in the microwave. This is, of course, very useful when preparing a meal (see page 22). Some dishes – a cake or a pudding, for example – should be removed from the oven while the top is still slightly moist and left to stand until cooking is complete. Whether food is left to stand inside or outside the cooker is entirely up to you. It may be that you wish to leave the dish inside the oven out of the way, or you may have other food to cook in the meantime.

Appearance of food

With experience you will be able to tell if food is cooked by its appearance even though it does not take on the traditional golden-brown colour normally asssociated with conventionally cooked foods. You will find that the fact the foods are cooked so quickly compensates for the lack of browning, and anyway this can be overcome very easily by garnishing and decorating dishes more attractively. Have available some ready-prepared toppings such as browned crumbs, chopped nuts, crushed cereals, brown sugar, apricot glaze, paprika, dried herbs, parmesan cheese, etc. When a cake is cooked in only a few minutes and coated in frosting or dusted with icing sugar when cool, this surely outweighs the fact that it is not golden brown in colour underneath, for it is virtually indistinguishable from one cooked conventionally.

Some longer cooking joints and poultry will brown to a degree but this can be enhanced by sprinkling with paprika before cooking or by the use of microwave seasonings and colourings or gravy brownings or sauces. If extra browning is required, food can be placed under a hot grill or in a preheated conventional oven for a few minutes at the end of the microwave cooking time. This is a way of combining speed of microwave with the browning acquired by cooking conventionally, and there are references to this throughout the book where appropriate.

Keeping foods hot

Dishes can be kept warm after heating or cooking by covering with aluminium foil (shiny side inside) or by simply leaving in the covered container during the final standing period. Remember that foods carry on cooking for a short while during this time so that it is possible to cook several items one after another and serve them all together when required. If the temperature of the food has dropped slightly, dishes can easily be put back into the oven for another minute or two to boost the serving temperature.

It is often quicker to heat or cook foods in small amounts rather than to overfill the oven with food, but if a large quantity of items are to be cooked, it is advisable to use the warming compartment or oven on your conventional cooker on a low setting to keep foods hot for an extended period prior to serving.

Cooking by temperature

If your microwave cooker includes a temperature probe, the instructions supplied with your particular model will give detailed specific information on its use and care although I have included here some basic information for your guidance.

Generally, a probe gives best cooking results with foods of the same density, ie solid joints of meat (preferably without bone), or all liquid; for example, a casserole consisting of cubes of meat in a light stock is not recommended although of course a temperature probe can be used successfully when reheating foods of this type.

When using the temperature probe for dishes which need to be covered, clingfilm is the ideal covering material as it can easily be pierced to allow the insertion of the probe into the food.

Positioning the probe: The pointed end of the metal thermometer should be inserted into the leanest/thickest part of the food and usually to a depth of at least 2.5cm (1in). When cooking meat, insert the probe into the centre of the joint – avoid inserting through fat and ensure that it is not in

A browning dish in use

contact with bone as these tend to give false temperature readings.

For poultry, the probe should be positioned between the body and inner thigh of the bird. Minced meat casseroles and bolognaise sauces can be cooked successfully using the probe which should be placed in the centre of the dish. Cook on a low 30 or 50% power level to allow flavours to blend during the cooking period. Alternatively, some models have a facility whereby you can cook by temperature followed by time. Once food has reached the preset probe temperature, the food can be held at that temperature for a determined period of time to allow flavours to blend and sauces to thicken until ready for serving.

Temperature cooking chart: With the exception of meat and poultry items, all the temperatures given are intended as a guide, as much depends on personal preference and the particular recipe for each food type. Whether your oven is equipped with a temperature probe or you wish to use a separate microwave thermometer, the following gives recommended temperatures at the end of cooking for a variety of foods. Remember that the internal temperature of foods (particularly meat

and poultry) will increase a further 5–10°C (9–18°F) during the standing time at the end of the cooking period.

Food	Internal Temperature at End of Cooking	
Beverages	70–80°C	160–175°F
Fish	65°C	150°F
MEAT		
Beef—boneless roast		
rare	55–60°C	130–140°F
medium	65–70°C	150–160°F
well done	75–80°C	167–175°F
Lamb—top leg roast		
medium	70–75°C	160–167°F
well done	75–80°C	167–175°F
Pork—loin roast	75–80°C	167–175°F
Veal	75–80°C	167–175°F
Meat loaf	70–75°C	160–167°F
Minced meat casserole, eg savoury mince, bolognaise sauce	70–75°C	160–167°F
POULTRY		
Chicken, whole	80–85°C	175–185°F
joint	80–85°C	175–185°F
Turkey, whole	80–85°C	175–185°F
boneless roast	70–75°C	160–167°F
Reheating, eg left-overs, canned foods, casseroles	70–80°C	160–175°F
Soups	75–80°C	167–175°F

Variable power control

The advantage of the variable power control featured on some models is that it enables a greater flexibility and control of the cooking speed. When a setting other than 100% (full) has been selected on the variable power control, the microwave energy is automatically cycled on and off at varying rates depending on the setting chosen. At the lower setting the energy is off longer than it is on. As the control is moved to the higher settings the energy is on for longer periods and at 100% (full) setting, the energy is on all of the time. In some models the energy is not cycled on and off at the reduced levels, but has a continuous lower power level.

Choosing the setting is similar to selecting the oven temperature on your conventional cooker – the lower the setting or temperature, the longer the cooking time; the higher the setting, the shorter the cooking time. When a variable power setting has been selected, the timer does not stop and start, but continues to move while the energy switches on and off in the oven.

It is important to understand the percentage outputs or power levels of your own microwave cooker and how these relate to the descriptions of the settings. This information should be given in the manufacturer's instructions to users.

Description of settings
There are many different ways that manufacturers portray the variable power control settings on the control panels of their microwave cookers. In addition, the electronic touch-control models enable any percentage level or setting to be selected just by touching the appropriate part of the control panel.

Below are a few examples of the description of settings used together with the approximate power (watts) outputs and percentage levels at those settings.

Description of settings

Power levels
Some foods require slower cooking to help tenderise them, such as the less expensive cuts of meat. Slower cooking also allows food flavours to blend thoroughly, meat sauces and curries for example, and some foods are heated through more evenly by using a lower power level. The following may be a useful guide as to the use of the variable power control percentage levels:

10–20% This low setting may be used for defrosting joints very slowly and for keeping foods warm for up to half an hour.
30–40% This setting is often used for defrosting, cooking less tender joints, slow-simmering cheaper cuts of meat and for softening butter or cream cheese.
50–60% Use this setting for faster defrosting and simmering. It may also be used for de-

1	2	3	4	5	6	7
KEEP WARM	SIMMER/DEFROST	STEW	DEFROST	BAKE	ROAST	HIGH
LOW	LOW	MED–LOW	MEDIUM	MED–HIGH	HIGH	FULL
150 WATTS	200 WATTS	250 WATTS	300 WATTS	400 WATTS	500 WATTS	650 WATTS
(20–25%)	(30%)	(40%)	(50%)	(60%)	(75%)	(100%)

frosting and reheating frozen casseroles.
70–80% Most precooked foods and left-overs may be reheated using this setting. Use it also for roasting joints and for cooking foods which contain cheese or cream.
100% – Use for bringing liquids to the boil and for preheating a browning dish. Most joints of meat and poultry, vegetables and fish can be cooked on this setting. However, many dishes may have a better flavour, texture and appearance if one of the lower settings is used, in which a longer cooking period would be required.

Power levels time chart
By using the chart given below, it is possible to adapt the cooking times given in this book to suit your own particular model. However, the timings given in the chart are intended only as a guide for much depends on the shape, density, texture and temperature of the food. The calculations have been based on a microwave cooker with an average power output of 650 watts and, of course, this may vary between different models. Allow slightly extra time if using a microwave cooker with a lower output and slightly less time if using a cooker with a higher output (see page 16).

Unless otherwise stated, the recipes in this book have microwave cooking times given for 100% (full) setting.

If you wish to slow down the heating or cooking cycle by using one of the lower settings on the variable power control, this chart will give you the approximate times for the other percentage outputs. Remember to check with your instruction booklet for the description of settings/power levels and the percentage outputs of each one on your particular model. For times greater than 10 min, simply add together the figures in the appropriate column.

Defrost control

When defrosting food by microwave, it is so fast compared with normal methods that there is less flavour loss and the risk of bacterial growth is minimal by comparison.

In some models, the defrost control may be incorporated as part of the variable power control (page 20), or it may be a separate switch or setting when the microwave cooker features just one or two different power levels.

Check with your instruction booklet for the percentage output of the defrost control as this may vary according to the model.

When the defrost control is operated, the microwave energy is either cycled on and off in the oven or is on a continuous low power output to slow down the heating process. Otherwise, if frozen food were subjected to microwave energy until it was completely defrosted, the outer edges would begin to cook before the centre was thawed. Therefore, the defrost control allows the heat to equalise within the frozen food by gradual conduction and no surface cooking should take place.

Defrosting
When defrosting some foods – joints of meat or poultry for example – additional standing periods are required to give a perfect thaw with no overheating of the outside edges. The food is then at an even temperature throughout, which ensures that when it is subsequently cooked, a good, even result is obtained. The number of heating and resting periods depends on the size or amount of food being defrosted, but generally the larger the item, the longer the periods of heating and of rest, with a final resting period being allowed before cooking or reheating.

Quicker defrosting is possible by simply placing frozen food into the microwave on defrost control until it is completely thawed, with one standing period halfway through; however, with

Power levels time chart *(cooking time in minutes)*

10%	20%	30%	40%	50%	60%	70%	80%	90%	100% (full)
10	5	3¼	2½	2	1¾	1½	1¼	1	1
20	10	7	5	4	3¼	2¾	2½	2¼	2
30	15	10	7½	6	5	4	3¾	3¼	3
40	20	13	10	8	7	5¼	5	4¾	4
50	25	17	12	10	8	7	6	5½	5
60	30	20	15	12	10	8	7½	6½	6
70	35	23	17	14	12	9¼	8¾	7¾	7
80	40	27	20	16	13	11	10	9	8
90	45	30	22	18	15	12	11	10	9
100	50	33	25	20	16	13	12	11	10

this method less even results may be obtained. Alternatively, frozen food can be defrosted until it is warm to the touch on the outside edges and then left to stand at room temperature until it is completely thawed.

These defrosting methods are purely a matter of preference and time available, and with experience you will be able to determine which method you prefer. You will also find that many items – vegetables, small cakes, rolls, bread slices, for example – may be thawed in a matter of seconds or minutes by using a 100% (full) setting.

Most frozen foods should be placed in a suitable cooking container, first ensuring that it is large enough to hold the food once it has thawed – particularly important when defrosting soups, sauces, casseroles, etc – and allowing sufficient room for stirring the food without spillage. Commercially frozen foods in foil trays or containers should be removed and placed in a dish suitable for microwave cooking.

Foods should be covered during the defrosting period where necessary. In the case of pastry dishes and bread, kitchen paper towels can be used to absorb any moisture. Small, smooth pieces of aluminium foil (page 13) will protect the narrower ends of poultry, meat or fish for part of the defrosting cycle to prevent any cooking of these thinner parts.

You can check whether food is defrosted either by feel or by using a thermometer; if it needs a little extra time, just put it back into the oven for a short while longer. It is important that meat and poultry are completely thawed and at an even temperature throughout before cooking.

Defrosting and resting times are covered in more detail within the various recipe sections but the Convenience Foods Guide (page 32) deals with a range of commercially frozen foods and may be used as a general guide.

Heating and cooking
Some microwave cookers feature a defrost setting as the only alternative to 100% (full) power level. In addition to using it for defrosting, the control may be used for heating and cooking those foods which benefit from a slower heating or cooking period:

1 Softening butter, melting method cake mixtures, melting chocolate, combining butter and sugar for caramelising, melting jellies, melting cheese.
2 Cooking casseroles, either when using tougher cuts of meat or when it is important that seasoning and spices blend well, eg curries.
3 Cooking tougher joints of meat.

4 Heating or cooking egg-based custards or cream sauces and setting the fillings in pre-baked flan cases, eg quiches.
5 Reheating larger casseroles thereby eliminating some of the need to stir as heating of the centre will be through conduction.
6 Cooking larger, flatter dishes to prevent the outsides drying out before the centre is cooked, eg cheesecake, bread pudding.
7 Poaching large fruits, eg plums, greengages, peaches.
8 Warming bread or rolls in a basket.
9 Cooking richer cake mixtures.
10 Poaching more delicate fish fillets or cutlets, eg salmon.

Whether you use the defrost control for some of the above items is a matter of choice. I have included some recipes for dishes which may be cooked on a 'defrost' setting, but if adapting your own recipes, allow approximately double the cooking time given for 100% (full) setting and refer to the Power Levels Time Chart on page 21.

Meal planning

A microwave oven will cook anything, in that it will turn food from the raw state into a cooked state. Through experience though I have found that some foods are better for being cooked conventionally. Yorkshire puddings and roast potatoes are good examples and, therefore, it makes sense if cooking a traditional Sunday lunch to cook the beef, potatoes and yorkshire pudding in the normal way, leaving the microwave free for the vegetables, sauces, gravy and dessert. Foods which require deep fat frying must be cooked conventionally – eg fish in batter and chips. Frozen chips, however, can be thawed in the microwave while the fat is being heated conventionally and this will help to shorten the frying time.

Complete two-, three- or four-course meals can be cooked in the microwave with a little thought and planning. With experience, you will get more familiar with cooking and standing times. Dishes can be prepared in advance, so that they only need to be placed back in the oven to be reheated or to boost the serving temperature without any harm to the food or loss of flavour.

For many of us, Christmas lunch is possibly the most important meal of the year, with family and friends gathered together to enjoy this annual feast. Unfortunately, for the housewife, it could mean weeks of preparation culminating in her spending a great many hours slaving in a hot kitchen and consequently missing most of the

A selection of microwave cookware (Lakeland Plastics)

festivities. With the aid of the microwave, Christmas lunch need not be a headache at all.

Most food items required for Christmas will freeze for a period of at least 3 months, so by the end of September food can be bought, prepared by microwave and frozen, then on the day it just needs to be defrosted and reheated. Many of the dishes required at Christmas are contained within the recipe section of the book. Do try the Christmas Pudding recipe (page 114) which really does save that day of 'steaming the puddings'.

A few tips

1 When first planning your menus cook each course separately, then gradually progress until a complete meal is cooked by microwave. You will find that organising a time plan will help.

2 As the microwave will not cook roast potatoes successfully, it is possible to roast potatoes and a joint together conventionally, leaving the microwave free for all the other items.

3 Defrost all foods first, except vegetables which can be cooked from frozen. When a large number of vegetables are required, some may be partly cooked then left to stand while the rest are cooked.

4 When cooking a joint of meat or poultry, the vegetables should be cooked during its final standing time.

5 Try to serve one cold course – either a starter or sweet – which can be prepared by microwave then refrigerated.

6 Soups, casseroles, sauces and gravies may be prepared in advance, placed in serving dishes and then heated when required.

7 While eating one course, the next can be heating or cooking.

8 Where practicable, use clingfilm to cover dishes; also, use roasting bags which can be thrown away afterwards.

23

9 Line up in order all the foods to be cooked in the microwave and clear the kitchen of any washing up.

10 Have aluminium foil ready so that you can wrap cooked items to keep them warm, or if there are a lot of dishes to be served, use the warming compartment in your conventional cooker.

Plate meals

With the microwave, you really can cook just once a day – an enormous help where members of the family require meals at different times. Whether refrigerated to reheat later or frozen to use next week, plate meals are ideal standbys for those members of the family who need to cook a meal for themselves when you are not there – and only one plate to wash up.

When arranging a meal on a plate for reheating, place the food within the well of the place as evenly as possible; if thin slices of meat are to be served, it is better to place them in the very centre with the gravy poured over and the vegetables around. All items of food on the plate should be at the same temperature and cooked to the same degree to ensure evenness of reheating.

The plate should be covered with a plate cover or pierced clingfilm while heating. The average plate meal (350–450g-/12–16oz) using 100% (full) will take approximately 3–4 min to reheat from room temperature and 4–5 min from a re-frigerator; with a frozen plate meal, more even re-sults will be achieved if it is defrosted for 10–12 min using a 30–50% setting before reheating. Allow about a minute standing time before un-covering and serving.

If you are heating two plate meals, one after the other, pop the first one back after the second one has heated and give it an extra ½–1 min to boost the temperature before serving. Alternatively, use a plate stacking ring but allow half to three-quarters extra time for reheating.

Baby's food

Once prepared, baby's bottles and feeds may be quickly heated in the microwave (see page 29). However, sterilisation of the bottles by micro-wave is not advised.

Converting conventional recipes

There is no real mystery or problem in converting favourite conventional recipes for cooking by microwave. Most conventional recipes adapt very well, provided they are within the micro-wave oven's capabilities. There is no definite for-mula as much depends on the type of recipe.

Experience in the use of your microwave cooker is the most important factor, and be prepared to experiment at first. Little will happen from the addition of different flavourings or herbs, but quantities can be important. Here are a few guidelines.

Ingredients and methods

1 Make sure you are familiar with general microwave cooking techniques and methods of preparing, arranging and cooking foods. Bear them in mind when converting recipes.

2 Choose a microwave recipe closest to the con-ventional one you wish to convert and be guided by the ingredients and methods.

3 Butter, margarine or oil quantities can be reduced if preferred when 'sautéing' foods such as vegetables and meat in the micro-wave, and remember that the food will not brown as when sautéing conventionally.

4 Cut down on liquid quantities if thickening relies on reduction during cooking, eg cas-seroles, jams, chutneys. Fast boiling without covering on 100% (full) will help to reduce liquid quantities at the end of cooking if necessary.

5 When casseroling, ensure that whole joints, poultry or game birds are turned regularly so that they are cooked in the liquid because meat exposed above the surface may overcook and toughen.

6 Always pre-bake a flan case for a quiche or tart before adding the filling when cooking it in the microwave.

7 Use the finer sugars, and take care not to over-cream sugar with the butter for light sponge cakes otherwise the mixture will rise during cooking but sink back at the end.

8 Wetter cake and pudding mixtures give the best results as the microwave cooker is in-clined to dry the cake more than conventional cooking or baking. Adjust the liquid quantity to ensure that the mixture is a soft dropping consistency before cooking in the microwave.

Power levels and timings

1 Always be guided by power levels and timings for a microwave recipe closest to the one you wish to convert.

2 For timings in microwave cookers with differ-ent outputs, the chart on page 16 should be a useful guide.

3 Get to know what the various power levels are for – 30% = simmer, 60% = bake, 75% = roast etc. If your microwave has variable power control, refer to the information given on page 20.

4 If your microwave cooker has a defrost control as the only alternative power level, refer to its use under 'Heating and Cooking' on page 22.

Adjusting quantities

Reducing or increasing the quantities of food given in a particular microwave recipe is not too difficult to achieve if you follow a few simple rules. As when cooking conventional recipes, there is no exact formula as much depends on the type of food and cooking method. Be prepared to experiment a little at first and use the following recommendations as a guide.

1 Adjust the quantities given in the ingredients list to suit when either reducing or increasing the recipe.
2 Use a dish which is smaller or larger in proportion to the one required for the original recipe.
3 Follow the advice given in the method of the original recipe with reference to covering the dish and stirring and turning the food.
4 Increase the timings for larger quantities allowing about half as much time again when doubling the food to be cooked. Reduce timings by a third when halving the quantities or by two thirds when cooking a quarter of the ingredients. Give minimum time at first, check the results and cook for a little longer if necessary.
5 Be aware of the factors which affect cooking times such as the starting temperature, the type and density of the food and the size and shape of the container.
6 Adjust the standing times given in the original recipe.

7 Keep a note of the adjusted recipe and timings for future reference.

Combination cooking

The advantage of combining convection and microwave cooking in one compartment is that it ensures the crisp results normally associated with traditional browning, while the efficiency of microwave energy speeds up normal cooking times. However, the time saving is not as significant as when cooking by microwave energy alone. Most combination cookers are supplied with a range of accessories such as baking racks, roasting trivets, grids, shelves and turntables. Some of these may be metal and in some models metal containers can be used; you can be assured that where the manufacturer recommends them for cooking, the oven in those models is fitted with a special guard which protects the magnetron from damage by reflected microwave energy.

Foods such as pies, tarts, quiches, cakes, breads, puddings and roasts benefit from the combination method of cooking but do refer to the instructions and cookery book supplied with your particular cooker as the operation and cooking methods vary between the different models. With experience you will find that, using the manufacturer's handbook as a guide, you will soon have no problem in adapting the recipes in this book. Basically there are two types of combination cookers available:

Microwave/Convection cooking in sequence
There are usually two ways in which this type of cooker can be used. Firstly, convection cooking followed by microwave – a sequence which can normally be programmed for automatic opera-

tion. Secondly, microwave cooking followed by convection – for those dishes requiring defrosting first, or which are prepared by microwave and then finished off by convection to achieve a brown finish. This latter process is operated manually and enables both modes of cooking to be operated entirely independently of each other.

Microwave/Convection cooking in unison
With this type of combination cooker both microwave and convection cooking can be carried out completely independently of each other but in addition they can be operated at the same time. When used in this way, it is important to ensure that the oven is not preheated first. It is the gradual build up of heat to the set temperature while microwave energy is cooking the food which ensures a crisp brown result at the end of the cooking time. Therefore foods which normally have a very short cooking time such as small biscuits and scones are not suitable for cooking by this method as the build up of heat is insufficient to brown the food before it is cooked.

●GUIDELINES AT-A-GLANCE

●Choose foods which particularly benefit from the crisp brown finish achieved by combination cooking.

●Refer to the manufacturer's instructions for the correct use of the oven accessories supplied.

●Before using metal containers and utensils, ensure that they are recommended for use during a particular combination sequence or process.

●Always use heatproof containers and utensils when cooking by the combination method or convection alone. Some plastic specialist microwave cookware will withstand oven temperatures up to 200°C (400°F).

●Be guided by the manufacturer's recommendations whether or not to preheat the convection oven when cooking by the combination method.

●It is not normally necessary to stir, turn or rearrange food when combination cooking or using convection only.

The following recipes are intended as a guide to the sorts of foods and cooking methods particularly suitable for combination cookers. The cooking times may vary depending on the particular model and microwave power levels used.

Roast beef *(serves 6)*
POWER LEVEL: 70%
CONVECTION TEMPERATURE: 190°C
METHOD: convection followed by microwave

1½kg (3lb) topside
oil or melted dripping for brushing
salt and pepper

1 Place the meat on the turntable, on the meat roasting rack or in a roasting tin on the turntable. If the roasting rack is used, a shallow ovenproof dish may be placed under the meat to collect the drippings.
2 Brush the meat with a little oil or dripping and sprinkle lightly with salt and pepper.
3 Programme the convection temperature and set the timer, allowing 50 min (16–17 min per 450g/1lb plus 15 min for a medium result).
4 Set the microwave power level and timer, allowing 15 min (5 min per 450g/1lb.)
5 Commence the cooking sequence and at the end of the microwave cooking time test the meat. Allow it to stand for 10 min wrapped in foil. If not cooked sufficiently for your liking, allow another minute or two using microwave alone.
6 During the standing time, prepare the gravy using the drippings from the meat. Vegetables may also be cooked during this time by microwave alone.
7 Carve the meat and serve.

Roast potatoes *(serves 6)*
POWER LEVEL: 100% (FULL)
CONVECTION TEMPERATURE: 230°C
METHOD: microwave followed by convection

900g (2lb) potatoes, cut into even pieces
6 x 15ml (6 tbsp) salted water
5 x 15ml (5 tbsp) oil or dripping

1 Place the potatoes into a large casserole dish or bowl with the salted water. Cover with a lid or clingfilm and cook for 13–14 min, stirring once halfway through. Allow to stand.
2 Put the oil or dripping in a roasting tin and place in the cooker on the convection rack. Turn on the oven and preheat for about 10 min.
3 Drain the potatoes and place on kitchen paper towel to dry. Toss them in the hot fat and then cook for 20–25 min until golden brown, turning the potatoes over in the hot fat halfway through cooking.
4 Drain on kitchen paper to absorb some of the grease before serving.

DO NOT FREEZE

Apple tart (serves 4–6)

POWER LEVEL: 70%
CONVECTION TEMPERATURE: 220°C
METHOD: convection followed by microwave

225g (8oz) shortcrust pastry
675–900g (1½–2lb) cooking apples, sliced
sugar to taste

1 Divide the pastry into two. Roll out one piece and line the base of a shallow pie dish.
2 Place the prepared fruit into the dish and sprinkle with sugar to taste. Dampen the edges of the pastry base. Roll out the remaining pastry to fit and cover the pie. Trim and seal the edges then knock up or crimp. Make a slit in the middle of the pie.
3 Set the convection temperature and the timer for 25–30 min. Bake the pie until golden brown and then cook by microwave for 2 min.

Individual yorkshire puddings (makes 6)

POWER LEVEL: 50%
CONVECTION TEMPERATURE: 250°C
METHOD: convection/microwave simultaneously

100g (4oz) plain flour
pinch salt
2 eggs
275ml (½pt) milk
oil for brushing

1 Sift the flour and salt into a bowl. Add the eggs and mix well together to make a thick paste. Add the milk gradually, beating well after each addition and finally whisking to make a smooth batter.
2 Lightly oil 6 individual ramekin dishes. Divide the batter between dishes and place them on a wire rack on the turntable.
3 Cook at combination medium (50%) at temperature setting 250°C for 16–18 min until well risen and golden brown. Serve straight away.

DO NOT FREEZE

Victoria sandwich (serves 6)

POWER LEVEL: 50%
CONVECTION TEMPERATURE: 250°C
METHOD: convection/microwave simultaneously

175g (6oz) butter or margarine
175g (6oz) caster sugar
3 eggs, beaten
175g (6oz) self-raising flour
4 x 15ml tbsp (4 tbsp) jam
icing sugar for dusting
oil for brushing

1 Cream together the butter or margarine with the caster sugar until light and fluffy. Add the eggs gradually, beating well after each addition. Finally fold in the flour.
2 Lightly oil two 17.5cm (7in) cake dishes and line the bases with circles of greaseproof paper. Divide the mixture evenly between each dish and smooth the surface.
3 Place one dish on the turntable and one on the wire rack above. Cook at combination medium (50%) at temperature 250°C for 10–12 min until risen and golden brown.
4 Remove the cakes from the oven when cooked – usually the top cake should be removed first to avoid overbrowning. Allow them to cool slightly, then turn out of the dishes onto a cooling rack.
5 When quite cold, sandwich the cakes together with the jam and dust the top with icing sugar.

Useful information

The quantities for recipes in this book are given in metric and imperial measurements; in the following tables, American measurements are also given for comparison. Exact conversions do not always give acceptable working quantities and so the metric equivalents are rounded off into units of 25g. This may mean that the overall volume of the cooked product varies very slightly, but from experience I have found that this has little effect on the final result.

Measurement of ingredients

	Metric	Imperial
Weight	25g	1oz
Weigh and measure as	50g	2oz
accurately as possible and	75g	3oz
do not mix metric and	100g	4oz
imperial weights in one	150g	5oz
recipe as all measurements	175g	6oz
are proportionate.	200g	7oz
Imperial and American	225g	8oz
measurements in weight	250g	9oz
and length are the same	275g	10oz
	300g	11oz
	350g	12oz
	375g	13oz
	400g	14oz
	425g	15oz
	450g	16oz (1lb)
	475g	17oz
	500g (½kg)	18oz
	550g	19oz
	575g	20oz (1¼lb)

	Metric	Imperial
Length	1.25cm	½in
	2.5cm	1in
	15.0cm	6in
	17.5cm	7in
	20.0cm	8in
	22.5cm	9in
	25.0cm	10in

	Metric	Imperial	American
Liquid	150ml	¼pt	⅔ cup
Measurements in	275ml	½pt	1¼ cups
liquid and volume	425ml	¾pt	2 cups
are different and	550ml	1pt	2½ cups
these charts show	850ml	1½pt	3¼ cups
the equivalents	1000ml (1l)	1¾pt	4½ cups
using the American	1150ml	2pt	5 cups
8 oz measuring cup			
Volume			
butter	225g	8oz	1 cup
sugar	225g	8oz	1 cup
flour	225g	8oz	2 cups
icing sugar	225g	8oz	1½ cups
rice	225g	8oz	1 cup
dried fruits	225g	8oz	1½ cups
breadcrumbs	225g	8oz	4 cups
grated cheese	225g	8oz	2 cups
Spoon measures			
All spoon meas-	5ml tsp	1tsp	1tsp
ures used in	15ml tbsp	1 tbsp	1tbsp
recipes throughout	1½ × 15ml		
the book are level	tbsp	1½tbsp	2tbsp
unless otherwise	2 × 15ml tbsp		
stated and are best	(or 30ml)	2tbsp	3tbsp
used only for small	4 × 15ml tbsp		
quantities	(or 60ml)	4tbsp	5tbsp

Conventional oven temperature chart

Oven temperatures		°C	°F	Gas
For those	VERY COOL	110	225	¼
microwave users		130	250	½
who wish to com-	COOL	140	275	1
bine microwave		150	300	2
and conventional	MODERATE	160	325	3
cooking this chart		180	350	4
gives the compara-	MODERATE/	190	375	5
tive temperature	HOT	200	400	6
and settings be-	HOT	220	425	7
tween electric		230	450	8
and gas ovens	VERY HOT	240	475	9

Cleaning and care

The manufacturer's instruction leaflet supplied with your cooker will give detailed information on the cleaning and care of your particular model and should be read thoroughly. Any particular recommendations regarding the installation and siting of the appliance must be carefully followed.

Oven cavity
It is important that the oven cavity is kept clean for maximum efficiency. Soilage which is left in the oven will absorb microwave energy, slow down the cooking times and become more difficult to remove.

Microwave cooking is clean because most dishes are covered while heating or cooking in the oven. In addition, with no radiant heat, the oven cavity remains relatively cool so that any splashing on the interior is normally easy to remove with a warm, soapy or just a damp cloth. Splashes which are more difficult to remove can be loosened by placing a cup of water in the oven and allowing it to boil for a few minutes. The steam will soften the soilage, which can then be wiped away more easily. Afterwards, rinse the surfaces and dry with a soft, dry cloth or kitchen paper towel.

Abrasive cleaning materials must not be used as they can scratch the interior surface finish.

Condensation
Condensation may occur during cooking some foods but providing it is wiped away with a dry cloth or kitchen paper towel afterwards, no harm should occur; alternatively, a piece of kitchen paper towel can be placed in the oven during cooking – this will assist by absorbing any moisture from the food.

Door seals
One of the most important areas to keep clean inside the oven is the door seal which should be frequently wiped to clear any soilage which may have been deposited.

Combination models
If your oven incorporates a browning element, or is a microwave-convection model, then soilage may require more vigorous rubbing to remove. Avoid using abrasive cleaners other than those suggested by the manufacturer to avoid scratching.

Oven shelves and turntables
Removable oven shelves or turntables may be easily washed in the sink and dried before replacing in the oven; do read the manufacturer's instructions and recommendations before placing such items in the dishwasher.

Cabinet exterior
The exterior of the cabinet normally only requires the occasional wipe over with a damp cloth and afterwards a dry and polish with a clean duster. If you wish to use a little spray polish, do not direct it straight onto the appliance but spray onto the

duster instead, before applying it to the cabinet. This will ensure that polish is not inadvertently sprayed into any inlet or outlet air vent, which should also be kept clear of any dishes, tea towels, etc while the microwave cooker is operating.

Servicing

Most reputable manufacturers produce cookers which do not leak microwave energy even after many years use, but should you require reassurance, servicing checks are usually available on request. However, it is advisable to check periodically that the door hinges are not faulty or rusty through neglect or lack of service. In the unlikely event of the glass or plastic front panel fracturing, do not use the cooker but contact your service engineer as soon as possible.

Cooking hints and tips

The cooking times are for a 650 watt oven using 100% (full) setting unless otherwise stated (see page 16 for conversion table).

Almonds   To blanch, just cover 100g (4oz) almonds with cold water in a jug or bowl and heat for 3–3½ min until boiling (hot water will shorten the boiling time). Leave to cool before removing the skins by rubbing between the finger and thumb. If the skins are difficult to remove, heat for a few seconds longer.

To toast almonds, place blanched and split, flaked or chopped almonds on a heatproof plate and cook for 5–6 min or until evenly toasted, stirring once or twice throughout.

Fry almonds by tossing them in sufficient melted butter or oil to coat them and cook on a heatproof plate for 5–6 min, stirring once or twice throughout. Drain on absorbent kitchen paper towel.

Baby's bottles   Sterilization of bottles should be carried out using conventional methods, but baby's milk can be made for the day and placed into sterilized bottles for heating later in the microwave. To heat the milk, remove the teat and cap from the bottle and, depending on the type of milk, a 100ml (4oz) bottle-feed will heat in 30–45 sec and a 225ml (8oz) feed in 50–60 sec on 100% (full) setting. Replace the cap and teat and shake well before testing the temperature. Heat for a few seconds longer if necessary.

Baby's food   Heating times for solid food will vary according to the type and quantity. Canned baby's food should be turned into a suitable microwave dish, but jars can be heated in the microwave. Remove the lid and heat a 128g (4½oz) jar

for about 45 sec. Two jars or one 175g (6oz) jar will take approximately 60 sec. Stir well before testing the temperature.

Baked eggs   When cooked in the microwave, baked eggs may be used as hard-boiled eggs. Chop or slice them for use in salads or adding to sandwich fillings. Refer to page 40 for recipe and method.

Barbecue   Meat or poultry can be part-cooked in the microwave before placing on the barbecue to help prevent it from scorching on the outside before the centre of the meat is cooked through.

Blanching   Small quantities of vegetables can be blanched in the microwave before freezing (page 91). In addition, peeled potatoes may be blanched prior to roasting or frying conventionally. Place 450g (1lb) peeled and cut or chipped potatoes in a bowl or dish with 4 x 15ml tbsp (4 tbsp) salted water, cover with a lid or pierced clingfilm and cook for 5–6 min until hot. Stir well halfway through.

Breadcrumbs   To dry breadcrumbs, spread about 50g (2oz) fresh crumbs on a double thickness of kitchen paper towel and heat in the microwave for approximately 2 min. Check every minute and toss them over if necessary. To toast them in butter, stir the fresh crumbs in 25g (1oz) melted butter in a large shallow dish. Cook them, uncovered, for 3–4 min, checking and stirring every minute.

Bread rolls   Warm rolls in wicker baskets before serving at a lunch or dinner party. Line the basket with a napkin or paper serviette and arrange the rolls evenly in the basket. Heat 6 rolls for ¾–1 min depending on the type of bread, or heat 12 for 1½–2 min. Leave for about 1 min before serving.

Butter and margarine   Soften 250g (8.8oz) butter from the refrigerator by placing it unwrapped on a plate or dish and heating for 12 sec. Check and heat for a few seconds longer if necessary. Defrost it from the freezer by heating on 30% setting for 1¼–1½ min, turning it over halfway through. Stand for 10–12 min before using.

Melt 25g (1oz) butter by placing it in a bowl or dish and heating for 45-60 sec, or 50g (2oz) for about 1½ min, depending on the starting temperature. Cover the dish to prevent splattering if necessary.

Cheese   To ripen brie, heat 225g (8oz) brie on 30% setting for 30 sec at a time until soft, but remove it from the microwave as soon as it is warm or beginning to melt. For general information on cheese, see page 35.

Liver Pâté (page 58) and Quick Poor Man's Cassoulet (page 86)

Chestnuts　To shell chestnuts, first slit the skins with a sharp knife, place 10–12 at a time on a plate and heat for 1–1½ min. Leave to cool slightly before peeling.

Chips　Frozen oven chips can be cooked in the microwave by using a browning dish which gives the better result. Alternatively, place 225g (8oz) frozen oven chips onto a plate or dish lined with a double layer of kitchen paper towel and heat, uncovered, for 5–6 min, tossing them over halfway through. Deep-fat frying must not be attempted in the microwave but frozen chips for frying can be quickly defrosted before cooking conventionally to cut down on the frying time.

Chocolate　Melt chocolate for cake toppings by breaking 100g (4oz) into a bowl or dish and heating for 1½ min. Stir well and heat for a further 30–60 sec if necessary.

Citrus fruits　To obtain maximum juiciness before squeezing, heat oranges, lemons, limes or grapefruits in the microwave until warm. One will take 20–30 sec, two 45–60 sec and three 1–1½ min, depending on the type and size of the fruit.

Coffee　Filtered coffee can be made in advance and reheated in the microwave when required. Refer to page 36 for heating times.

Cream　Frozen cream sticks can be defrosted in the microwave but care must be taken not to overheat otherwise they will melt. Place 227ml (½pt) cream sticks in a jug or bowl, cover and heat on 30% setting for 3–4 min. Break down the sticks with a fork and heat for a further 30–60 sec if necessary. Leave to stand for about 30 min until completely thawed, stirring frequently during the standing time.

Croûtons　Cut 25g (1oz) bread into small dice and toss well in 25g (1oz) melted butter in a shallow dish. Cook, uncovered, for 1 min, turn the bread over and cook for a further 1 min. Drain on absorbent paper before serving sprinkled with paprika.

Desiccated coconut　To toast, spread 40–50g (1½–2oz) desiccated coconut over a heatproof plate or dish. Heat for 5–6 min until browned, stirring twice throughout.

Dried fruits To soak dried fruits, place in a bowl, and add sufficient cold water to cover. Cover the bowl and heat in the microwave until boiling, then cook for a further 2 min. Leave for up to 1 hr to swell and soften. Heat currants, sultanas and raisins until warm to plump and soften them before cake making.

Fats Do not attempt deep-fat frying in the microwave as the temperature of the fat or oil cannot be controlled. When cooking in the microwave, it is possible to cut down on the amount of fat or oil normally added to food. For fat free diets, the majority of foods may be cooked without additional fat but do make sure dishes are covered when appropriate to keep in the moisture.

Flour Warm the flour and liquid ingredients in the microwave when bread making. This ensures that the dough is at a warm, even temperature throughout which assists the proving process.

Herbs Small quantities of herbs may be quickly dried in the microwave. Refer to page 92 for method and timings.

Icings To soften refrigerated or frozen icings, warm in the microwave for 10–12 sec at a time until soft, then stir or beat well before using.

Jams, syrups, honey Remove the cap from the jar or place a quantity into a bowl. Heat for 15 sec at a time until warm. This will make spreading and measuring by the spoonful much easier.

Jelly To melt a table jelly, cut or break it into cubes and place in a bowl or measuring jug with 2 x 15ml tbsp (2tbsp) water or fruit juice. Heat for 30–45 sec until melted and stir well until completely dissolved. Add remaining liquid with some ice cubes to the amount required to set it quickly.

Lemon zest To dry, spread finely grated lemon rind between kitchen paper towels and heat for 30 sec at a time until dry and crumbly. Leave to stand, uncovered, until cool and completely dry before storing.

Mars bars To make a topping for cakes or ice cream, cut a Mars bar into pieces and place in a bowl with 2 x 15ml tbsp (2tbsp) water or milk. Heat for 30 sec at a time until melted, stirring well until smooth.

Marzipan and fondant icing Prepared marzipan and fondant icings can be stored in the refrigerator to be used when required. To make them more pliable, soften in the microwave by heating 175g (6oz) until warm then knead well.

Milk Heat milk for drinks or cereals by removing the cap from the glass bottle or pouring a quantity into a jug or bowl. Refer to the timings given on page 36.

Onions Slice and cook them, covered, in the microwave to prevent smells in the kitchen. A large sliced onion with 25g (1oz) butter or 2 x 15ml tbsp (2tbsp) oil will take about 4 min.

Pancakes and waffles To reheat pancakes and waffles, 4 from room temperature will take 30–45 sec, from the refrigerator 45–60 sec and from the freezer 1¼–1½ min. Larger quantities from the freezer are best defrosted first.

Pastry dishes When reheating sausage rolls, quiches, flans etc, place them on or cover with paper towel to absorb moisture and retain crispness.

Plate meals Reheat a meal on a plate for a late homecomer. Cover with pierced clingfilm or a plate cover and heat for 3–4 min from room temperature (see also page 24).

Plates Warm plates or dishes (suitable for the microwave) by rinsing in cold water and heating in the microwave for 1–2 min until hot, then dry them before using.

Proving Yeast doughs can be proved in the microwave by giving short heating times of 15 sec interspersed with 5–15 min standing time (page 134).

Sauces, gravies Make them in advance and place in their serving jugs to be quickly reheated when required; 275ml (½pt) sauce will take 2–3 min. Stir well before serving.

Scones, buns, doughnuts Whether home-made or shop bought, serve them warm for tea by reheating in the microwave. Heat 1 for 10–15 sec or 6 (arrange in a circle) for about 1 min.

Spirits and liqueurs For flambé dishes, hot toddies and liqueur coffees, pour 2–4 x 15ml tbsp (2–4tbsp) into a glass and heat for 10–20 sec.

Sugar and salt To soften hard or damp sugar or salt, heat in the microwave for 30–60 sec.

Toffees To serve with ice-cream or use as a cake topping, heat 100g (4oz) caramel or chocolate toffees with 3 x 15ml tbsp (3tbsp) cream, milk, water or liqueur for 3 min until melted. Stir well halfway through and again before using.

Tomatoes and peaches To remove the skins from tomatoes or peaches, first slit the skin then heat in the microwave for 30–60 sec until just hot. Leave to stand for a few minutes before peeling. If skinning a quantity of fruit, the traditional boiling water method will be more convenient.

Convenience foods guide

Not all convenience foods are included, but use this chart as a handy reference guide.

Food	Quantity	Method	Defrost 30–50%	Cook 100% (full)	Special points
CANNED FOODS *Reheat* Soup	275ml (½pt)	Pour into mug or soup bowl		3 min	Stir once during cooking
	2 mugs or bowls			5–6 min	
Pasta eg macaroni cheese	425g (15oz)	Place in a bowl or serving plate, cover		4–5 min	Stir twice during cooking
Spaghetti in tomato sauce	440g (15½oz)	Place in bowl or serving plate, cover		3–4 min	Stir once during cooking
Baked beans	220g (7¾oz)	Place in a bowl, or on a plate, cover		1–1½ min	Stir once during cooking
	425g (15oz)			3–4 min	
Peas or other small vegetables	425g (15oz)	Place in bowl, cover		4–4½ min	Stir twice during cooking
Custard or milk puddings	440g (15½oz)	Place in serving jug or bowl		3 min	Stir once during cooking
Sponge pudding	298g (10½oz)	Place in bowl or on a plate		2 min	Turn once during cooking
MEAT *Reheat* Cornish pasty	1	Stand on kitchen paper towel		¾–1¼ min	Stand 2–3 min before serving
Individual meat pie	1	Remove from foil tray, stand on kitchen paper towel		¾–1¼ min	Stand 2–3 min before serving
Family size meat pie or quiche	450g (1lb)	Remove from foil dish and place on serving dish		6 min	Stand 4 min halfway through and after cooking
4 Beefburgers, canned	283g (10oz)	Place on dish or serving plate, cover		4 min	Turn over halfway through cooking
Steak and kidney pudding, canned	440g (15½oz)	Remove from can, place in a bowl, cover		4–5 min	Stand 5 min after cooking
Soya protein mince or chunks, canned	425g (15oz)	Place in a bowl, cover		3–4 min	Stir once during cooking
Frozen Roast meat in gravy	113g (4oz)		5 min, stand 4 min	1½ min	Separate slices after defrosting
	340g (12oz)		10 min, stand 9 min	3½ min	
Individual steak and kidney puddings	125g (5oz)	Remove from foil dish and place on serving plate	2 min, stand 5 min 3 min stand 2 min	2½ min	Stand 2 min before before serving
Shepherd's pie	454g (16oz)	Remove from foil dish and place on serving plate or dish	6 min, stand 6 min 3 min, stand 6 min	5–6 min	Turn once during cooking

Food	Quantity	Method	Defrost 30–50%	Cook 100% (full)	Special points
Beefburgers	4	Place on kitchen paper towel		3–4min	Turn over once during cooking
Individual meals 'boil in bag'	227g (8oz)	Slit bag and place on serving plate	6 min, stand 6 min	2–2½ min	Flex bag during defrosting. Stand 2 min before serving
Moussaka or Lasagne	454g (1lb)	Remove from foil dish and place on serving plate or dish, cover	8 min, stand 6 min 4–5 min	9 min	Stand 1 min before serving
Sausage rolls (cooked)	1 4	Place on kitchen paper towel	30–60 sec, stand 1 min 1½–2 min, stand 3 min	15 sec 30–60 sec	
FROZEN FISH 2 Cod steaks	225g (8oz)	Place on plate or dish, cover	6 min, stand 6 min	3 min	Turn over halfway through defrosting
'Boil in bag' fish, eg smoked haddock	187g (7oz)	Slit top of bag and place on plate	6 min, stand 4 min	6 min	Separate fillets after defrosting
Fish steak in sauce 'boil in bag'	170g (6oz)	Slit top of bag and place on plate	4 min, stand 4 min 2 min, stand 5 min	1½ min	Flex bag during defrosting. Shake contents of bag before serving
Fish fingers	10	Arrange in circle on plate	6 min, stand 4 min	1½–2½ min	Dot with butter before cooking
2 Fish cakes	each 50g (2oz)	Place on plate	4 min, stand 4 min	1–1½ min	Dot with butter before cooking
CAKES AND PUDDINGS *Frozen* Homemade cake	1 slice	Place on serving plate	1–2 min		Time varies with size and type of cake
Cream sponge	250g (10oz)	Place on serving plate	1–1½ min, stand until cream is completely thawed		Times given are sufficient to thaw the sponge only
Cream doughnut	1 4	Place on kitchen paper towel	30 sec, stand 4 min 1¼ min, stand 5 min		
Jam doughnut	1 4	Place on kitchen paper towel	1½ min, stand 2 min 4 min, stand 4 min		
Cheesecake with fruit topping		Place on serving plate	4 min, stand 5 min 2 min, stand 5 min		
Reheat Mince pies, (cooked)	1 4	Place on kitchen paper towel		10–15 sec 45–60 sec	Stand 1–2 min before serving
Christmas pudding	1 whole 550–850ml (1–1½pt) 1 portion	In pudding basin On serving plate or dish		2–3 min 30–60 sec	Stand 1 min before serving Stand 1 min before serving

Seafood Flan (page 73)

Food	Quantity	Method	Defrost 30–50%	Cook 100% (full)	Special points
BREAD PRODUCTS					
Frozen					
Roll or large slice of bread	1 3	Place on kitchen paper towel or an oven shelf		10–25 sec 20–35 sec	Thawing time depends on density and type of bread
Croissant	4	Place on kitchen paper towel	1½–2 min, stand 2 min		
Small loaf	1	Place on oven shelf	4–5 min, stand 8–10 min		
Large loaf	1		7–9 min, stand 12–16 min		
Pizza, large small	1 1	Place on serving plate		5–6 min 3 min	

Simple beginnings

This section is intended as a guide to help you get to know your microwave cooker, starting off with some of the easier dishes and working towards more complicated ones. It will also assist you in getting familiar with cooking times and the appearance of foods when cooked by microwave. Recipes are included for drinks, snacks and light meals, egg and cheese dishes, all of which are easy to prepare so that members of your family will also be encouraged to start cooking by microwave.

●GUIDELINES AT-A-GLANCE

●**Arrange** foods as evenly as possible in the container and on the cooking shelf. Individual dishes and small items are best arranged in a circle when possible to ensure even heating or cooking.

●**Bacon** rashers and sausages can be placed on a microwave rack or trivet to keep them out of the juices during cooking. Cover with kitchen paper towel to absorb moisture and prevent splashes onto the oven interior.

●**Baked eggs** from the microwave may be used as hard-boiled eggs when required chopped or sliced for use in salads or fillings.

●**Boiled eggs** in their shells should not be attempted in the microwave without first piercing the shell with an egg piercer or safety pin or wrapping smoothly in aluminium foil (see recipe page 41).

●**Browning dishes** are useful for cooking sausages, beefburgers, fish fingers etc if a browned result is required (page 14).

●**Cover** large dishes or family size snacks with a lid or pierced clingfilm also when it is important to retain moisture during cooking, reheating and defrosting. It is not normally necessary to cover quickly reheated individual snacks or servings.

●**Eggs and cheese** are both high protein foods and as such are sensitive to heat – both will become leathery in texture if overcooked. Yolks set before the whites and cheese melts quickly, so allow a little less time at first and cook for a few seconds longer if necessary or leave to stand (see below). If a brown finish is required, put cheese dishes under a conventional hot grill for a few minutes before serving.

●**Egg yolks** should always be pricked with a sharp pointed knife before cooking otherwise steam build-up inside the membrane will cause them to explode.

●**Overcooking** causes dry or hard results so, if in doubt, remove food from the microwave when barely done and pop back if necessary for a few seconds or minutes longer to finish cooking. Some food items will finish cooking or setting during the standing period (see below).

●**Pastry** items such as sausage rolls and servings of quiche should be placed on or covered with kitchen paper towel before heating in the microwave to absorb moisture and help retain a crisp result.

●**Soufflés** and light omelettes do not brown and crisp due to the lack of dry heat in the microwave. Individual soufflés and 'spanish' type omelettes with plenty of filling give acceptable results, but otherwise cook conventionally.

●**Standing times** are important for eggs and egg-based dishes (except omelettes and soufflé type) and these food items are best removed from the microwave when barely set and allowed to finish cooking during the standing time. If after standing for 1 min the eggs are not set sufficiently for your liking, return them to the oven for a further 10–15 seconds.

●**Stir** dishes when appropriate to bring the food from the sides of the dish to the centre and vice versa for even cooking. Scrambled eggs need frequent stirring or whisking during cooking.

●**Toast** should be made conventionally. Toppings can be placed on the toast before heating through in the microwave although the toast will absorb moisture from the topping and will not remain crisp. Alternatively, heat the topping separately and pile onto the hot toast before serving.

●**Turn** dishes occasionally during cooking if necessary and when it is not possible to stir. In addition, thicker foods (large jacket potatoes for example) will require turning *over* halfway through cooking.

Drinks

Preparing drinks in the microwave is quick and easy. It can even be used to reheat that forgotten half cup of tea or coffee or refresh left-over percolated or filtered ground coffee without loss of flavour. When making a milky drink in a mug or cup, just heat it until it is at a hot serving temperature. Be careful of boil-overs when adding ingredients to hot liquids. Here is a guide to heating times from cold using a 100% (full) power level.

Quantity	Cooking time
150ml (¼pt) milk	1–1¼ min
275ml (½pt) milk	2–2½ min
550ml (1pt) milk	4½–5 min
275ml (½pt) black coffee	3–3½ min
550ml (1pt) black coffee	4½–5½ min
1.1 litre (2pt) black coffee	6–7½ min
1 mug or cup	1½–2½ min
2 mugs or cups	3–3½ min
3 mugs or cups	4–4½ min
4 mugs or cups	5–5½ min
5 mugs or cups	6½–7 min
6 mugs or cups	7½–8½ min

Hot chocolate or coffee *(for 1 cup)*
POWER LEVEL: 100% (FULL)

1–2 x 5ml tsp (1–2 tsp) drinking chocolate or instant coffee
sugar to taste, optional
175ml (6fl oz) milk or milk and water

1 Blend the chocolate or coffee with the sugar and a little of the liquid in a cup or mug.
2 Stir in the rest of the milk and heat for 1¾min. Stir well before serving.

Note: *Heat 2 cups for 3 min.*

Tea *(for 1 cup)*
POWER LEVEL: 100% (FULL)

175ml (6fl oz) water
1 teabag
sugar and milk or lemon, to taste

1 Heat the water in a cup for 2 min.
2 Add the teabag and leave to 'brew' for 1 min.
3 Remove the teabag and add sugar and milk or lemon to taste.

Note: *Heat 2 cups for 3½ min.*

Hot Bovril *(for 1 cup)*
POWER LEVEL: 100% (FULL)

175ml (6fl oz) water
1 x 5ml (1tsp) Bovril

1 Heat the water in a cup for 2 min.
2 Stir in the Bovril and serve straight away.

Note: *Heat 2 cups for 3½ min.*

Egg nog *(serves 1)*
POWER LEVEL: 100% (FULL)

175ml (6fl oz) milk
1 egg
1 x 15ml tbsp (1 tbsp) sugar
grated nutmeg or few drops of vanilla essence

1 Heat the milk in a small jug, in the microwave, for 1½ min.
2 Beat together the other ingredients. Whisk in the warm milk and serve.

DO NOT FREEZE

Hot apricot cider cup *makes about 1¾l (2¾pt)*
POWER LEVEL: 100% (FULL)

1l (1¾pt) strong cider
15cm (6in) cinnamon stick
15g (½oz) blanched almonds
1 × 822g (1lb 13oz) can apricots
2 × 241ml (8½fl oz) bottles tonic water

1 Heat 275ml (½pt) cider with the cinnamon and almonds in a large bowl for 5 min.
2 Blend the apricots and juice in a liquidiser or rub through a nylon sieve. Add the apricots to the hot liquid.
3 Add the remaining cider and the tonic water. Heat in the microwave for 10–15 min. Stir well and remove the cinnamon stick before serving.
DO NOT FREEZE

Mulled wine *makes about 1l (1¾pt)*
POWER LEVEL: 100% (FULL)
colour page 51

275 ml (½pt) water
100g (4oz) sugar
4 cloves
7.5cm (3in) cinnamon stick
1 orange
1 lemon
1 bottle red wine
few lemon slices

1 Place the water, sugar and spices in a bowl and heat in the microwave for 4 min.
2 Slice the orange and lemon thinly and add to the spiced water. Leave to stand for 10 min.
3 Add the wine and reheat for 4 min. Strain the wine and heat for 2 min.
4 Garnish with extra lemon slices and serve hot.

DO NOT FREEZE

Spicy apple juice *makes about 700ml (1¼pt)*
POWER LEVEL: 100% (FULL)

450g (1lb) cooking apples
2 × 15ml tbsp (2tbsp) water
sugar, to taste
150ml (¼pt) white wine
generous pinch cinnamon
275ml (½pt) cider

1 Place apples, water and sugar in a roasting bag, cover and cook in the microwave for 5 min.
2 Blend the apples with the white wine and cinnamon in a liquidiser or food processor.
3 Stir in the cider and serve – warm or cold.

DO NOT FREEZE

Eggs mornay *(serves 2 or 4)*
POWER LEVEL: 50%

butter
4 eggs
275ml (½pt) cheese sauce (page 65)
1 × 15ml tbsp (1tbsp) grated cheese
1 × 15ml tbsp (1tbsp) browned breadcrumbs

1 Lightly grease a shallow dish with a little butter. Break the eggs into the dish, arranging them around the edge. Prick the yolks.
2 Heat the sauce if necessary for 3–4 min. Coat the eggs with the cheese sauce. Mix the grated cheese with the breadcrumbs and scatter over the top of the sauce.
3 Cook in the microwave for 10–12 min until the eggs are set. Serve straightaway.

DO NOT FREEZE

Porridge *(serves 1–2)*
POWER LEVEL: 100% (FULL)

4 × 15ml tbsp (4tbsp) porridge oats
150ml (¼pt) water or milk and water
pinch salt
For serving:
sugar and milk or cream

1 Mix the porridge with the water (or milk and water) and salt in a serving bowl or dish.
2 Cook for 1¾ min, stirring twice throughout.
3 Allow to stand for 1–2 min.
4 Serve hot with sugar and milk or cream.

DO NOT FREEZE

Corned beef hash *(serves 4–6)*
POWER LEVEL: 100% (FULL)

A substantial supper dish.

25g (1oz) butter or margarine
1 large onion, peeled and finely chopped
225g (8oz) can corned beef
450g (1lb) potatoes, cooked
225g (8oz) can baked beans
salt and freshly ground black pepper
½–1 × 5ml tsp (½–1tsp) worcestershire sauce
paprika for sprinkling, optional

1 Melt the butter or margarine in a large pie dish for 1 min, toss in the onion, cover and cook for 4–5 min until soft and transparent.
2 Dice the corned beef and potato. Add the corned beef and half the potato to the onion with the baked beans, seasonings and worcestershire sauce. Mix well together and smooth the top. Scatter the remaining potato over the top.
3 Cover and cook for 3–4 min until heated through.
4 Brown the potato under a grill or sprinkle with paprika. Serve hot.

Tomatoes on toast *(serves 1–2)*
POWER LEVEL: 100% (FULL)

4 tomatoes, cut into halves
salt and pepper
slivers butter
2 slices hot buttered toast

1 Place the tomato halves in a circle on a plate. Sprinkle with salt and pepper and add a sliver of butter to each half.
2 Cook for 3–4 min, turning the plate halfway through.
3 Serve on slices of hot buttered toast.

DO NOT FREEZE

Jacket potatoes *(serves 2–4)*
POWER LEVEL: 100% (FULL)

2 potatoes (each 225–250g/8–9oz)
knob butter
salt and pepper

1 Scrub the potatoes then dry and prick them with a fork or score them.
2 Cook for 10–12 min, or until soft. Cut the potatoes in half and scoop out the soft potato.
3 Mix with the butter and seasoning, then pile the filling back into the potato skins. Reheat for 1½ min before serving.

Variations: Add the following to the cooked potato and reheat as above.

Cheese:
50g (2oz) cheese, grated
15g (½oz) butter
½ × 5ml tsp (½tsp) milk

Bacon:
50g (2oz) cooked bacon, chopped
½ × 5ml tsp (½tsp) milk

Soured cream and chives
2 × 15ml tbsp (2tbsp) soured cream
1 ×5ml tsp (1tsp) chives, chopped

DO NOT FREEZE

Courgettes Maison (page 56) Mushrooms à la Grecque (page 57), Creamy Haddock and Sweetcorn (page 56), Minestrone Soup (page 61) and Miniature Meatballs (page 57)

Quick crumpet pizzas
POWER LEVEL: 100% (FULL)

Ingredients for each pizza:
1 crumpet
knob butter
½ slice cooked ham
2 thin slices tomato
pinch mixed herbs
salt and pepper
few onion rings
15–25g (½–1oz) cheese, grated
For garnish:
sliced green olives

1 Heat the crumpet in the microwave until hot (½–1½ min depending on quantity).
2 Lightly butter the crumpet. Place the ham on the crumpet and top with tomato, herbs, seasoning, onion and grated cheese.
3 Cook 1 crumpet 1 min; 2 crumpets 1½ min; 4 crumpets 2½ min; or until the cheese is melted.
4 Garnish with sliced green olives.

DO NOT FREEZE

Bacon sandwich (serves 1)
POWER LEVEL: 100% (FULL)

3 rashers bacon, trimmed
2 large slices bread
butter optional

1 Place the bacon rashers on a plate, cover with kitchen paper and cook for 2½–3 min.
2 Butter the bread slices or brush with the bacon fat.
3 Make up the sandwich and reheat for 30 sec; cut and serve.

Sausage and egg crisp (serves 4–6)
POWER LEVEL: 100% (FULL) OR 70%

1 medium onion, grated or finely chopped
450g (1lb) sausagemeat
1 × 15ml tbsp (1tbsp) mixed dried herbs
50g (2oz) white breadcrumbs
2 eggs, beaten
milk for mixing
salt and pepper
60–75g (2½–3oz) potato crisps

1 Mix the onion with the sausagemeat, herbs and breadcrumbs.
2 Stir in the eggs and sufficient milk to form a soft mixture. Add seasonings to taste.
3 Place the mixture in a 17.5–20cm (7–8in) shallow dish. Smooth the top and cover.
4 Cook for 4 min on 100% (full) setting. Allow to rest for 4 min, turn the dish and cook for a further 4–5 min. Alternatively cook on 70% setting for 10–12 min, turning 2–3 times.
5 Drain off any fat. Crumble the potato crisps and scatter over the top of the sausagemeat.
6 Heat for 1 min and serve immediately.

DO NOT FREEZE

Scrambled egg (serves 2)
POWER LEVEL: 100% (FULL)

4 eggs
4 × 15ml tbsp (4tbsp) milk
pinch salt
25g (1oz) butter
2 slices hot buttered toast

1 Beat the eggs, milk and salt together.
2 Melt the butter in a bowl for 1 min. Pour in the egg mixture and cook for 1 min.
3 Stir well and cook for 2–2½ min, stirring every 30 sec. Serve with hot buttered toast.

Note: *Halve the above cooking times for 2 scrambled eggs.*

Soft roe savoury (serves 1–2)
POWER LEVEL: 100% (FULL)

12 soft herring roes (about 100g/4oz)
25g (1oz) butter
salt, black pepper
chopped parsley
few drops lemon juice
2 slices hot buttered toast

1 Wash the roes and dry with kitchen paper.
2 Melt the butter in a shallow dish, in the microwave, for 1 min.
3 Add the roe, cover with a lid or clingfilm and cook for 1½ min.
4 Turn the roe and cook for a further 1 min. Season and add chopped parsley and lemon juice.
5 Serve on hot buttered toast.

DO NOT FREEZE

Cheese on toast (serves 1)
POWER LEVEL: 100% (FULL)

1 slice toast
thin slices cheese
chutney, sweet pickle or tomato slices, optional

1 Put the toast on a plate and cover with thin slices of cheese, making sure the layer of cheese is even.
2 Cook for 1–1¼ min until the cheese is soft. Do not overheat otherwise the cheese will melt and run off the toast.
3 Top with chutney, sweet pickle or tomato slices and serve immediately.

DO NOT FREEZE

Sautéed kidneys on toast (serves 1–2)
POWER LEVEL: 100% (FULL)

4 lambs' kidneys
2 × 15ml tbsp (2tbsp) seasoned flour
25g (1oz) butter
1 small onion, finely chopped
seasoning
2 slices hot buttered toast

1 Remove and discard the skin and cores from the kidneys. Chop finely and toss in the seasoned flour.
2 Melt the butter in a shallow dish for 1 min. Add the onion and cook for 1½ min.
3 Add the kidneys, stir, cover and cook for 4½ min stirring once during cooking.
4 Adjust seasoning and serve on hot buttered toast.

DO NOT FREEZE

Poached eggs *(serves 2–4)*
POWER LEVEL: 100% (FULL) AND 50%

boiling water
4 eggs
4 slices hot buttered toast

1 Pour the boiling water into individual cups, ramekin dishes or small bowls to a depth of about 2.5cm (1in).
2 Place the dishes in a circle in the microwave and heat on 100% (full) setting until boiling. Carefully break the eggs into each dish and prick the yolks.
3 Cook on 50% setting for 3–3½ min, until the whites are set, turning the dishes halfway through.
4 Serve on hot buttered toast.

Note: *Cook 1 egg on 50% setting for 1–1½ min, 2 eggs for 1½–2 min.*

Strawberry jelly mousse *(serves 4–6)*
POWER LEVEL: 100% (FULL)
colour page 42

1 × 298g (10oz) can strawberries
1 × 135g (4¾oz) strawberry jelly
1 small can evaporated milk, chilled

1 Drain the strawberries, reserving the juice. Break the jelly into squares and place in a 550ml (1pt) measuring jug.
2 Melt the jelly with 2 × 15ml tbsp (2tbsp) of the strawberry juice in the microwave for 30–40 sec and stir well.
3 Add the juice from the strawberries and make the jelly up to 550ml (1pt) with cold or chilled water. Mix well.
4 Pour the jelly into a large bowl and leave in the refrigerator until nearly set.
5 Whisk the jelly, gradually adding the evaporated milk in a thin stream. Whisk well together.
6 Stir in the strawberries and pour the mousse into clean moulds or a bowl and leave in the refrigerator until set.

Fried eggs *(serves 1–2)*
POWER LEVEL: 100% (FULL)

15g (½oz) butter or margarine
2 eggs

1 Melt the butter in 2 small shallow dishes or saucers. Break the eggs into the hot butter and pierce the yolks.
2 Cover and cook for 30 sec. Stand for 1 min, then turn the dishes and cook for 15–30 sec.

Baked eggs *(serves 1–2)*
POWER LEVEL: 50%

butter or margarine
2 eggs

1 Lightly grease 2 small dishes or bowls with the butter or margarine.
2 Break the eggs into the dishes and prick the yolks.
3 Cover and cook for 2–2½ min, turning the dishes once halfway through.

Note: *Baked eggs may be used in place of hardboiled eggs when required chopped for use in salads or fillings.*

Toffee mallow crunch *(makes about 20–25)*
POWER LEVEL: 100% (FULL)
colour page 42

100g (4oz) soft toffees
100g (4oz) butter
100g (4oz) marshmallows
150g (5oz) rice krispies

1 Unwrap the toffees and put them into a large mixing bowl with the butter. Cover and cook for 3 min.
2 Stir the toffee mixture and add the marshmallows. Cover and heat for another 2 min, then stir again.
3 Add half the rice krispies to the mixture and stir well, making sure all the krispies are covered with toffee. Add the rest of the krispies and stir well again.
4 Press the mixture into greased square or oblong tins or dishes and leave to cool before cutting into squares. Alternatively, make small rock shapes from spoonfuls of the mixture on trays and leave to cool and set.

DO NOT FREEZE

Swiss toast *(serves 2–4)*
POWER LEVEL: 100% (FULL)

4 slices toast
butter
4 slices cooked ham
4 slices swiss cheese
For serving:
scrambled eggs (page 39)

1 Butter the toast, put a slice of ham on each and cover with a slice of cheese.
2 Cook 2 slices together for 1–1½ min.
3 Serve with scrambled egg.

DO NOT FREEZE

Macaroni cheese *(serves 3–4)*
POWER LEVEL: 100% (FULL)

100g (4oz) macaroni
275ml (½pt) boiling water
1 × 15ml tbsp (1tbsp) oil
1 × 5ml tsp (1tsp) salt
1 small onion, chopped
pinch salt
25g (1oz) butter
25g (1oz) plain flour
425ml (¾pt) milk
1 egg yolk
75g (3oz) cheddar cheese, grated
salt and freshly ground black pepper
For garnish:
tomato, sliced

1 Place the macaroni in a large, bowl or dish. Pour over the boiling water and stir in the oil and salt. Cook for 10 min, then separate with a fork. Drain.
2 Place the onion and a pinch of salt in a bowl, cover and cook for 3 min.
3 Melt the butter in a bowl for 1 min. Blend in the flour and gradually stir in the milk. Cook for 5–6 min, stirring every minute. Beat in the egg yolk, cheese, seasoning and cooked onion.
4 Pour the sauce over the macaroni and mix well.
5 Cook for 3 min and serve immediately, garnished with the sliced tomato. Alternatively sprinkle with a little extra grated cheese and brown the top under a hot grill.

Boiled eggs *(serves 2–4)*
POWER LEVEL: 100% (FULL) OR 50%

While this recipe does not save cooking time, it is the only method by which eggs may be boiled in the microwave cooker. The timings will depend on how soft or well done the eggs are preferred.

4 eggs
boiling water

1 Wrap the eggs tightly in pieces of smooth foil to reflect the microwave energy and thus prevent the eggs from exploding.
2 Place the eggs in a bowl and just cover with boiling water.
3 Cover and cook for 2–4 min, stand for 1–2 min.
4 Drain and unwrap the eggs and serve straight away.
5 Alternatively, pierce the rounded ends of the eggs with an egg piercer or safety pin and cover with water just off the boil. Cover the dish and cook on 50% setting for 2–4 min. Stand for 1–2 min before serving.

Piperade *(serves 4)*
POWER LEVEL: 100% (FULL)

3 × 15ml tbsp (3tbsp) cooking oil
2 medium onions, peeled and finely sliced
2 cloves garlic, crushed
2 red peppers, deseeded and sliced
4 tomatoes, skinned
4 eggs
· salt and freshly ground black pepper
For serving:
triangles fried or toasted bread or
fresh bread and butter

1 Heat the oil in a large bowl or dish for 1½ min. Add the onions and garlic, cover and cook for 3 min. Add the peppers and continue to cook for 3 min.
2 Chop the tomatoes and add them to the onions and peppers. Season lightly, cover and cook for a further 3–4 min until the vegetables are tender, stirring occasionally.
3 Whisk the eggs lightly in a bowl and pour over the vegetables; stir lightly as for scrambled eggs, cover and cook for 1 min, stir then cook for a further 1–2 min. When the eggs begin to thicken, the piperade is cooked.
4 Serve immediately with triangles of fried or toasted bread, or with fresh bread and butter.

DO NOT FREEZE

Eggs en cocotte *(serves 4)*
POWER LEVEL: 50%

150ml (¼pt) double cream
salt and pepper
garlic salt
paprika
25g (1oz) butter
4 eggs
For garnish:
parsley sprigs

1 Mix the cream with the seasonings, to taste. Whip the mixture lightly until the cream is thick but not stiff.
2 Divide the butter between 4 ramekin or individual soufflé dishes and melt for 1 min. Brush the butter around the dishes and break an egg into each dish.
3 Pierce the yolk of each egg, then spoon over the cream mixture.
4 Cover and cook for 2–2½ min and stand for 1 min.
5 Sprinkle with more paprika and garnish with parsley before serving.

DO NOT FREEZE

Double deckers *(makes 6)*
POWER LEVEL: 100% (FULL)
colour photograph above

6 squares chocolate
12 digestive biscuits
6 marshmallows

1 Place the 6 squares of chocolate on top of 6 of the biscuits. Arrange in a circle on a plate or on the microwave shelf.
2 Cook for 2–2½ min, remove from the oven and spread the chocolate over the biscuits with a knife.
3 Place the 6 marshmallows on top of the remaining 6 biscuits and arrange in the microwave. Cook for ¾–1¼ min until the marshmallows have 'puffed up'.
4 To make the double deckers, put a chocolate-covered biscuit on top of each melted marshmallow. Leave to cool slightly before serving.

DO NOT FREEZE

42

Strawberry Jelly Mousse (page 40), Cheeseburgers (below), Toffee Mallow Crunch (page 40) and Double Deckers (below)

Beefburgers and cheeseburgers *(makes 4)*
POWER LEVEL: 100% (FULL)
colour photograph above

4 beefburgers
4 baps or soft round rolls
butter
3–4 × 15ml tbsp (3–4tbsp) fried onions, optional (page 98)
4 cheese slices, optional

1 Cook the beefburgers on a plate covered with a piece of kitchen paper, for 2½–3 min.
2 Cut the rolls in half and spread with butter.
3 Place the onions, beefburgers and cheese slices in the rolls and heat through for 1½–2 min.

Baked egg custard (serves 4–5)
POWER LEVEL: 100% (FULL) AND 50%

425ml (¾pt) milk
3 eggs, lightly beaten
50g (2oz) sugar
few drops vanilla essence
ground nutmeg for sprinkling

1 Heat the milk in a measuring jug or bowl for 3 min on 100% (full) setting. Add the eggs, sugar and vanilla essence and whisk lightly.
2 Strain and pour the mixture into individual bowls or ramekin dishes. Sprinkle with nutmeg and cover.
3 Arrange in a circle in the microwave and cook on 50% setting for 10–12 min, turning the dishes halfway through. If not quite set, allow an extra 1–2 min, or leave to stand.
4 Serve warm or leave to chill in the refrigerator.

DO NOT FREEZE

Spanish omelette (serves 2)
POWER LEVEL: 100% (FULL) AND 50%

100g (4oz) frozen mixed vegetables
1 cooked potato, chopped
1 tomato, chopped
1 × 15ml tbsp (1tbsp) oil
4 eggs
seasoning

1 Place the vegetables and tomato in a shallow dish with the oil. Cover and cook on 100% (full) setting for 1½–2 min.
2 Whisk the eggs and seasoning together and pour over the vegetables. Cook uncovered on 50% setting for 8 min.
3 Leave to stand for 1 min.
4 Do not fold the omelette but serve on a warm plate with a green salad.

Welsh rarebit (serves 1–2)
POWER LEVEL: 100% (FULL)

100g (4oz) cheddar cheese, grated
25g (1oz) butter
1 × 5ml tsp (1tsp) dry mustard
1 × 15ml tbsp (1tbsp) brown ale
salt and pepper
2 slices toast

1 Place the ingredients for the topping in a small bowl and cook for 20 sec. Stir well.
2 Spoon the topping on to the slices of toast and cook for 15–30 sec. Serve immediately.

DO NOT FREEZE

Eggs florentine (serves 2)
POWER LEVEL: 100% (FULL) AND 50%

450g (1lb) spinach, washed
15g (½oz) butter
salt and pepper
2 eggs
150ml (¼pt) cheese sauce (page 65)
25g (1oz) cheese, grated
paprika for sprinkling

1 Cook the spinach with just the water that clings to its leaves in a covered dish or boiling bag for 6–8 min on 100% (full) setting. Leave to stand for a few minutes. Drain well, chop roughly and stir in the butter and seasoning. Place in a dish and keep warm.
2 Poach the eggs in small dishes (page 40) on 50% setting for 1½–2 min. Leave to stand for 30 sec.
3 Drain the eggs and place them on top of the spinach. Coat with the cheese sauce and sprinkle with the grated cheese and paprika.
4 Reheat the dish on 100% (full) setting for 30–60 sec or brown the top under a hot grill.
5 Serve straight away.

DO NOT FREEZE

Flan case: rich shortcrust pastry for a
20cm (8in) flan case
POWER LEVEL: 100% (FULL)

175g (6oz) plain flour
pinch salt
75g (3oz) butter or margarine
2 × 5ml tsp (2tsp) caster sugar, optional
1 egg yolk
2 × 15 ml tbsp (2tbsp) water

1 Sift the flour with the salt and rub in the butter or margarine finely. Stir in the sugar if using.
2 Beat the egg yolk with the water and add to the flour. Mix well, then knead together lightly.
3 Chill before rolling out.

To line a flan dish
Roll out the pastry into a circle 5cm (2in) larger than the dish. Wrap the pastry loosely around the rolling pin and lift into the flan dish. Ease the pastry into shape removing any air from under the base, pressing well into the sides and taking care not to stretch the pastry. Cut the pastry away but leave 6mm (¼in) above the rim of the flan dish. Carefully ease this down into the dish, or flute the edges and leave slightly higher than the rim of the dish (this allows a little extra height to the sides of the flan case to compensate for any shrinkage during cooking). Alternatively, run the rolling

pin across the top of the flan to cut off surplus pastry. Prick the base well.

To bake blind
Using a long, smooth strip of aluminium foil measuring approximately 3.75cm (1½in) wide, line the inside, upright edge of the pastry flan case to protect this section from overcooking in the microwave. Place two pieces of absorbent kitchen paper over the base, easing around the edge and pressing gently into the corner between base and side to help keep the foil strip in position. Place in the microwave and cook on 100% (full) setting for 4–4½ min, giving the dish a quarter turn every minute. Remove the kitchen paper and foil and cook for a further 1–2 min.

Alternative conventional bake
Line the pastry flan case with a circle of lightly greased greaseproof paper (greased side down) or kitchen paper. Half fill the paper with uncooked beans, lentils, small pasta or rice which may be specially kept for this purpose. Alternatively, line the pastry flan case with foil only. Cook in a pre-heated oven at 200°C (400°F) Mark 6 for 15–20 min, until the pastry is nearly cooked. Remove the lining and bake for 5–10 min until the base is firm and dry.

Light wholewheat pastry
Half the plain flour is replaced by wholewheat flour.

Cheese pudding *(serves 4)*
POWER LEVEL: 100% (FULL)

6 medium slices brown bread
25g (1oz) butter
150ml (¼pt) milk
2 eggs, beaten
150ml (¼pt) dry white wine
salt and freshly ground black pepper
100g (4oz) cheese, grated
paprika for sprinkling

1 Lightly grease a 15–17.5cm (6–7in) soufflé dish.
2 Remove the crusts from the bread, cut into dice and place in the greased dish.
3 Add the butter to the milk and warm for 2 min. Stir until the butter is melted.
4 Beat the eggs with the butter and milk, add the wine and season well. Pour over the bread.
5 Sprinkle over the cheese and paprika.
6 Cook for 4–5 min, turning every 2 min.
7 Serve immediately.

DO NOT FREEZE

Cheese and ham au gratin *(serves 4)*
POWER LEVEL: 100% (FULL) AND 50%

25g (1oz) butter or margarine
1 medium onion, peeled and chopped
2 cloves garlic, crushed or finely chopped
100g (4oz) ham, cut into strips
2 eggs, beaten
275ml (½pt) milk
100g (4oz) emmenthal or gruyère cheese, grated
salt and freshly ground black pepper
pinch nutmeg
450g (1lb) potatoes
25g (1oz) parmesan cheese, grated
paprika for sprinkling

1 Lightly grease a shallow ovenware or au gratin dish.
2 On 100% (full) setting, melt the butter or margarine for 1 min in a bowl, add the onion and garlic, toss well in the fat and cook for 3–4 min. Add the ham and cook for 1½ min.
3 Add the egg to the milk with threequarters of the cheese, seasoning and nutmeg. Stir into the onions and ham.
4 Peel and coarsely grate the potatoes, squeeze and drain off any liquid. Add to the egg mixture. Mix well and pour into the greased dish.
5 Cover and cook on 50% setting for 18–20 min, turning every 5 min, until cooked and set.
6 Sprinkle with the remaining cheese, the parmesan cheese and paprika.
7 Cook on 100% (full) setting for 1–1½ min until the cheese is melted.
8 Serve hot with crusty french bread.

Sausage and bacon rolls *(serves 2–8)*
POWER LEVEL: 100% (FULL)

Serve as a main course with creamy mashed potatoes or as an accompaniment to poultry or game.

8 chipolata sausages
8 lean rashers bacon

1 Prick the sausages and remove the rind from the bacon. Wind the bacon around the sausages and secure each one with a wooden cocktail stick. Alternatively thread the sausage and bacon rolls onto skewers. (If metal skewers are used, they must not touch each other or the interior of the microwave.)
2 Place the rolls on a plate or suitable-sized dish and cover with kitchen paper towel. Cook for 9–10 min, turning the rolls over halfway through. Allow them to stand for 3 min before serving.

Kipper and vegetable bake (serves 2–3)
POWER LEVEL: 100% (FULL)

225g (8oz) kipper fillets
100g (4oz) mushrooms, sliced
2 courgettes, sliced
4 eggs, beaten
pepper and salt
25–50g (1–2oz) wholewheat breadcrumbs
For garnish:
tomato slices

1 Cook the kippers on a plate or in a shallow dish, covered with pierced clingfilm, for 3–4 min. Stand for a few minutes, then skin and flake the fillets.
2 In a 20cm (8in) oval or round dish, cook the mushrooms and courgettes, covered, for 5–6 min, stirring once during cooking. Stir in the flaked kippers.
3 Beat the eggs with a little pepper, adding salt only if necessary. Pour the eggs over the fish and vegetables. Cook for 4–5 min or until set, stirring after 2 min.
4 Sprinkle with the breadcrumbs and heat for a further 1–1½ min. Garnish with tomato slices before serving hot.

DO NOT FREEZE

Jacket potatoes stuffed with cheese, apple and tuna (serves 2)
POWER LEVEL: 100% (FULL)

2 large potatoes (each 225–250g/8–9oz)
1 small onion, chopped
100g (4oz) curd cheese
1 red eating apple, cored and diced
lemon juice
90g (3½oz) can tuna fish in brine, drained
sprig fresh mint, chopped
salt and paprika

1 Prepare and cook the potatoes as given on page 38.
2 Cook the onion in a small covered dish for 2–3 min until soft, stirring once. Beat the curd cheese into the onion.
3 Toss the apple in the lemon juice and add to the cheese and onion mixture. Flake the tuna fish and add it to the filling with the chopped mint. Season to taste with salt and paprika.
4 Cut the potatoes through the cross about 1.25cm (½in) and carefully open them. Pile the filling into the potatoes and reheat, uncovered, for 2–3 min. Serve immediately.

DO NOT FREEZE

Cheese and onion flan (serves 6)
POWER LEVEL: 100% (FULL) AND 60%

225g (8oz) light wholewheat pastry (page 44)
25g (1oz) butter or margarine
450g (1lb) onions, peeled and finely sliced
175g (6oz) strong cheddar cheese, grated
salt and freshly ground black pepper
paprika for sprinkling

1 Roll out the pastry, line a 20cm (8in) flan dish and bake blind (page 44). Reserve the trimmings.
2 Melt the butter in a large bowl for 1 min. Add the onions and toss well in the butter.
3 Cover and cook for 8–9 min until soft, shaking or stirring twice throughout.
4 Add the cheese to the onions with the salt and black pepper. Mix well together and place into the flan case.
5 Roll out the trimmings from the pastry and cut into thin strips. Lay the strips of pastry over the filling in a lattice style.
6 Reduce to 60% setting and cook, uncovered, for 12–15 min or until the lattice is set and cooked. Turn the dish once or twice throughout.
7 Leave to stand for a few minutes and then sprinkle with paprika.
8 Serve hot or cold as a snack or main course.

Pot meal soup (serves 2–3)
POWER LEVEL: 100% (FULL)

1 onion, chopped
1 carrot, diced
1 stick celery, chopped
4 tomatoes, skinned and chopped
550ml (1pt) boiling vegetable stock
salt and pepper
2 × 15ml tbsp (2tbsp) tomato purée
75g (3oz) lentils
100g (4oz) cooked meat, ie chicken, lamb, diced
3–4 × 15ml tbsp (3–4tbsp) grated parmesan cheese

1 Cook the onion, carrot and celery in a large covered dish for 5 min, stirring once.
2 Add the tomatoes, stock, salt and pepper and tomato purée and mix well together. Add the lentils, cover and cook for 10–15 min.
3 Stir in the cooked meat and continue to cook, uncovered, for a further 5 min.
4 Check and adjust the seasoning. Spoon into bowls or soup dishes and sprinkle with parmesan cheese before serving.

Note: *This basic recipe for a substantial soup can be varied according to ingredients available. Add extra cooked vegetables, pasta or rice as required.*

Bananas and bacon on toast (serves 2)
POWER LEVEL: 100% (FULL)

4 rashers bacon, derinded and chopped
2 slices wholewheat toast, buttered or spread with margarine
2 small bananas, thinly sliced
For garnish:
chopped parsley

1 Cook the bacon in a small dish, covered with kitchen paper, for 3–4 min.
2 Place the prepared toast on a serving plate or individual plates. Arrange the banana slices on the toast and top with the bacon.
3 Heat, uncovered, for 2½–3 min until hot through. Garnish with chopped parsley.

DO NOT FREEZE

Gammon steaks with pineapple (serves 2)
POWER LEVEL: 70% AND 100% (FULL)

2 gammon steaks, weighing about 175g (6oz) each
8 cloves, optional
2 × 5ml tsp (2tsp) brown sugar
freshly ground black pepper
200g (7oz) can pineapple rings
1 tomato, halved
2 × 5ml tsp (2tsp) cornflour
For garnish:
sprigs of watercress
For serving:
creamed potatoes (page 97)

1 Snip the fat off the gammon steaks with scissors and stick the cloves into the steaks. Place a single layer in a large shallow dish or plate.
2 Sprinkle the steaks with brown sugar and freshly ground black pepper. Drain the pineapple and pour the juice into the dish.
3 Cover and cook for 6–8 min on 70% setting, turning the dish or rearranging the steaks halfway through. Test with a skewer and if not quite tender allow another 2–3 min. Leave to stand for 3 min.
4 Place a ring of pineapple on the top of each steak and place a halved tomato into each ring. Cook, uncovered, for 2–3 min to heat through.
5 Remove the steaks from the dish with a draining spoon and place on a serving dish or platter. Blend the cornflour with a little water and stir into the juices.
6 Cook for 1–2 min on 100% (full) until thickened and boiling, stirring once halfway through. Pour the sauce over the steaks and garnish with sprigs of watercress. Serve hot with creamed potatoes.

Pork chops with apple and mace (serves 2)
POWER LEVEL: 100% (FULL) AND 70%

2 pork chops, about 175g (6oz) each
1 onion, grated
1 cooking apple, grated
salt and pepper
1 bay leaf
1 blade mace
1 × 15ml tbsp (1tbsp) dark demerara sugar

1 Preheat a browning dish on 100% (full) for 8 min. Press the chops onto the hot surface of the dish with a heatproof spatula, turn the chops over and cook in the microwave for 2 min. Leave on the browning dish to keep warm.
2 Place the grated onion and apple in a large dish with salt and pepper to taste, the herbs and sugar. Cover and cook for 3 min.
3 Add the chops to the dish and toss in the apple mixture. Cover with a lid or pierced clingfilm and cook for 6 min on 70% setting. Allow to stand for 3–4 min before serving hot.

Bacon and egg sandwich (serves 2)
POWER LEVEL: 100% (FULL) AND 50%

The sandwiches are lightly 'fried' in the browning dish.

4 rashers lean bacon, derinded
4 slices bread
butter
2 eggs

1 Place the bacon rashers on a plate, cover with kitchen paper and cook on 100% (full) setting for 2½–3 min. Allow a little longer if the bacon is preferred more crispy.
2 Preheat the browning dish for 6–8 min, depending on size.
3 Brush the slices of bread with the bacon fat or use butter. Make up the bacon sandwiches with the greased side outwards.
4 When the browning dish is preheated, quickly place the sandwiches on the hot base of the dish and press down well with a heatproof spatula to brown the first side lightly.
5 Turn the sandwiches over, press down again and place in the microwave; cook, uncovered for 1½–2 min. drain on kitchen paper towel and keep warm.
6 Place the eggs in 2 lightly buttered small dishes and prick the yolks. Cook on 50% setting for 2–2½ min, turning the dishes halfway through.
7 Top each sandwich with an egg and serve straightaway.

DO NOT FREEZE

Herb omelette *(serves 1–2)*
POWER LEVEL: 100% (FULL)

15g (½oz) butter
4 eggs
2 × 15ml tbsp (2 tbsp) milk
salt and pepper
1 × 15ml tbsp (1tbsp) mixed dried herbs

1 Melt the butter in a 20cm (8in) shallow dish for
   30 sec. Mix all the other ingredients together in
   a separate bowl.
2 Brush the melted butter around the base and
   sides of the dish. Pour in the egg mixture.
3 Cover and cook for 1 min, stir gently, cook for
   1 min. Uncover and cook for 1 min. Turn out of
   the dish and serve immediately.

Variations
Any of the following ingredients can be substi-
tuted in place of the herbs. Cook as above.

2 × 15ml tbsp (2tbsp) cheese, grated
2 × 15ml tbsp (2tbsp) cooked ham, chopped
2 × 15ml tbsp (2tbsp) cooked onion, chopped.

*Cheesy Spinach Flan (below) and Rich Fruit Cake
(page 120)*

Cheesy spinach flan *(serves 4–6)*
POWER LEVEL: 100% (FULL) AND 50%
colour photograph above

1 17.5cm (7in) baked flan case (page 43)
For the filling:
1 small onion, peeled and chopped
225g (8oz) cream cheese
2 egg yolks
225g (8oz) cooked fresh or frozen spinach, chopped
salt and pepper

1 Place the onion in a small dish, cover with
   clingfilm or a lid and cook on 100% (full) setting for 2 min.
2 Cream the cheese until soft, then add the egg
   yolks, beating well together.
3 Stir in the onion and spinach then season to taste.
4 Spoon the mixture into the precooked flan case
   and cook on 50% setting for 12–14 min until
   the filling is set.
5 Serve hot or cold.

47

Fondue *(serves 4)*
POWER LEVEL: 50%
colour page 51

1 clove garlic, crushed
100g (4oz) gruyère cheese, grated
100g (4oz) emmenthal cheese, grated
black pepper
grated nutmeg
175–225ml (6–8fl oz) dry white wine
squeeze of lemon juice
2 × 5ml tsp (2tsp) cornflour
1 liqueur glass kirsch
For serving:
crusty bread

1 Rub the garlic round the inside of a heatproof dish. Place the cheese, seasonings, wine and lemon juice in the dish.
2 Melt the cheese in the microwave for 10 min. (The cheese and wine will not combine at this stage.)
3 Blend the cornflour with the kirsch, add to the fondue, stir and cook for 6 min until slightly thickened, stirring twice.
4 Serve with crusty bread, keeping the fondue warm over a spirit lamp or dish warmer.

DO NOT FREEZE

Beef fillet florentine *(serves 2)*
POWER LEVEL: 100% (FULL)

This very simple steak dish is marinated first, cooked in the browning dish and served with lemon.

2 × 15ml tbsp (2tbsp) oil
salt and freshly ground black pepper
2 × 200g (7oz) fillet steaks, about 2.5cm (1in) thick
2 × 5ml tsp (2tsp) lemon juice
For garnish:
parsley sprigs
For serving:
lemon wedges

1 Mix together the oil and seasoning and brush over the steaks on both sides. Leave to marinate in a cool place for 2 hr.
2 Preheat a browning dish for 6–8 min depending on size. Quickly add the steaks, press down against the hot base of the dish with a heatproof spatula and then cook, uncovered, for 1½ min. Turn the steaks over and again press down against the base of the dish. Cook for a further 1–1½ min.
3 Serve straightaway sprinkled with the lemon juice. Garnish with parsley sprigs and hand the lemon wedges separately.

Cottage cheese and ham cocottes
(serves 2–4)
POWER LEVEL: 60%

oil
225g (8oz) cottage cheese
175g (6oz) cooked ham, diced
2 eggs, beaten
salt and pepper
1 × 15ml tbsp (1tbsp) chopped chives
paprika or chopped parsley
For serving:
freshly cooked spinach or a salad

1 Lightly oil 4 small ramekin dishes.
2 Beat the cottage cheese in a bowl, add the ham and eggs and mix well. Season to taste with salt and pepper and add the chopped chives.
3 Spoon the mixture into the greased ramekin dishes and cook, uncovered, for 8–10 min on 60% setting until set.
4 Sprinkle with paprika or chopped parsley and serve hot with freshly cooked spinach or a salad.

DO NOT FREEZE

Herby toad in the hole *(serves 4)*
POWER LEVEL: 100% (FULL)
OVEN TEMPERATURE: 220°C (425°F), MARK 7

The sausages are partly cooked in the microwave before being added to the batter and finally cooked in the conventional oven.

25g (1oz) lard
450g (1lb) pork sausages
100g (4oz) plain flour
pinch salt
1 egg
275ml (½pt) milk or milk and water mixed
2 × 15ml tbsp (2tbsp) chopped mixed fresh herbs or 2 × 5ml tsp (2tsp) dried mixed herbs

1 Place the lard in a 17.5 × 27.5cm (7 × 11in) shallow tin and heat in the preheated conventional oven.
2 Prick the sausages and arrange on a plate. Cook in the microwave for 5–6 min, turning the plate or rearranging the sausages halfway through.
3 Make the batter by mixing the flour and salt together; add the egg and, beating or whisking well, add the milk or milk and water. Stir in the herbs.
4 When the fat is hot pour the batter into the tin and arrange the sausages in the mixture. Cook for 35–45 min in the conventional oven until well risen and golden brown.

Beef and walnut burger *(serves 4–6)*
POWER LEVEL: 100% (FULL)
OVEN TEMPERATURE: 180°C (350°F), MARK 4

25g (1oz) butter
2 medium onions, finely chopped
2 tomatoes, skinned and finely chopped
675g (1½lb) lean braising steak, finely minced
75g (3oz) walnuts, chopped
1 × 5ml tsp (1tsp) paprika
salt and freshly ground black pepper
1–2 eggs, beaten
For garnish:
tomato slices and parsley sprigs
For serving:
jacket potatoes and coleslaw

1 Melt the butter in a large bowl in the micro-wave for 1 min. Stir in the onions, cover and cook for 5–6 min until softened.
2 Mix in the remaining ingredients and shape into a mound. Place on a greased baking tray and flatten the top slightly.
3 Cook in a preheated oven for about 1–1¼ hr until firm and well browned. Garnish with tomato slices and parsley sprigs and serve hot, cut into wedges with jacket potatoes and coleslaw.

Baked beans or spaghetti on toast *(serves 1)*
POWER LEVEL: 100% (FULL)

1 slice hot buttered toast
3–4 × 15ml tbsp (3–4 tbsp) canned baked beans or spaghetti

1 Place the toast on a plate. Add the topping.
2 Heat through uncovered for 1½–2 min. Serve immediately.

Note: *Alternatively, the topping can be heated separately in a dish or bowl for 1–1¼ min before adding to the toast.*

DO NOT FREEZE

Mushroom pudding *(serves 4)*
POWER LEVEL: 100% (FULL)

450g (1lb) button mushrooms
75g (3oz) butter
75g (3oz) fresh white breadcrumbs
1 × 15ml tbsp (1tbsp) chopped parsley
1 × 15ml tbsp (1tbsp) double cream
salt and freshly ground black pepper
2 eggs, beaten
For serving:
mushroom sauce (page 65), optional, and crusty bread and butter

1 Thinly slice 2–3 of the mushrooms to give about 8–10 even pieces. Chop the rest.
2 Melt 25g (1oz) of the butter for 1 min in a bowl or dish and add the sliced mushrooms. Cover and cook for ½–1 min until softened but not overcooked.
3 Remove the slices from the dish, drain on kitchen paper towel and reserve. Add the chopped mushrooms to the dish, toss well in the butter, cover and cook for 4–4½ min, stirring halfway through. Drain off the juices.
4 Melt the remaining butter for 1½ min and add to the chopped mushrooms with the breadcrumbs, parsley, cream and seasoning.
5 Stir well and add the beaten eggs. Place the mixture in a lightly greased 850ml (1½pt) pudding basin and cover with clingfilm slit with the point of a sharp knife.
6 Cook for 4–5 min, turning once halfway through. Allow to stand for a few minutes before inverting onto a serving platter.
7 Arrange the reserved mushroom slices around the top of the pudding and serve hot with the mushroom sauce handed separately.

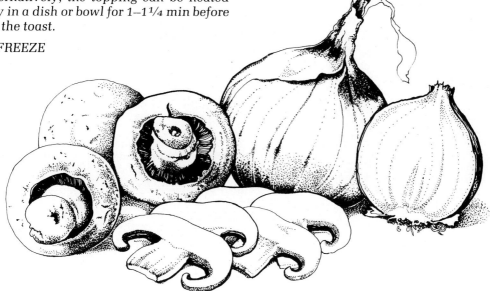

Tomatoes with cheese (serves 3–4)
POWER LEVEL: 100% (FULL)

450g (1lb) tomatoes, skinned
salt and freshly ground black pepper
1 onion, finely chopped
1 × 15ml tbsp (1tbsp) oil
75g (3oz) cheese, gruyère and parmesan mixed
3 × 15ml tbsp (3tbsp) browned breadcrumbs
slivers butter
For garnish:
1 × 15ml tbsp (1tbsp) chopped parsley

1 Slice the tomatoes and sprinkle with salt and freshly ground black pepper.
2 Mix the onion with the oil in a small bowl, cover and cook for 4 min until tender.
3 Layer the tomatoes, onion and cheese in a dish, ending with a layer of cheese. Cover and cook for 4–5 min, turning the dish halfway through.
4 Sprinkle with the browned breadcrumbs and top with slivers of butter. Cook, uncovered, for 1–1½ min until the butter has melted.
5 Sprinkle with chopped parsley before serving.

Spinach au gratin (serves 3)
POWER LEVEL: 100% (FULL) AND 60%

The dish is browned under a hot grill before serving.

900g (2lb) fresh spinach
salt and pepper
2 eggs, beaten
100g (4oz) cheddar cheese, grated
275ml (½pt) soured cream or natural yoghurt
For serving:
fresh buttered toast

1 Wash the spinach well and break off the thick stalks. Shake it dry and place in a large covered dish. Cook for 9–12 min, stirring once during cooking.
2 Drain the spinach well in a colander and chop with a metal spoon while squeezing out the water. Season well with salt and pepper and arrange in the bottom of a shallow serving dish.
3 Beat the eggs with 75g (3oz) of the grated cheese and add the soured cream or natural yoghurt, mixing well together. Pour the mixture over the spinach.
4 Cook, uncovered, for 10–12 min on 60% setting or until the topping has set. Meanwhile, cook the toast under a hot grill.
5 When the gratin topping is set, sprinkle over the remaining cheese and brown under the hot grill before serving with the toast.

DO NOT FREEZE

Soufflé rarebit (serves 2)
POWER LEVEL: 100% (FULL)

1 egg, separated
75g (3oz) cheese, finely grated
25g (1oz) butter, softened
salt and pepper
pinch dried mustard
2 thick slices toasted bread
paprika for sprinkling

1 Mix together the egg yolk, 50g (2oz) of the cheese and the butter until blended. Stir in the seasoning and mustard.
2 Whisk the egg white until stiff and fold into the cheese mixture. Pour over the slices of toast and sprinkle with the remaining cheese and paprika.
3 Cook uncovered, for 1½–2 min until hot through and lightly risen. Serve straightaway.

DO NOT FREEZE

Beef with peppers (serves 2–3)
POWER LEVEL: 100% (FULL)

This is an impressive dish, quick to prepare using left-over cooked meat, and makes a substantial supper dish.

1 onion, chopped
1 red pepper
1 green pepper
25g (1oz) flour
275ml (½pt) boiling vegetable or beef stock
350g (12oz) cooked beef, diced
salt and pepper
½ × 5ml tsp (½tsp) paprika
2 × 15ml tbsp (2tbsp) yoghurt
  or soured cream
For garnish:
paprika
For serving:
crisp lettuce or a green salad

1 Place the onion in a large casserole dish. Deseed the peppers and cut them into thin 5cm (2in) strips. Add them to the dish and cook, covered, for 5–6 min, stirring once throughout.
2 Stir the flour into the vegetables, gradually add the stock mixing well together. Cook, uncovered, for 4–5 min until boiling, stirring every minute.
3 Add the diced beef, salt and pepper to taste and the paprika. Cover the dish and heat for 5–6 min.
4 Stir in the yoghurt or soured cream and check the seasoning. Sprinkle with paprika to garnish and serve with crisp lettuce or a green salad.

Fondue (page 48) and Mulled Wine (page 37)

Scallop kebabs (serves 2)

POWER LEVEL: 100% (FULL)

The scallops are marinated for 1 hour before cooking.

5 scallops, cut into halves
3 × 15ml tbsp (3tbsp) oil
1 × 15ml tbsp (1tbsp) wine vinegar
1 × 15ml tbsp (1tbsp) lemon juice
salt and freshly ground black pepper
½ ×5ml tsp (½tsp) each paprika and dried basil
4 rashers streaky bacon
25g (1oz) butter
50g (2oz) mushrooms, chopped
50g (2oz) frozen peas, thawed
75g (3oz) long-grain rice, cooked (page 102)

For garnish:
chopped fresh parsley or dried basil

1 Place the scallops in the marinade, made by combining the oil, vinegar, lemon juice, seasonings and basil. Leave for 1 hr.
2 Derind the bacon and cut each rasher into half. Roll each half into a small bacon roll.
3 Drain the scallops and thread onto skewers, alternating each piece of fish with the bacon rolls. (If metal skewers are used, they must not touch each other or the interior of the microwave.)
4 Place the skewers into the microwave and cook, uncovered, for 4½–5½ min. Cover and allow to stand for 5 min.
5 Melt the butter for 1 min, add the mushrooms and peas and cook for 3 min. Stir in the rice and cook for a further 2 min, stirring after 1 min.
6 Place the rice on a serving plate and arrange the kebabs on top. sprinkle with the herbs and serve straightaway.

Cheese and apple toasties *(serves 2–4)*
POWER LEVEL: 70%

3 dessert apples
½ lemon, juice
175g (6oz) cheddar cheese, grated
1 × 15ml tbsp (1tbsp) natural yoghurt
1 × 15ml tbsp (1tbsp) peanut butter
1 × 15ml tbsp (1tbsp) chopped parsley
salt and pepper
4 slices freshly cooked toast
For garnish:
watercress

1 Core one of the apples and slice it into 4 rings. Brush the rings with the lemon juice. Grate the remaining two apples.
2 Mix together the grated apples, cheese, yoghurt, peanut butter, parsley and salt and pepper. Spread the mixture on the freshly made toast.
3 Place the toasties on a serving plate and cook for 3–4 min on 70% setting until the cheese is melted.
4 Garnish each slice with an apple ring and watercress, and serve immediately.

DO NOT FREEZE

Vienna roll *(serves 2–3)*
POWER LEVEL: 100% (FULL)

1 small vienna loaf
8 lean bacon rashers, derinded and chopped
75g (3oz) butter
100g (4oz) mushrooms, chopped
1 green pepper, deseeded and diced
8–10 stuffed olives, sliced
1 clove garlic, crushed
salt and freshly ground black pepper

1 Cut the loaf lengthways through the centre. Leaving a 1.25cm (½in) crust, carefully remove and crumb the soft bread.
2 Cook the bacon for 5–6 min until crisp, stirring once halfway through. Add the breadcrumbs, 25g (1oz) of the butter and the remaining ingredients. Cover and cook for 3 min.
3 Butter the inside of the loaf with the remaining butter and fill with the bacon mixture.
4 Place the loaf on kitchen paper towel and then directly on to the oven shelf or a plate. Cook, uncovered, for about 3 min until heated through. Serve hot cut into slices.

Leek and ham rolls *(serves 2 or 4)*
POWER LEVEL: 100% (FULL)

450g (1lb) leeks, washed and trimmed
2 × 15ml tbsp (2tbsp) salted water
4 large, thin slices of ham
275ml (½pt) cheese sauce (page 65)
3 × 15ml tbsp (3tbsp) grated cheese
paprika for sprinkling

1 Cut the leeks in half lengthways, or if they are very large, cut into quarters.
2 Place the leek halves or quarters in a casserole dish with the salted water. Cover and cook for 7–10 min until tender. Drain well.
3 Keeping the leeks in strips, divide between the slices of ham. Roll up each slice and place back in the dish.
4 Cover and cook for 2 min until the ham is heated through.
5 Heat the cheese sauce, if necessary, and pour over the rolls.
6 Sprinkle with the grated cheese and paprika and cook uncovered for 2–3 min until the cheese is melted. Alternatively, brown under a hot grill.

Haddock with bacon *(serves 2)*
POWER LEVEL: 100% (FULL)

This makes a substantial breakfast, lunch or supper dish. .

2 medium-sized smoked haddock
4 rashers lean bacon
butter
freshly ground black pepper

1 Rinse the haddock well in cold water and place in a large shallow dish. Cover and cook for 6–8 min, turning each haddock halfway through the cooking time. Leave to stand covered, for 5 min.
2 Remove the rinds from the bacon and place in a single layer on a plate or dish. Cover with kitchen paper towel and cook for about 3 min, allowing an extra ½–1 min if the bacon is preferred more crispy. Drain well on kitchen paper towel.
3 Uncover the haddock, drain well and place on to serving plates. Add a knob of butter to each fish and sprinkle with ground black pepper.
4 Place the bacon rashers on top of the haddock and serve hot.

Starters

The recipes in this section include a variety of appetising hot and cold dishes. They make excellent starters to a meal but some may also be used for snacks or supper dishes. Most of them can be prepared in advance and refrigerated until required; those to be served hot can be quickly reheated when you and your guests are ready.

●GUIDELINES AT-A-GLANCE

●**Advance** preparation and cooking is ideal when entertaining and with a little careful thought and planning many starters can be prepared beforehand, leaving the cook ample time to get the rest of the meal together.

●**Cover** dishes with lids or clingfilm to prevent drying out and store in the refrigerator until required. If food is to be served hot it can be quickly reheated in the microwave when you and your guests are ready. Remember to pierce clingfilm covering before reheating.

●**Defrost** any frozen starters in advance using a 30 or 50% power setting and then refrigerate until required.

●**Pastry** items such as cooked quiches should be placed on, or covered with, kitchen paper towel to absorb moisture when reheating. This will help prevent the pastry from becoming soggy although a few minutes in a warm hotcupboard or left to stand in a warm room will help pastry to retain crispness. Puff or flaky pastry items are best freshly cooked or reheated conventionally.

●**Refrigerated** starters which have been prepared and cooked in advance should be removed from the refrigerator and allowed to come up to room temperature if to be served cold rather than chilled.

●**Reheat** starters to serving temperature when required. If heating a number of individual servings a few at a time, pop the first ones back in the microwave for a few seconds to boost the serving temperature. The power level setting required depends on the food type and quantity.

●**Sauces** are best prepared and reheated separately when cooked in advance if to be used to coat a main ingredient such as a vegetable or fish. This will ensure that a skin does not form over the sauce when it is not possible to stir the food – an au gratin dish for example. Finish and garnish the dish just before serving.

●**Undercook** food slightly for dishes which are to be served hot to ensure food does not overcook when reheating before serving.

Quick kipper pâté (serves 4)
POWER LEVEL: 100% (FULL)

1 × 175g (6oz) pkt frozen kipper fillets
100ml (4fl oz) natural yoghurt
1 small onion, chopped
salt and pepper
squeeze lemon juice
1 × 15ml tbsp (1tbsp) chopped parsley
For garnish:
parsley sprigs
For serving:
buttered toast

1 Slit the kipper bag. Heat the kippers for 2 min, stand for 5 min.
2 Cook the kippers for 3 min. Skin the fillets and flake the fish. Place in a liquidiser goblet or food processor. Blend until well mixed.
3 Cook the onion in a small, covered dish for 1½–2 min, then add to the kipper mixture. Add the other ingredients, seasoning to taste.
4 Pack the mixture into a serving dish and garnish with parsley. Cover and chill in the refrigerator for at least an hour before serving. Serve with hot buttered toast.

DO NOT FREEZE

Potted shrimps *(serves 4)*
POWER LEVEL: 100% (FULL)

225g (8oz) frozen shrimps (or prawns), thawed
225g (8oz) unsalted or clarified butter
½ × 5ml tsp (½tsp) dried basil
pepper to taste
For garnish:
parsley sprigs and lemon slices

1 Put the shrimps in a bowl, cover and heat in the microwave for 30 sec. Stand for 1 min, then heat for 1 min.
2 Place about 150g (5oz) of butter in a bowl and melt for 3 min. Liquidise or blend the shrimps, melted butter and seasonings to give a smooth paste.
3 Press mixture firmly into a small dish and chill for ½ hr.
4 Melt the remaining butter for 2 min. Smooth the top of the shrimp mixture and pour over the butter. Cover and leave to chill in the refrigerator.
5 Serve garnished with parsley sprigs and lemon slices.

DO NOT FREEZE

Globe Artichokes (above) with Hollandaise Sauce (page 68)

Artichokes with vinaigrette dressing
(serves 4)
POWER LEVEL: 100% (FULL)

An excellent starter when you have time to linger over a meal.

4 medium globe artichokes
150ml (¼pt) salted water
2 × 15ml tbsp (2tbsp) lemon juice
For the vinaigrette dressing:
150ml (¼pt) oil
3 × 15ml tbsp (3tbsp) wine vinegar
salt and freshly ground black pepper
1 × 15ml tbsp (1tbsp) chopped fresh herbs

1 Wash the artichokes and trim off the lower leaves if necessary.
2 Place in a large roasting bag or covered casserole dish with the salted water and lemon juice. Cook for 15–20 min, turning the dish or rearranging the artichokes twice throughout. Test whether cooked by removing one of the leaves – it should pull away quite easily. Drain and leave to cool.
3 Blend the oil, vinegar and seasoning by whisking together in a bowl or placing in a screw-top jar and shaking vigorously. Alternatively, blend in a liquidiser. Beat in the chopped herbs.

Melon with Port Jelly (below)

4 Serve the artichokes on individual dishes or plates, pour over a little dressing and hand the rest separately.

Note: *The artichokes may also be served hot with hollandaise sauce (page 68) or with melted butter.*

DO NOT FREEZE THE VINAIGRETTE DRESSING

Melon with port jelly *(serves 4)*
POWER LEVEL(100% (FULL)
colour photograph above

A really delicious, refreshing but simple starter.

1 lemon table jelly to make 550ml (1pt)
150ml (¼pt) water
1 lemon, thinly pared rind and squeeze of juice
2.5cm (1in) cinnamon stick
275ml (½pt) port, approximately
2 small melons
For serving: crushed ice and mint or lemon

1 Break up the table jelly into a bowl or measuring jug. Add the water, lemon rind and juice and the cinnamon stick. Stir well.
2 Heat for about 1–1½ min, then stir until the jelly cubes are dissolved. Make up to 550ml (1pt) with the port and allow to cool.
3 Cut the melons in half, and remove a thin slice of the peel from the base of each half so that it will stand firm. Remove the seeds.
4 When the jelly is nearly cold, strain through a sieve and divide between the four halves of melon. Refrigerate until the jellies are set.
5 Serve on beds of crushed ice on individual serving plates or dishes. Garnish with sprigs of mint or lemon twists.

Note: *If there is any jelly left over, allow it to set, chop finely,and pile it up in the centre of the melon halves.*

DO NOT FREEZE

Courgettes maison (serves 4 or 8)
POWER LEVEL: 100% (FULL) AND 50%
colour page 38

8 small courgettes, trimmed and washed
25g (1oz) butter
1 onion, finely chopped
4 tomatoes, skinned
1 × 5ml tsp (1tsp) paprika
salt and freshly ground black pepper
225g (8oz) shelled prawns
275ml (½pt) béchamel sauce (page 65)
50g (2oz) parmesan cheese, grated
paprika for sprinkling

1 Place the courgettes in a large dish, cover and cook on 100% (full) setting for 4–5 min. Rinse in cold water.
2 Cutting lengthways, remove a thin slice from the top of each courgette. Discard the slices. Scoop out the flesh from each courgette and chop finely.
3 Melt the butter in a bowl for 1 min on 100% (full) setting. Add the onion, cover and cook for a further 2 min.
4 Remove the seeds from the tomatoes, chop the flesh and add to the onions with the flesh from the courgettes, paprika and seasonings. Cover and cook on 100% (full) setting for 3 min.
5 Stir the prawns into the mixture and divide between the courgette cases.
6 Cover the dish and cook on 100% (full) setting for a further 3–5 min.
7 Mix the béchamel sauce with half the cheese and spoon over the courgettes. Sprinkle the remaining cheese and paprika over the top of the sauce.
8 Cook, uncovered, for 5 min on 50% setting until heated through.

FREEZE THE SAUCE SEPARATELY. FINISH AND GARNISH JUST BEFORE SERVING

Creamy haddock and sweetcorn (serves 4)
POWER LEVEL: 100% (FULL)
colour page 38

450g (1lb) potatoes, creamed (page 97)
knob butter
1 × 15ml tbsp (1tbsp) chopped parsley
20g (¾oz) butter
20g (¾oz) plain flour
175ml (6fl oz) milk
225g (8oz) haddock, cooked and flaked
50g (2oz) frozen sweetcorn
salt and pepper
2 × 15ml tbsp (2tbsp) single cream
paprika for sprinkling

1 Cook and mash the potatoes. Mix in a large knob of butter and the parsley. Using a large rosette pipe, pipe a border of potato onto 4 scallop shells.
2 Place butter, flour and milk in a bowl. Cook for 1 min, beat thoroughly, cook for 1 min. Repeat this operation until the sauce thickens (about 3 times).
3 Add the fish and corn to the sauce and season to taste. Cook for 1 min, stir, cook for 1 min. Add the cream, adjust the seasoning and spoon the mixture into the scallop shells.
4 Heat the scallops for 4–5 min. Sprinkle with paprika and serve immediately.

DO NOT FREEZE

Baked avocados with walnut cheese
(serves 4)
POWER LEVEL: 100% (FULL)
colour page 87

This is an unusual way of serving avocado pears as a starter and makes a change from the normal 'vinaigrette' or 'with prawns'.

2 avocado pears, ripe
few drops lemon juice
50g (2oz) butter
100g (4oz) cream cheese
50g (2oz) walnuts
freshly ground black pepper
For serving:
lemon wedges

1 Cut the avocados in half, remove the stones and sprinkle each half with a little lemon juice.
2 Place the avocado halves in a microwave dish with the narrow ends towards the centre. Cover with a lid or clingfilm slit with the pointed end of a sharp knife.
3 Place in the microwave and cook for 5–7 min until soft, depending on the ripeness of the pears. Allow to stand for a few minutes. (The avocado flesh will darken slightly during the cooking process).
4 Meanwhile, cream the butter and cheese together until light. Reserving 4 walnut halves, chop the remainder very finely and mix into the creamed butter and cheese. Add freshly ground black pepper to taste.
5 Uncover the avocados and divide the walnut and cheese mixture between the 4 halves. Heat for 1 min – just long enough to warm the topping.
6 Add a walnut half to each avocado and serve hot with lemon wedges.

DO NOT FREEZE

Chinese cucumber starter (serves 4)
POWER LEVEL: 100% (FULL)
colour page 67

1 large cucumber, washed
40g (1½oz) butter
100g (4oz) button mushrooms, washed
1 × 5ml tsp (1tsp) cornflour
75ml (2½fl oz) chicken stock
75ml (2½fl oz) single cream
few drops soy sauce
100g (4oz) shelled prawns
For garnish:
freshly chopped chives or dill
lemon or cucumber twists

1 Cut the cucumber into 1.25cm (½in) dice, place in a dish, cover and cook for 3 min. Drain.
2 Melt the butter in a bowl for 1–1½ min, add the mushrooms, cover and cook for 2 min. Add the cucumber and cook for 3 min until the vegetables are tender but crisp.
3 Blend the cornflour with the stock, add the cream and soy sauce. Pour over the vegetables and heat for 1–2 min. Stir in the prawns and continue to heat for 1–2 min.
4 Divide the mixture between 4 individual serving dishes and garnish with the chopped herbs and lemon or cucumber twists.
5 Serve hot.

Note: *Tiny, button mushrooms are best but if the mushrooms are large, cut them into slices before cooking.*

DO NOT FREEZE

Hot cinnamon grapefruit (serves 2)
POWER LEVEL: 100% (FULL)

1 large grapefruit
pinch cinnamon
25g (1oz) demerara sugar
2 × 15ml tbsp (2tbsp) sherry or rum, optional
1 glacé cherry

1 Halve the grapefruit, remove the pips and loosen around the flesh of the fruit. Place each half grapefruit in an individual bowl.
2 Mix the cinnamon and sugar together. If using the sherry or rum, pour 1 × 15ml tbsp (1tbsp) over each half grapefruit, then sprinkle with the sugar mixture. Place half a glacé cherry in the centre of each half grapefruit.
3 Heat the grapefruit halves in the microwave for 1–1½ min, turn, heat for 1–1½ min. Serve immediately.

DO NOT FREEZE

Mushrooms à la grecque (serves 6)
POWER LEVEL: 100% (FULL)
colour page 38

2 × 15ml tbsp (2tbsp) olive oil
1 small onion, peeled and finely chopped
1 clove garlic, crushed
450g (1lb) button mushrooms, sliced
4 tomatoes, skinned and deseeded
salt and freshly ground black pepper
1 × 15ml tbsp (1tbsp) tomato purée
1 wine glass white wine
2 × 15ml tbsp (2tbsp) chopped parsley

1 Place the oil in a large serving dish with the onion and garlic. Cover and cook for 2 min.
2 Add the mushrooms, tomatoes, salt and freshly ground black pepper, cover and cook for 3 min.
3 Blend the tomato purée and wine together and add to the mushrooms. Stir, cover and cook for 2½ min.
4 Stir half the parsley into the dish and allow to cool, then chill for 2 hr.
5 Serve cold, sprinkled with the rest of the parsley.

Miniature meatballs (makes about 40)
POWER LEVEL: 100% (FULL)
colour page 38

100g (4oz) butter, softened
1 × 15ml tbsp (1tbsp) onion, finely chopped
3 cloves garlic, finely chopped
2 × 15ml tbsp (2tbsp) chopped parsley
pinch pepper
1 onion, finely chopped
450g (1lb) minced beef
50g (2oz) breadcrumbs
salt and pepper
1 egg, beaten
1 × 15ml tbsp (1tbsp) tomato purée
1 × 5ml tsp (1tsp) worcestershire sauce
For garnish:
chopped parsley

1 Prepare garlic butter by blending the first five ingredients thoroughly. Cover and chill until hard.
2 Place the onion in a large bowl and cook for 1½ min. Add the other ingredients and mix thoroughly.
3 Shape about 1 × 15ml tbsp (1 tbsp) meat mixture around ¼ × 5ml tsp ¼tsp) of garlic butter, sealing in the butter completely.
4 Place the meatballs in a single layer in the serving dish 12–18 at a time. Cook uncovered for 3 min, turn the dish, cook for 2 min.
5 Garnish with extra chopped parsley, before serving.

Tomato and Mushroom Crumble (page 97) and Baked Stuffed Tomatoes (below)

Baked stuffed tomatoes *(serves 6)*
POWER LEVEL: 100% (FULL)
colour photograph above

12 large, firm tomatoes
40g (1½oz) butter or margarine
1 onion, peeled and finely chopped
175g (6oz) cooked meat, minced
100g (4oz) cooked rice
1 × 15ml tbsp (1tbsp) single cream or top of the milk
2 × 5ml tsp (2tsp) worcestershire sauce
2 × 15ml tbsp (2tbsp) chopped parsley
salt and freshly ground black pepper
50g (2oz) cheese, grated
1 × 15ml tbsp (1tbsp) fresh breadcrumbs
For garnish:
parsley sprigs

1 Cut a thin slice from the top of each tomato and scoop out the flesh.
2 Melt the butter or margarine in a bowl for 1½ min, toss in the onion and cook for 3–4 min.
3 Stir in the meat, rice, cream or top of the milk, worcestershire sauce and the chopped parsley. Season to taste.
4 Fill the tomato cases with the meat mixture and place in a shallow, round serving dish.
5 Cover and cook for 4–5 min until heated through.
6 Mix together the cheese and breadcrumbs and sprinkle over the top of the tomatoes. Cook uncovered for 1½–2 min until the cheese has melted.
7 Serve hot, garnished with parsley sprigs.

Liver pâté *(serves 8–12)*
POWER LEVEL: 50%
colour page 30

350g (12oz) lamb's liver
50g (2oz) chicken livers
1 slice bread
1 small onion, peeled
100g (4oz) pork fat
½ × 5ml tsp (½tsp) garlic salt
½ × 5ml tsp (½tsp) ground black pepper
1 × 5ml tsp (1tsp) mixed herbs
1 × 5ml tsp (1tsp) lemon juice
1 egg
75ml (3fl oz) red wine
For garnish:
gherkin, tomato, juniper berries or olives
For serving:
hot toast

1 Mince the livers, bread, onion and pork fat. Stir in all the other ingredients.
2 Grease a suitable deep round dish. Pile the pâté mixture into the dish and press down firmly.
3 Cover and cook on 50% setting for 10 min, stand for 5 min, cook for 5 min. Allow to cool slightly, then cover and place weights on top of the pâté. Leave in the refrigerator overnight.
4 Turn out and garnish before serving with hot toast.

Soups

Whether used as a starter to a meal or as a snack, home-made soups are always welcome and when prepared with a good stock are particularly nourishing and full of flavour. A soup can be served cold or chilled in the summer, or hot on a cold winter's day and, whether home-made or commercially prepared, when heated in the microwave it will retain its full flavour and colour.

Home-made soups can be made in advance and, if preferred, frozen in individual portions. If frozen in larger quantities, the soup should be broken down and stirred frequently during the defrosting process so that the outside liquid does not overheat before the centre portion is thawed. When reheating soups, ensure that the dish or bowl is covered for faster results and is large enough to allow for the expansion of the liquid; this is particularly important when heating milk based soups.

Soups can be heated on 100% (full) as follows:

Individual bowls or mugs	Large bowls or jugs
1 3 min	550ml (1pt) 5–7 min
2 4–5½ min	675ml (1½pt) 8–9 min
3 7–8 min	1.1 litre (2pt) 10–12 min
4 9–10 min	

Canned condensed soups
Add hot water and whisk thoroughly before heating in a large jug or dish or soup tureen. The 275g (10oz) size will take 6–7 min on 100% (full) to come to boiling point but do not allow to overheat. Stir thoroughly halfway through the cooking time and whisk well before serving.

Packet soups
Empty the packet of soup mix into a large bowl or jug and gradually stir in the amount of water recommended on the packet. Stir well, cover the bowl or jug and bring to the boil in the microwave. This will take 8–10 min on 100% (full) setting depending on the quantity of soup. Cook for 1–2 min, stir or whisk well and leave to stand for 2-3 min before serving with a knob of butter or a spoonful of cream as preferred.

●GUIDELINES AT-A-GLANCE

●**Boil-overs** occur if the container is not large enough to allow for the expansion of the liquid, particularly with milk-based soups. As a general guideline, ensure the container is twice the capacity of the soup.

●**Boiling stock** or water added to the basic ingredients will cut down on the overall cooking time.

●**Containers** should be large enough to allow for stirring as well for the expansion of liquids when defrosting, cooking and reheating soups. Jugs or bowls with pouring lips are ideal for serving when heating or cooking larger quantities.

●**Cooking** times and power levels will depend on quantity and types of food used in the soup, although most soups can be cooked using 100% (full) setting.

●**Cover** dishes with pierced clingfilm or a lid to quicken cooking times. A lid is preferable to clingfilm when cooking or reheating cream soups as more frequent stirring is required.

●**Cream soups** and those thickened with cream and/or egg yolks should be defrosted and reheated using a 50–70% power level to ensure that no separation or curdling of the liquid occurs. Do not allow cream soups to boil.

●**Defrosting** can be carried out on 100% (full) setting for most soups. The exception to this is cream soups (see above).

●**Food processors** and blenders are ideal for puréeing soups at the end of the cooking time. Thickenings added to the soup at this stage while puréeing will lessen the amount of stirring required when reheating to thicken.

●**Heating** most prepared soups can be carried out using a 100% (full) setting. The exception to this is cream soups (see above).

●**Individual servings** in bowls or mugs can be heated in the microwave without covering, but stir well before serving.

●**Separation** in the liquid may occur with some soups during defrosting and reheating. This can usually be corrected by whisking thoroughly at intervals during the heating process.

- **Stir** occasionally when reheating and cooking to ensure even results are obtained. Cream soups will require more frequent stirring to ensure the outside edges of the soup do not overheat and start to boil before the centre is heated through.

- **Temperature probes** can be used when heating soups; the temperature should be 75–80°C (167–175°F).

- **Thickenings** may be added to the soup at the end of the cooking period. Stir or whisk well or add if appropriate when puréeing in a food processor or blender (see above). Continue to stir or whisk frequently during the final heating time until thickened.

Chilled avocado soup *(serves 4)*
POWER LEVEL: 100% (FULL)

Serve as a first course for a special luncheon menu.

15g (½oz) butter
1 small onion, peeled and finely chopped
1 large avocado pear, ripe
1 × 15ml tbsp (1tbsp) lemon juice
150ml (¼pt) chicken stock
150ml (¼pt) milk
150ml (¼pt) double cream
salt and freshly ground black pepper
a little green food colouring, optional

1 Melt the butter in a large dish for 30 sec. Add the onion, cover and cook for 3 min until soft.
2 Halve the avocado pear, remove the stone and scoop out the flesh with a spoon. Add to the onion with the lemon juice and mix together until blended.
3 Add chicken stock, milk and half the cream. Purée in a liquidiser or blender or pass through a sieve. Add seasoning and the colouring if desired.
4 Chill thoroughly and just before serving swirl in the remainder of the double cream.
5 Serve with melba toast.

DO NOT FREEZE

French onion soup *(serves 4)*
POWER LEVEL: 100% (FULL)

50g (2oz) butter
450g (1lb) onions, peeled and thinly sliced
25g (1oz) flour
salt and freshly ground black pepper
1 × 5ml tsp (1tsp) sugar
550ml (1pt) boiling beef stock

For serving:
4 slices french bread, toasted
grated cheese

1 Heat the butter in a large, shallow serving dish for 2 min. Toss the onion in the butter and cook for 5 min.
2 Add the flour and mix into the butter and onion. Add salt and pepper and sugar.
3 Add the stock gradually, mix well together. Cover and cook for 25 min.
4 Place the toasted bread on top of the soup and sprinkle with the grated cheese.
5 Heat in the microwave for 2–3 min until the cheese is melted, or alternatively brown the cheese under a hot grill.
6 Serve immediately.

Note: *For a 'special' soup, 2 × 15ml tbsp (2 tbsp) brandy may be added to the cooked soup before garnishing with the toast and cheese.*

DO NOT FREEZE WITH THE TOAST

Cream of turnip soup *(serves 6)*
POWER LEVEL: 100% (FULL)

Use early turnips for this delicious vegetable soup.

50g (2oz) butter
350g (12oz) young turnips, peeled and diced
225g (8oz) potatoes, peeled and diced
1 leek, trimmed, washed and chopped
1 onion, peeled and chopped
25g (1oz) flour
2l (3½pt) boiling chicken or vegetable stock
salt and freshly ground black pepper
2 egg yolks
2 × 15ml tbsp (3tbsp) double cream
For garnish:
croûtons (page 30)

1 Melt the butter in a large bowl for 1½–2 min. Add all the vegetables, toss well in the butter. Cover and cook for 12–15 min, shaking or stirring every 5 min.
2 Stir in the flour and blend in the boiling stock. Season to taste.
3 Cook for 15–20 min until the vegetables are tender. Purée the soup in a blender or food processor or pass through a sieve.
4 Beat the egg yolks with the cream, add a little of the soup and stir until well blended. Add this to the soup and mix well. Adjust seasoning.
5 Heat without boiling. Serve hot, garnished with croûtons or hand them separately.

DO NOT FREEZE

Celery and pea soup (serves 4–6)
POWER LEVEL: 100% (FULL)

1 onion, peeled and chopped
½ head celery, trimmed and roughly chopped
225g (8oz) frozen peas
550ml (1pt) boiling chicken stock
salt and pepper
1 bay leaf
bouquet garni
1 × 15ml tbsp (1tbsp) cornflour
150ml (¼pt) milk
150ml (¼pt) single cream
For garnish:
freshly chopped parsley

1 Place the onion, celery, peas and stock into a large casserole dish or bowl. Add salt and pepper, bay leaf and bouquet garni.
2 Cover and cook for 12–15 min until the vegetables are tender.
3 Remove bay leaf and bouquet garni. Purée the soup in a blender or food processor or pass through a sieve.
4 Blend the cornflour with the milk and then add to the soup in the bowl. Heat for 3–4 min or until slightly thickened and boiling.
5 Stir in the cream to give a swirled effect and serve sprinkled with chopped parsley.

Minestrone soup (serves 4–6)
POWER LEVEL: 100% (FULL)
colour page 38

25g (1oz) butter
1 carrot, peeled and diced
1 onion, peeled and finely chopped
1 small leek, finely sliced
1 stick celery, finely chopped
1 clove garlic, finely chopped
550ml (1pt) boiling chicken stock
15g (½oz) long-grain rice
salt and pepper
225g (8oz) tomatoes, skinned and chopped
2 × 15ml tbsp (2tbsp) baked beans
For garnish:
1 × 5ml tsp (1tsp) chopped parsley
For serving:
grated parmesan cheese

1 Melt the butter in a large bowl for 1 min. Add the carrot, onion, leek, celery and garlic. Toss well in the butter, cover and cook for 3 min.
2 Add boiling stock, rice and seasoning. Cover and cook for 5–6 min, stirring once halfway through.
3 Add the tomatoes and baked beans and continue to cook, covered, for a further 5–6 min.

4 Sprinkle with parsley and serve with grated parmesan cheese.

Borsch (serves 4–6)
POWER LEVEL: 100% (FULL)

This beetroot soup can be served hot or cold, with soured cream swirled over the top to give a good colour contrast.

1 onion, peeled and finely chopped
1 large carrot, peeled and finely chopped
2–3 parsley sprigs
1 bay leaf
salt and freshly ground black pepper
1l (1¾pt) boiling chicken stock
450g (1lb) cooked beetroot, chopped
150ml (¼pt) soured cream
For garnish:
chopped chives or mint

1 Place the onion, carrot, herbs, seasoning and boiling stock in a large serving dish. Cover and cook for 5 min.
2 Add the beetroot and cook for 10 min.
3 Purée the soup in a blender or food processor, then strain through a sieve into the serving dish.
4 Wipe the edges of the dish, stir in the soured cream and serve hot. If serving cold, chill in the refrigerator and stir in the cream just before serving.
5 Serve sprinkled with chopped chives or mint.

DO NOT FREEZE

Lentil and ham soup (serves 4–6)
POWER LEVEL: 100% (FULL)

1 large onion, chopped
2 sticks celery, sliced
1 large carrot, chopped
2–3 × 15ml (2–3 tbsp) oil
100g (4oz) lentils
825ml (1½pt) boiling vegetable stock
salt and pepper
1 bay leaf
100g (4oz) cooked ham, diced
1 × 15ml tbsp (1tbsp) chopped parsley

1 Cook the onion, celery and carrot with the oil in a large covered dish for 6–8 min, stirring once.
2 Add the lentils, stock and seasoning. Add the bay leaf, cover and cook for 15–20 min until the lentils are tender and have thickened the soup.
3 Stir in the ham and continue to cook for a further 2–3 min. Adjust the seasoning, stir in the parsley and serve hot.

Greek Lemon Soup (below) and Stuffed Cabbage Leaves (page 96)

Vichyssoise soup *(serves 4)*
POWER LEVEL 100% (FULL)

675g (1½lb) leeks, washed and trimmed
225g (8oz) potatoes, peeled
40g (1½oz) butter
1 stick celery, finely sliced
550ml (1pt) boiling chicken stock
salt and pepper
550ml (1pt) milk
275ml (½pt) double cream
freshly grated nutmeg

1 Slice the leeks finely and cut the potatoes into small dice.
2 Melt the butter for 1½ min, add the leeks, potatoes and celery. Mix well together, cover and cook for 5–6 min.
3 Pour on the boiling chicken stock, add salt and pepper. Cover and cook for 12–14 min, until the vegetables are tender.
4 Purée the mixture in a blender or food processor or pass through a sieve.
5 Add the milk, cover and cook for 5–6 min until heated through.

6 Cool, check seasoning and stir in the cream.
7 Serve chilled, sprinkled with freshly grated nutmeg.

Greek lemon soup *(serves 4)*
POWER LEVEL: 100% (FULL)
colour photograph above

1l (1¾pt) jellied chicken stock
4 × 15ml tbsp (4tbsp) cooked rice
2 eggs
1 lemon, grated rind and juice
salt and freshly ground black pepper
For garnish:
a little finely grated lemon rind

1 Heat the chicken stock in a large bowl until boiling, about 8–10 min. Add the rice.
2 Beat the eggs, with the lemon rind and juice and seasoning.
3 Add a little of the hot stock to the eggs, beating well until smooth and then pour the mixture back into the stock, stirring continuously.
4 Heat without boiling for approximately 2–3 min, whisking every 15 sec to incorporate the egg mixture thoroughly into the stock.
5 Adjust seasoning and serve hot sprinkled with a little finely grated lemon rind.

Sauces

At first glance you may think that it is hardly worth cooking sauces in the microwave as the time saved is negligible. However, providing the mixture is stirred at intervals during the heating stage, the result is a very smooth sauce and the advantage is that other ingredients can be added for heating or cooking during or after the sauce has cooked, and of course there will be only one dish or bowl to wash.

When heating dishes which have a sauce as part of the main ingredient, ie au gratin dishes, always use a lower 50–70% setting otherwise the sauce will be bubbling and overcooking before the rest of the food is heated through.

•GUIDELINES AT-A-GLANCE

•**Advance** preparation and cooking of most sauces can be carried out. Place into sauce jugs or boats (suitable for microwave use) and cover until required. Reheat in the microwave and stir well before serving.

•**Au gratin** dishes and other dishes which use a sauce as part of the main ingredient should be defrosted using a 30% setting and reheated on 50–70% setting to ensure the sauce does not overheat and bubble too quickly before the main ingredient has heated through.

•**Boil-overs** can occur if the container is not large enough to allow for the expansion of the liquid when heating, particularly with milk-based sauces. As a general guideline ensure the container is twice the capacity of the sauce.

•**Butter and margarine** melt very quickly and can sometimes spatter when melting at 100% (full) setting. A lower power setting will overcome this or cover the dish with a lid or plate to prevent splashing onto the oven interior.

•**Containers** such as jugs or bowls with curved corners will make stirring and whisking easier during cooking. Remember to have a container large enough to allow for expansion of liquid.

•**Cooking** traditional white sauces or fruit or vegetable based sauces is usually carried out at 100% (full), stirring frequently throughout. Meat and curry sauces should be reduced to a 30–50% setting to allow food flavours to blend during a longer cooking time. Egg custard sauces should be cooked using 50% setting and must not be allowed to boil otherwise curdling may occur.

•**Cover** with a lid or pierced clingfilm for longer cooking time but quick sauces which require frequent whisking or stirring may be left uncovered. Sauces which are prepared in advance should be covered until required.

•**Defrosting** power level is dependent on the type of sauce. Most sauces (suitable for freezing) can be started off on 100% (full) to commence the thawing process and then reduced to 50–70% setting to ensure an even result. Break down lumps as soon as possible and stir occasionally.

•**Flour** should be blended thoroughly with the butter (then called the roux) before adding milk or liquid gradually, beating well after each addition.

•**Food processors** and blenders are ideal for puréeing fruit or vegetable sauces. They are also useful for correcting a lumpy sauce should this occur.

•**Heating** most sauces which have been prepared in advance can be carried out using 100% (full), stirring well before serving. Delicate sauces such as hollandaise should be heated for 5–10 sec only at a time and then beaten well. Egg sauces and those which form part of a composite dish should be heated on a 50–70% setting.

•**Lumpy** sauces should not happen if the roux and liquid ingredients have been blended together sufficiently before cooking and the sauce has been beaten or whisked every 30–60 sec during the cooking period. If lumpiness does occur, rub the sauce through a sieve or purée in a food processor or blender.

- **One stage** white sauces may be started off on a 30 or 50% power setting to warm the ingredients and melt the butter. Beat or whisk well to combine the ingredients then cook on 100% (full), beating or whisking every 30–60 sec until thickened and cooked.

- **Separation** in the liquid may occur in white sauces after defrosting. This can be corrected by whisking or beating well at intervals during the heating process.

- **Sieve** sauces such as raspberry or tomato after puréeing to remove pips (and skins if appropriate). Ingredients may also be sieved if no food processor or blender is available to obtain a smooth, puréed sauce and to remove lumps.

- **Skin** can be prevented from forming on white sauces when made in advance by placing a piece of damp greaseproof paper onto the surface of the sauce.

- **Temperature probes** can be used when cooking minced meat sauces such as bolognaise sauce when the temperature should be set to 70–75°C (160–167°F). When reheating sauces, the temperature should be 70–80°C (160–175°F) depending on the type of sauce and ingredients.

Quick white sauce *makes about 275ml (½pt)*
POWER LEVEL: 100% (FULL)

When in a hurry, try this one-stage sauce; although it needs attention whilst cooking, it makes a good quick substitute for the béchamel sauce.

25g (1oz) butter or margarine cut into pieces
25g (1oz) flour
¼ × 5ml tsp (¼tsp) garlic purée
pinch dry mustard
salt and freshly ground black pepper
275ml (½pt) milk

1 Place all the ingredients into a bowl or serving jug and stir briskly or whisk. The ingredients will not combine at this stage.
2 Heat for 3–4 min, stirring or whisking every 15 sec, until cooked and thickened. As the butter or margarine melts it will absorb the flour and, providing the mixture is stirred or whisked frequently, a smooth sauce will be obtained. Adjust seasoning if necessary.

Rum or brandy butter *makes about 225g (½lb)*

Also called hard sauce, this is traditionally served with Christmas pudding, but could also be served with any special hot dessert.

100g (4oz) unsalted butter
100g (4oz) caster sugar
2–3 × 15ml tbsp (2–3tbsp) rum or brandy

1 Cream the butter, add the sugar gradually, beating well together until the mixture is soft and fluffy.
2 Add the rum or brandy a little at a time, beating well after each addition.
3 Place in the serving bowl and chill in the refrigerator until hard. To make the sauce more decorative, it can be piped into the serving bowl in swirls before chilling.

Apple sauce *makes about 275ml (½pt)*
POWER LEVEL: 100% (FULL)

450g (1lb) cooking apples
15g (½oz) butter
sugar, to taste
1 strip lemon peel
1 × 15ml tbsp (1tbsp) water

1 Peel and core the apples and slice thinly. Cook with the other ingredients in a covered dish or roasting bag for 6 min.
2 When cooked, remove lemon peel, beat well, purée in a blender or sieve.
3 Serve hot or cold with rich meat or poultry, eg pork or duck.

Jam sauce *makes about 425ml (¾pt)*
POWER LEVEL: 100% (FULL)

275ml (½pt) water or fruit juice
225g (8oz) jam
1 × 15ml tbsp (1tbsp) cornflour or arrowroot
4 × 15ml tbsp (4tbsp) cold water
lemon juice

1 Warm the water or fruit juice for 2–2½ min and stir in the jam.
2 Blend the cornflour or arrowroot with the cold water and stir into the jam. Cook for 2–3 min, stirring every minute.
3 Add lemon juice to taste.

Syrup sauce
Follow the ingredients and method for jam sauce substituting syrup for the jam.

Béchamel sauce *makes about 275ml (½pt)*
POWER LEVEL: 50% AND 100% (FULL)

This is basic white sauce but with an excellent flavour.

1 small onion
6 cloves
1 bay leaf
6 peppercorns
1 blade mace
275ml (½pt) milk
25g (1oz) butter
25g (1oz) flour
salt and pepper

1 Peel the onion and stick with the cloves. Place in a bowl with the rest of the spices and milk.
2 Heat at 50% setting for 10–11 min. This allows the infusion of the flavours from the spices into the milk.
3 Melt the butter for 1 min on 100% (full) and stir in the flour and the seasonings. Strain the milk and add a little at a time to the butter and flour mixture (called the roux), stirring continuously.
4 Cook for 1½–2 min, stirring every ½ min until thickened and bubbling. Adjust seasoning if necessary.

Bread sauce *makes about 425ml (¾pt)*
POWER LEVEL: 100% (FULL)
colour page 79

1 medium-sized onion
2 cloves
425ml (¾pt) milk
pinch salt
6 peppercorns
1 bay leaf
25g (1oz) butter
75g (3oz) breadcrumbs

1 Peel the onion but leave it whole. Place in a bowl with the cloves, milk and salt. Heat for 3 min.
2 Add the other ingredients and cook for 5 min, stirring once during cooking.
3 Remove the onion, cloves, peppercorns and bay leaf, then beat well. Beat in an extra 15g (½oz) butter if required.

Meat or poultry gravy
POWER LEVEL: 100% (FULL)

While the joint is in its final standing period, pour off the meat juices into a jug or gravy boat. Add the usual flavourings or thickening and stock. Heat until cooked, stirring every minute.

Savoury white sauce *makes about 275ml (½pt)*
POWER LEVEL: 100% (FULL)

25g (1oz) butter
25g (1oz) plain flour
275ml (½pt) milk
salt and pepper

1 Melt the butter in a medium-sized glass bowl for 1–1½ min. Blend in the flour and gradually stir in the milk.
2 Add the seasonings and cook for 4–5 min, stirring every minute. Use as required.

Variations
One of the following ingredients may be added to the sauce 2 min before the end of the cooking time:

Prawn sauce: 100g (4oz) peeled prawns
Cheese sauce: 50–75g (2–3oz) cheese, grated (*colour page 103*)
Mushroom sauce: 50g (2oz) mushrooms, chopped
Onion sauce: 100g (4oz) cooked onion, chopped
Parsley sauce: 2 ×5ml tsp (2tsp) parsley, chopped
Egg sauce: 1 hard-boiled egg, chopped finely

White wine sauce

Follow the recipe above replacing a wine glass of dry white wine for the same measure of milk.

Tomato sauce *makes about 275ml (½pt)*
POWER LEVEL: 100% (FULL)

1 × 15ml tbsp (1tbsp) olive oil
1 large onion, peeled and finely chopped
1–2 cloves garlic, crushed or finely chopped
400g (14oz) can tomatoes, drained
1 × 15ml tbsp (1tbsp) tomato purée
1 glass red wine or juice from tomatoes
few sprigs fresh herbs, or
1 × 5ml tsp (1tsp) dried herbs, eg thyme or rosemary
salt and freshly ground black pepper

1 Place olive oil, onion and garlic into a bowl and toss well. Cook for 4–5 min until soft.
2 Roughly chop the tomatoes and add to the bowl with the remaining ingredients.
3 Cook uncovered until soft and the liquid quantity is reduced giving a fairly thick sauce, stirring every 3 min.
4 Use when referred to in recipes or where a good, well-flavoured tomato sauce is required, ie as a topping for pizzas or to mix with plain boiled pasta.

Butterscotch sauce *makes about*

150ml (¼pt)
POWER LEVEL: 100% (FULL) AND 50%
colour photograph opposite

50g (2oz) light, soft brown sugar
50g (2oz) butter
2 × 15ml tbsp (2tbsp) golden syrup
15g (½oz) chopped almonds, optional
squeeze lemon juice

1 Heat the sugar in a bowl on 100% (full) setting for 30 sec. Add the butter and syrup.
2 Heat on 50% setting for 1 min, then stir thoroughly adding almonds and lemon juice.
3 Heat on 50% setting for 3–4 min, stirring every minute, or until sugar dissolves.

Note: *Use as a topping for ice-cream and desserts.*

Chocolate sauce *makes about 425ml (¾pt)*

POWER LEVEL: 100% (FULL)
colour photograph opposite

175g (6oz) plain chocolate
1 × 5ml tsp (1tsp) butter
3–4 × 15ml tbsp (3–4tbsp) golden syrup
1 × 5ml tsp (1tsp) coffee essence
150ml (¼pt) single cream

1 Break up the chocolate and place in a bowl with the butter, golden syrup and coffee essence.
2 Heat until melted 2–3 min, stirring once halfway through.
3 Stir in the single cream and heat without boiling.
4 Serve hot or cold.

Egg custard sauce *makes about 275ml (½pt)*

POWER LEVEL: 100% (FULL) AND 50%

2 egg yolks
25g (1oz) caster sugar
15g (½oz) cornflour
275ml (½pt) milk
few drops vanilla essence

1 Place the egg yolks in a bowl with the sugar and mix well.
2 Blend the cornflour smoothly with the milk and heat in the microwave for 2–3 min on 100% (full) setting, stirring every minute.
3 Pour the milk onto the egg and sugar mixture and stir well. Add the vanilla essence and stir again. Cook on 50% setting for 4–4½ min, stirring every 30 sec. Do not allow to boil.

DO NOT FREEZE

Cornflour sauce *makes about 275ml (½pt)*

POWER LEVEL: 100% (FULL)

1 × 15ml tbsp (1tbsp) sugar
1 × 15ml tbsp (1tbsp) cornflour
275ml (½pt) milk
few drops vanilla essence

1 Mix the sugar and cornflour together with a little of the milk. Gradually add the rest of the milk and the vanilla essence.
2 Cook for 3–4 min until thick, stirring every minute.

Custard sauce
colour page 79
Follow the ingredients and method for cornflour sauce substituting custard powder for the cornflour.

Fennel sauce *(serves 4)*

POWER LEVEL: 100% (FULL)
colour page opposite

This sauce makes a good accompaniment to salmon or mackerel.

1 medium head fennel, washed and trimmed
2 × 15ml tbsp (2tbsp) salted water
For the sauce:
15g (½oz) butter
15g (½oz) flour
salt and pepper
275ml (½pt) milk and fennel juice, mixed
3 × 15ml tbsp (3tbsp) single cream

1 Cut the fennel into small pieces and cook with the salted water in a covered dish or boiling bag for 6–7 min. Drain off the juices and reserve.
2 Chop the fennel finely.
3 Melt the butter, add the flour and seasonings. Make the reserved juices up to 275ml (½pt) with milk and add gradually to the roux, stirring continuously. Stir in the fennel. (If preferred, the sauce may be puréed in a blender or food processor at this stage).
4 Heat the sauce for 4–5 min until thickened and bubbling, stirring every 30 sec.
5 Allow the sauce to cool slightly and stir in the cream. Serve hot with fish.

Chocolate Sauce and Butterscotch Sauce (above)
Chinese Cucumber Starter (page 57) and Fennel Sauce (above)

Hollandaise sauce *(serves 4)*
POWER LEVEL: 50%
colour page 54

Serve with freshly cooked asparagus, broccoli or globe artichokes as a starter to a meal.

100g (4oz) butter
2 × 15ml tbsp (2tbsp) wine vinegar
2 egg yolks
salt and pepper

1 Melt the butter on 50% setting for 2 min, add the vinegar and egg yolks and whisk lightly.
2 Cook on 50% setting for 1 min, whisk well, season and serve immediately.

DO NOT FREEZE

Barbecue sauce *makes about 275ml (½pt)*
POWER LEVEL: 100% (FULL)

15g (½oz) butter
1 onion, finely chopped
2 × 5ml tsp (2tsp) worcestershire sauce
6 × 15ml tbsp (6tbsp) tomato ketchup
225ml (8fl oz) water
salt and pepper

1 Melt the butter in the microwave for 1 min. Add the onion, cover and cook for 3 min.
2 Add the remaining ingredients, stir well and cook for a further 3 min.

Note: *Serve the sauce with beefburgers, chicken or any barbecued food.*

Curry sauce *makes about 550ml (1pt)*
POWER LEVEL: 100% (FULL) AND 30%

150ml (¼pt) milk
25g (1oz) desiccated coconut
50g (2oz) butter
1 onion, chopped
1 apple, peeled and diced
1–2 × 15ml tbsp (1–2tbsp) curry powder
2 × 15ml tbsp (2tbsp) plain flour
550ml (1pt) boiling stock
2 × 15ml tbsp (2tbsp) chutney
25g (1oz) sultanas
salt and pepper
pinch cayenne pepper

1 Heat the milk and coconut together in a small dish for 1½ min on 100% (full) setting. Stir, leave for 10 min to infuse the flavours.
2 Melt the butter in a medium-sized bowl for 1½–2 min. Add the onion and apple and cook for 3 min.
3 Stir in curry powder and flour, mixing

thoroughly. Cook for a further 1 min.
4 Add the boiling stock gradually, beating well after each addition.
5 Strain the coconut milk into the sauce through a sieve. Add the remaining ingredients.
6 Bring to the boil on 100% (full) setting, stirring every 2 min.
7 Cover and cook on 30% setting for 10–15 min to allow flavours to blend, stirring occasionally.

Cranberry sauce *makes about 275ml (½pt)*
POWER LEVEL: 100% (FULL)
colour page 79

450g (1lb) cranberries, washed
100g (4oz) sugar
1 × 15ml tbsp (1tbsp) water
25g (1oz) butter

1 Place the cranberries in a covered dish, roasting bag or boiling bag with the sugar and water.
2 Cook for 5–6 min or until the fruit is soft.
3 Add the butter, stir until melted, then cook uncovered for 1 min.
4 Serve hot or cold with roast turkey or chicken.

Bolognaise sauce *(serves 4)*
POWER LEVEL: 100% (FULL) AND 50%

2 × 15ml tbsp (2tbsp) oil
1 onion, chopped
2 cloves garlic, finely chopped
2 sticks celery, finely chopped
1 carrot, diced
4 rashers streaky bacon, diced
450g (1lb) minced beef
½ green pepper, diced
4 tomatoes, skinned and chopped
275ml (½pt) boiling stock
2 × 15ml 5tbsp (2tbsp) tomato purée
1 bay leaf
1 × 5ml tsp (1tsp) mixed herbs
pinch nutmeg
salt and pepper
For serving:
freshly cooked spaghetti (page 102)
grated parmesan cheese

1 Heat the oil in a large bowl for 2 min on 100% (full) setting. Add the onion, garlic, celery and carrot, cover and cooked for 3 min.
2 Add the bacon and cook for 2 min, then add the minced beef, stir well and cook for 2 min.
3 Stir in all the remaining ingredients and season well. Cook on 100% (full) setting for 10 min and stir, reduce to 50% setting, cook for 20 min. Adjust seasoning to taste. Serve with freshly cooked spaghetti and grated parmesan cheese.

Fish

All fish cooked by microwave is simply out of this world – full of flavour and cooked to perfection – whether it is frozen, fresh, canned or boil-in-the-bag fish. If steaming, baking or poaching fresh fish either whole or filleted, it should be cleaned and prepared in the normal way and covered during cooking. Although most fish is cooked using a 100% (full) setting, when reheating fish in a sauce use a lower setting to ensure the dish is evenly heated throughout.

●GUIDELINES AT-A-GLANCE

●**Additional liquid** is not normally necessary although a few drops of lemon juice, a little melted butter or white wine can be used to enhance the flavour if preferred.

●**Aluminium foil** is used in small, smooth pieces, neatly wrapped around thin ends of fish fillets, heads and tails of whole fish and thin sides of flat fish to protect these thinner parts from overheating when defrosting and cooking.

●**Appearance** of microwave cooked fish is similar to steaming, poaching or baking conventionally. A sprinkling of paprika, chopped herbs or seasonings or garnishing with lemon slices, tomatoes or sprigs or parsley will enhance the appearance.

●**Arrangement** of the fish when cooking several fillets or whole fish together is important. Arrange in a single layer, head-to-tail and overlapping slightly to protect the thinner parts from overcooking. Alternatively, tuck the thinner ends of fillets under to achieve an even depth. Cutlets and steaks should be arranged in a circle with the thicker parts towards the outside of the dish and the narrow, thinner parts towards the centre.

●**Boil-in-the-bag** fish should be flexed slightly during defrosting to help the thawing process by breaking up the centre portion. Pierce the bag before cooking.

●**Breadcrumbed fish** may be brushed with oil or butter before cooking but the coating will not become crisp. A browning dish will help to attain a more crispy result. Battered fish is not successful in the microwave.

●**Browning dishes** are useful for cooking fish portions in breadcrumbs, fish fingers etc. Refer to page 14 for general guidance on the use of the browning dish.

●**Clean and prepare** fish in the normal way, ensuring that whole fish are gutted, thoroughly cleaned and washed. Slit the skin of whole fish at the thickest part to allow steam to escape.

●**Cooking** is usually carried out on 100% (full) setting although large whole fish and thicker steaks or cutlets may benefit from a lower 50–70% power level for more even results.

●**Cover** fish with pierced clingfilm or a lid on the dish when defrosting, cooking or reheating.

●**Deep-fat frying** must not be attempted in the microwave as the temperature of the fat or oil cannot be controlled.

●**Defrosting** should be carried out on 30% power setting and when evenly thawed the fish should be cold. If it is warm in parts it has started to cook and should be left to stand until completely thawed. Separate fillets as soon as possible and arrange in a single layer.

●**Frozen prepared** fish dishes should be defrosted using a 30–50% power setting depending on the quantity and type of ingredients.

●**Popping** or eruption in part of the fish during cooking *may* occur and is an indication of food overcooking. It is caused by heat build-up in small vessels or fat globules within the fish which eventually burst. This can be overcome by using a lower power setting but otherwise cannot be avoided.

Thatched Tuna Pie (page 71) and Cottage Pie (page 89)

- **Rearrangement** of fish when defrosting or cooking may be necessary to ensure even results. This involves moving centre portions or whole fish to the outside of the dish and outside ones to the centre. Thicker cutlets, steaks and whole fish may, in addition, need to be turned over halfway through.

- **Reheat** fish casseroles and entrées using a 50–70% power setting to ensure sauces do not overheat before the main fish ingredients have heated through.

- **Seasonings,** especially salt, should be kept to a minimum when cooking plain fish. Adjust seasonings to taste at the end of the cooking time.

- **Separate** defrosting fish fillets, shellfish and block fish into a single layer as soon as possible.

- **Shellfish** should be defrosted and cooked using the guidelines for fish above. Live shellfish such as lobsters and crabs should be killed by conventional methods.

- **Standing time** should be allowed after defrosting to ensure that fish is evenly thawed so that best results are obtained when it is cooked afterwards. When cooked, fish should be removed from the microwave when barely done and left to stand to finish cooking by residual heat.

- **Stir** the contents of a fish or shellfish casserole gently, from the outside of the dish to the centre and vice versa to ensure the fish is evenly cooked.

- **Temperature probe** or a thermometer can be used to measure the temperature of fish at the end of cooking; it should be 65°C (150°F).

- **Test** fish at regular intervals during cooking. When done, the flesh will flake easily and have a slightly opaque appearance. If it is still translucent it will require a little extra cooking time. If slightly translucent, it may be left to stand to finish cooking.

Fish defrosting and cooking chart

Fish	Defrost time 30%-50%	Cooking time 100% (full)
White fish, eg cod, haddock, coley fillets or cutlets, plaice or sole, 450g (1lb) prepared fillets	5–6 min, stand 5 min	4–5 min
Smoked fish, eg smoked haddock, cod, 450g (1lb) prepared fillets	5–6 min, stand 5 min	4–5 min
Mackerel 2 × 275–350g (10–12oz) fish, gutted but whole	5–6 min, stand 5 min 2–3 min, stand 3 min	8–10 min
Kipper, 1 medium	—	1–2 min
Herrings and trout 2 × 225g (8oz) fish, gutted but whole	4–5 min, stand 4 min 4–5 min, stand 5 min	6–8 min
Salmon steaks, 450g (1lb)	5–6 min, stand 5 min	4–5 min
Shell fish, eg scampi, prawns, 450g (1lb) prepared	4–6 min, stand 5 min	Use as recipe directs
Fish in sauce, 200g (7oz) bag	3–5 min, stand 5 min	3–4 min
Boil-in-the-bag fillets 200g (7oz)	3–5 min, stand 5 min	3 min
Kipper fillets 225g (8oz)	3–4 min, stand 5 min	3 min

Thatched tuna pie (serves 4–6)
POWER LEVEL: 100% (FULL)
colour photograph opposite

25g (1oz) butter or margarine
2 medium leeks, trimmed and finely sliced
275ml (½pt) béchamel sauce (page 65)
4 tomatoes, skinned and quartered
450g (1lb) canned tuna fish, approximately
1 × 15ml tbsp (1tbsp) chopped parsley
½ lemon, grated rind and juice
salt and freshly ground black pepper
50g (2oz) fresh brown breadcrumbs
50g (2oz) red leicester cheese, finely grated
grated nutmeg for sprinkling
For garnish:
parsley sprigs

1 Melt the butter or margarine in a large round, shallow dish for 1 min, toss in the leeks, cover and cook for 3–5 min. Add the sauce and the tomatoes.
2 Drain the flake and tuna and add to the sauce with the parsley, lemon rind and juice and seasoning. Mix well together, smooth the top and clean the edges of the dish.
3 Mix the breadcrumbs with the grated cheese and sprinkle over the top of the sauce mixture. Sprinkle with a little grated nutmeg.
4 Cook for 6 min, turning every 2 min, until heated through.
5 Serve hot garnished with parsley sprigs.

Fish pudding (serves 4–5)
POWER LEVEL: 100% (FULL)

This pudding is very light in texture and makes a good lunch or supper dish.

450g (1lb) white fish fillets, cooked
75g (3oz) fresh breadcrumbs
1 × 15ml tbsp (1tbsp) chopped parsley
1 lemon, grated rind
salt and freshly ground black pepper
50g (2oz) butter or margarine
2 eggs, beaten
For serving:
tomato sauce (page 65)

1 Lightly grease a 850ml (1½pt) pudding basin.
2 Flake the fish, discarding any skin or bones. Mix with the breadcrumbs, parsley, lemon rind and seasoning.
3 Melt the butter for 1–1½ min and add to the fish together with the beaten eggs. Mix thoroughly.
4 Place in the greased pudding basin. Cover with clingfilm making a slit with the pointed end of a sharp knife.
5 Cook for 4–5 min, turning once halfway through.
6 Remove clingfilm and invert onto the serving dish.
7 Serve hot with tomato sauce or cold with a dressed salad.

Roll mops *(serves 4)*
POWER LEVEL: 100% (FULL)

4 fresh herrings
1 blade mace
1 bay leaf
2 cloves
6 peppercorns
pinch salt
1 onion, chopped
150ml (¼pt) water
150ml (¼pt) vinegar

1 Clean and bone the herrings. Roll up tightly from the tail end. Secure with a wooden cocktail stick if necessary.
2 Place in a shallow dish with the herbs, seasoning and onion. Mix the water and vinegar together and pour over the fish. Cover the dish with a lid or clingfilm.
3 Cook in the microwave for 6–7 min. Allow to cool in the cooking liquor.
4 Serve cold as a starter or with salad.

Cod steaks with leek and corn stuffing
(serves 4)
POWER LEVEL: 100% (FULL)

1 leek, washed and trimmed
40g (1½oz) butter
50g (2oz) white breadcrumbs
40g (1½oz) cheddar cheese, grated
1 × 326g (11½oz) can sweetcorn
salt and pepper
2 tomatoes, skinned
1 egg, beaten
4 cod steaks, weighing about 175g (6oz) each

1 Slice the leek and place in a bowl with 2 × 15ml tbsp (2tbsp) salted water. Cover with pierced clingfilm and cook for 3 min.
2 Melt the butter in the microwave for 1–1½ min. Add to the leek with the breadcrumbs, cheese, sweetcorn and seasoning, reserving 2 × 15ml tbsp (2tbsp) of sweetcorn for garnish.
3 Chop one of the tomatoes and add it to the mixture. Bind the stuffing with the beaten egg.
4 Wash and trim the fish. Place in a large casserole with the thin ends towards the centre, and season lightly. Cover and cook for 5 min, then stand for 5 min.
5 Fill the cavity and cover the end of each steak with the stuffing.
6 Slice the remaining tomato and place one slice on each steak. Sprinkle on the reserved corn.
7 Cover and cook for 3 min, turn and cook for 3 min. Serve immediately.

Tomato fish charlotte *(serves 4)*
POWER LEVEL: 100% (FULL)

450g (1lb) cod or haddock fillet
25g (1oz) butter
½ lemon, juice and grated rind
100g (4oz) fresh breadcrumbs
5–6 × 15ml tbsp (5–6tbsp) oil
275ml (½pt) tomato sauce (page 65)
For garnish:
tomato slices

1 Lightly grease a large round dish or pie dish.
2 Skin the cod or haddock fillet, place in the greased dish, dot with the butter. Sprinkle with the lemon juice, cover and cook for 4–5 min, turning once. Drain the liquid from the fish.
3 Preheat a browning dish for 5–6 min.
4 Sprinkle the breadcrumbs with the oil, mix well to ensure they are coated with the oil.
5 Add the breadcrumbs to the preheated browning dish and cook uncovered for 1–2 min until lightly browned, stirring every ½ min. Stir in the grated lemon rind.
6 Heat the tomato sauce for 2–3 min and pour on top of the fish. Smooth the top and sprinkle on the breadcrumbs. Cook for 2–3 min until hot through.
7 Serve hot garnished with tomato slices.

Salmon with white wine sauce *(serves 2)*
POWER LEVEL: 50%

2 × 200–225g (7–8oz) salmon cutlets
salt and pepper
150ml (¼pt) white wine sauce (page 65)
1 egg yolk
3 × 15ml tbsp (3tbsp) single cream
For garnish:
shrimps or prawns
parsley and lemon butterflies

1 Wash the cutlets, place in a dish with the thin ends towards the centre and sprinkle with salt and pepper. Cover with a lid or pierced clingfilm and cook for 10–12 min, turning once.
2 Make up the white wine sauce as directed using the salmon juices. Cool the sauce slightly.
3 While the sauce is cooling, reheat the salmon steaks in a serving dish for 2 min.
4 Stir the egg yolk and cream into the sauce. Check and adjust the seasoning.
5 Pour the sauce over the salmon. Sprinkle with a few prepared shrimps or prawns and garnish with parsley and lemon butterflies.

FREEZE THE SAUCE SEPARATELY

Trout and almonds (serves 4)

POWER LEVEL: 100% (FULL)

4 trout (about 100–150g (4–5oz) each)
salt and pepper
few drops lemon juice
50g (2oz) butter
50–75g (2–3oz) flaked almonds, toasted
For serving:
lemon wedges

1 Clean the fish, leaving the heads on. Wash and dry. Place head-to-tail in the serving dish, season lightly and add a few drops of lemon juice. Protect heads and tails with small pieces of aluminium foil.
2 Melt the butter, in the microwave, for 2 min. Brush the trout with the butter, cover with kitchen paper and cook for 6 min.
3 Sprinkle almonds over the fish and cook for a further 2–4 min, depending on the size of the fish. Larger fish will take 1–2 min longer.
4 Serve hot with lemon wedges.

Seafood flan (serves 6)

POWER LEVEL: 100% (FULL)
colour page 34

175g (6oz) rich shortcrust pastry (page 43)
150ml (¼pt) béchamel sauce (page 65)
salt and pepper
225g (8oz) crabmeat, fresh or frozen
150ml (¼pt) mayonnaise
few drops lemon juice
2 hardboiled eggs, chopped
150ml (¼pt) double cream, whipped
For garnish:
thinly sliced cucumber and chopped parsley

1 Roll out the pastry, line a 20cm (8in) flan dish and bake blind (page 44). Leave to cool.
2 Beat the béchamel sauce and add seasoning. Mix in the crabmeat, mayonnaise, lemon juice and chopped hardboiled egg. Finally fold in the whipped double cream.
3 Pour the mixture into the cooled flan case and smooth the top. Chill until set.
4 Serve cold garnished with cucumber slices and chopped parsley as a starter to a meal or as a main course with mixed salad.

DO NOT FREEZE

Variations
Cooked and shelled prawns, scampi, mussels, scallops, lobster, fresh or canned tuna or salmon or a mixture of these can be used as alternatives to the crabmeat.

Coley and mushroom cobbler (serves 6)

POWER LEVEL: 100% (FULL)
OVEN TEMPERATURE: 220°C (425°F) MARK 7

1 large onion, chopped
225g (8oz) tomatoes, skinned and sliced
225g (8oz) mushrooms, thickly sliced
salt and pepper
½ × 5ml tsp (½tsp) ground mace
675g (1½lb) coley, skinned and cut into 6 evenly-
    sized pieces
25g (1oz) butter or margarine
25g (1oz) wholewheat flour
milk
For the scone topping:
175g (6oz) wholewheat flour
1 × 5ml tsp (1tsp) baking powder
pinch salt
pinch dried mustard
25g (1oz) butter or margarine
100g (4oz) cheddar cheese, grated
For garnish:
chopped parsley

1 Place the onion in a large casserole dish, cover and cook for 4 min, stirring once. Add the tomatoes and mushrooms and cook for a further 3 min.
2 Season the mixture with salt and pepper to taste and add the mace. Add the fish and cover with some of the vegetables. Cover and cook for 6–8 min until the fish is just cooked.
3 Melt the butter or margarine in a bowl for ½–1 min. Add the flour and beat well. Drain the liquid from the fish casserole and make up to 275ml (½pt) with milk. Add the liquid to the roux gradually, stirring well between each addition.
4 Heat the sauce for 4–5 min until boiling and thickened, stirring every minute. Adjust the seasoning and carefully mix the sauce into the fish casserole.
5 Prepare the scone topping by placing the flour in a bowl with the baking powder, a pinch of salt and pinch of dried mustard. Rub in the butter or margarine and add 50g (2oz) of the grated cheese. Mix into a workable dough with a little milk.
6 Knead the dough lightly on a floured surface and roll out to a thickness of 1.25cm (½in). Cut into 6 rounds using a scone cutter and place the scones on top of the coley casserole. Sprinkle with the remaining grated cheese.
7 Cook the cobbler in the preheated conventional oven for 10–12 min until the scones are cooked and the cheese is melted. Sprinkle with chopped parsley.

Scallop and mushroom pie *(serves 6–8)*
POWER LEVEL: 100% (FULL)

This makes an excellent fish course or main course for a dinner party.

16 scallops, cleaned
275ml (½pt) milk
salt and freshly ground black pepper
50g (2oz) butter
25g (1oz) flour
175g (6oz) mushrooms, washed and sliced
150ml (¼pt) dry white wine
450g (1lb) creamed potatoes (page 97)
For garnish:
parsley sprigs

1 Lightly grease a large shallow round ovenware dish.
2 Cut each scallop into 4, place with the milk and seasonings into a bowl and cook for 3–4 min. Drain and reserve the milk.
3 Melt 25g (1oz) butter for 1 min, stir in the flour until smooth. Gradually stir in the reserved milk.
4 Cook for 3–4 min until thick, stirring every minute. Beat well until smooth. Mix in scallops, mushrooms and wine.
5 Cover with piped creamed potatoes and top with slivers of the remaining butter.
6 Cook for 6–8 min or until hot through, turning every 2 min.
7 Garnish with parsley and serve hot with a side salad.

Variation
King-size prawns may replace the scallops. Peel the prawns and add to the sauce, made from the butter, flour and milk, with the mushrooms and wine. Continue as above.

Pancakes

Pancakes cannot be successfully cooked in the microwave, so are best cooked conventionally; this basic pancake batter is sufficient to make 8–10 thin pancakes.

100g (4oz) plain flour
pinch salt
1 egg, beaten
275ml (½pt) milk
oil for frying

1 Sift the flour and salt into a mixing bowl. Make a well in the centre and drop in the beaten egg.
2 Slowly pour on half the milk, mixing the egg and milk into the flour with a wooden spoon.
3 Beat the mixture with a wooden spoon or whisk until smooth and free of lumps.
4 Add the remaining milk, whisking continually until the mixture is bubbly and the consistency of single cream.
5 Heat a 17.5cm (7–8in) frying pan on a conventional hotplate or burner. Just sufficient oil should be added to prevent the pancakes from sticking.
6 The pan and oil should be really hot. Pour in just enough batter to allow a thin film to coat the base of the pan, tilting the pan to spread the mixture.
7 The base of the pancake should be cooked in about 1 min. Flip the pancake over with a palette knife or spatula and cook the other side for about 1 min. If the pancakes are taking too long to cook, adjust the heat or make sure that too much batter is not being used.
8 Layer the pancakes in absorbent kitchen paper and keep warm if to be used immediately. Alternatively, leave to cool, or freeze as they may be thawed and reheated most satisfactorily in the microwave.
9 Fill and use as required, allowing one per person if served as a starter to a meal or two if served as a snack or as a main course with vegetables.

Note: *The ingredients for the pancake batter may be blended in a liquidiser or food processor.*

Salmon-stuffed pancakes
POWER LEVEL: 70%
1 × 198g (7oz) can salmon, drained and flaked
1 × 5ml tsp (1tsp) mustard
1 × 15ml tsp (1tbsp) finely chopped onion
275ml (½pt) white sauce (page 65)
salt and pepper
8 × 20cm (8in) cooked pancakes (above)
2 × 15ml tbsp (2tbsp) lemon juice
150ml (¼pt) soured cream
For garnish:
2 × 15ml tbsp (2tbsp) chopped chives

1 Stir the salmon, mustard and onion into the white sauce. Season to taste.
2 Spread an equal amount of sauce on each pancake and roll up. Lay the pancakes in a shallow serving dish and moisten with the lemon juice.
3 Cover the dish with a lid or pierced clingfilm and cook in the microwave for 8–10 min until heated through, turning the dish 2–3 times throughout.
4 Top with soured cream and garnish with the chopped chives. Serve immediately.

Skate with Caper Butter (below) and Scampi Provençale (below)

Skate with caper butter *(serves 4)*
POWER LEVEL: 100% (FULL)
colour photograph above

2 wings of skate (about 450g (1lb) each)
50–75g (2–3oz) butter
1 × 15ml tbsp (1tbsp) capers
5 × 15ml tbsp (5tbsp) wine vinegar
1 × 15ml tbsp (1 tbsp) chopped parsley
salt and pepper

1 Cut each wing into 3 wedges. Place in a large, shallow dish with the thin ends towards the centre. Cover with pierced clingfilm or lid and cook for 5 min.
2 Melt and cook the butter for 5 min. Add the capers, vinegar, parsley and seasoning and cook for 2 min.
3 Skin the skate and lay the pieces in the serving dish. Pour the caper butter over the fish, cover and reheat for 3–4 min.
4 Serve hot.

Scampi provençale *(serves 4)*
POWER LEVEL: 100% (FULL)
colour photograph above

25g (1oz) butter
1 onion, chopped
1 clove garlic, chopped
1 × 397g (14oz) can tomatoes, drained
5 × 15ml tbsp (5tbsp) dry white wine
salt and pepper
pinch sugar
1 × 15ml tbsp (1tbsp) chopped parsley
225g (8oz) scampi

For serving:
boiled rice (page 102)

1 Melt the butter in a casserole dish for 1 min. Toss the onion and garlic in the butter and cook for 4 min.
2 Add tomatoes, wine, seasoning, sugar and parsley. Stir well and heat for 3 min.
3 Drain the scampi well, add to the sauce and cook for about 2 min or until just heated through. Serve with freshly boiled rice.

Rye and honey baked plaice *(serves 2)*
POWER LEVEL: 100% (FULL)

2 small plaice, cleaned and trimmed, each weighing
about 275–350g (10–12oz) when prepared
3 × 15ml tbsp (3tbsp) clear honey
75g (3oz) rye flakes
salt and pepper
2 × 15ml tbsp (2tbsp) chopped parsley
For serving:
salad or fresh vegetables

1 Place the cleaned plaice on a large plate. Heat
the honey in a small dish for about 45 sec, then
brush over the fish.
2 Mix together the rye flakes, seasoning and 1 ×
15ml tbsp (1tbsp) parsley and coat the plaice,
pressing the mixture well onto the surface of
the fish.
3 Pour any remaining honey over the fish and
sprinkle with any remaining rye flakes.
4 Cover the plate with pierced clingfilm and cook
for 7–9 min, rearranging the fish halfway
through if necessary.
6 Serve immediately with the remaining parsley
sprinkled over the top, and with a salad or fresh
vegetables.

Smoked fish flan *(serves 6)*
POWER LEVEL: 100% (FULL) AND 50%

175g (6oz) rich shortcrust pastry (page 43)
1 medium leek, washed and finely sliced
salt and pepper
225g (8oz) smoked cod or haddock, cooked
2 hardboiled eggs, sliced
275ml (½pt) béchamel sauce (page 65)
50g (2oz) cheese, finely grated
450 (1lb) creamed potatoes (page 97)
For garnish:
parsley sprigs

1 Roll out the pastry, line a 20cm (8in) flan dish
and bake blind (page 44).
2 Place the leek in a boiling or roasting bag or
covered casserole dish with a sprinkling of salt
and 2–3 × 15ml tbsp (2–3tbsp) water and cook

on 100% (full) setting for 4–5 min. Drain off the
water.
3 Flake the fish discarding any bones or skin and
place in the bottom of the flan with the leek.
4 Arrange the slices of hardboiled egg on the top,
sprinkle with salt and pepper and cover with
the béchamel sauce.
5 Beat half the cheese into the potato and place
the mixture in a forcing bag with a large star
nozzle. Pipe the potato around the edge and
across the middle of the flan.
6 Heat through on 50% setting for 9–10 min,
turning every 3–4 min.
7 Sprinkle with the remaining cheese and cook
on 100% (full) setting for 1 min until the cheese
is melted. Alternatively brown under a hot
grill.
8 Serve garnished with parsley.

DO NOT FREEZE

Fish pie
POWER LEVEL: 100% (FULL)

1 × 298g (10½oz) can condensed vegetable soup
150ml (¼pt) milk
3 × 15ml tbsp (3tbsp) frozen peas
450g (1lb) cooked fish
salt and pepper
75g (3oz) crisps
50g (2oz) cheddar cheese, grated
For garnish:
1 × 15ml tbsp (1tbsp) chopped parsley

1 Put the soup and milk into an ovenware dish.
Heat for 1 min, stir, heat for 2 min. Mix
thoroughly.
2 Add the peas and cooked fish and pour into a
850ml (1½pt) pie dish. Cook for 4 min, stirring
once during cooking.
3 Sprinkle half the crisps on top of the mixture,
cover with the cheese and top with the remaining crisps.
4 Cook for 1½ min, or until the cheese is melted.
Garnish with chopped parsley and serve.

DO NOT FREEZE

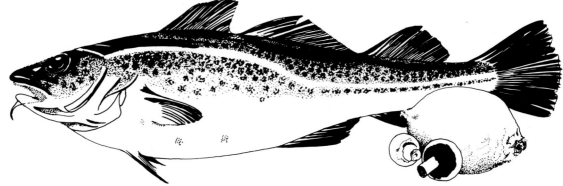

Meat and poultry

The microwave cooker produces excellent results whether you are cooking smaller cuts of meat or large joints but, as this cooking method does not tenderise meat in the same way as when roasting or grilling conventionally, prime cuts will give the best results. However, if you have a microwave cooker with variable power control giving 50% output or a lower 30% output (often a defrost setting) perfect results can be obtained, even when casseroling the tougher, cheaper cuts of meat.

If your microwave cooker does not have lower variable power control settings, cheaper cuts can be tenderised or marinated in oil and vinegar for several hours, or minced or cut into very small pieces before cooking. The fact that casseroles are often more tender if they are left to cool naturally after cooking and then reheated before serving means that dishes can be prepared well in advance – when you have the time – then refrigerated or frozen to be reheated when required.

The advantage of roasting joints by microwave is that while the joint is resting during its final standing period, vegetables, sauces and gravies can be cooked to produce a complete microwave meal.

Cooking

For best results, a joint should be regular in shape so that it will have a better appearance and cook more evenly – rolled joints or top leg of lamb or pork are ideal. Irregular-shaped joints such as shoulder or leg of lamb or poultry, may have the projecting part of the shoulder or narrow piece of the leg or drumsticks and wings protected with smooth small strips of aluminium foil for half the cooking time.

Seasoning should be limited to spices and herbs as salt attracts moisture and can have a toughening effect to the outside of the meat during cooking. The exception to this is pork crackling, when salt rubbed into the scored skin will help it to crisp. But, if in any doubt, leave the seasonings to the end of the cooking time.

Meat can be open roasted by placing it on to an upturned small, flat dish or plate which is used as a trivet inside the roasting dish. Special microwave roasting dishes are now available on the market. These serve a similar purpose as the trivet in keeping the meat out of the juices during cooking. Open roasting is ideal when cooking pork with crackling as this method allows moisture to escape and gives a more crisp finish to the outside of the meat. When open roasting, cover the dish with greaseproof paper or kitchen paper towel to help prevent splashings of fat on to the oven interior. Alternatively, roasting bags may be used to cook joints but remember that wire ties must not be used – string or rubber bands are suitable instead. The roasting bag should be pierced or slit at the base so that the juices will run out into the cooking container away from the meat.

Larger joints should be turned over at least once during the cooking period, and a joint which has fat on one side only should be placed fat side down at the beginning of cooking and turned over halfway through so that the fat is then on the top. If cooking joints on 100% (full) setting, a standing time of 10–25 minutes halfway throughout cooking will assist in a more even result, particularly important for joints over 2kg (4lb) in weight. If using a 50–80% setting on a variable power control model, this standing period halfway through is not necessary; although all joints should be allowed to stand for 5–20 minutes at the end of the cooking period, left in the roasting bag or covered in aluminium foil to retain the heat. However, if the joint is cooked to the desired degree on completion of the cooking time it is not necessary to let it stand.

If the total cooking time is 15 minutes or more the joint will brown naturally, but for extra browning the joint may be placed in a conventional oven at a high temperature for 10–15 minutes at the end of the microwave cooking period, or placed under a hot grill. The careful use of gravy brownings, sauces or paprika, or microwave seasonings painted or sprinkled on to the surface of the meat will give a more attractive colour if preferred. Steaks, chops, sausages and escalopes may be browned during cooking by using a browning dish (page 14) or alternatively finished off under a hot grill after cooking by microwave.

The cooking times given in the following charts are when using a 100% (full) setting and a 70% setting. For those microwave cookers with a 'roast' setting, it is advisable to check with the manufacturer's recommendations regarding cooking times. If you have a microwave with 'full' and 'defrost' settings only, the joint may be cooked for half the time on 100% (full) setting and then reduced to 'defrost' for the remaining time. Alternatively, some joints benefit from a slow cooking process using the 'defrost' setting in which case the cooking time will be almost double that for 100% (full) setting. Much depends on the time available and your own preferences.

The use of a meat thermometer is helpful to determine the temperature at the centre of the food, particularly when defrosting and cooking larger cuts and joints. Only specially designed thermometers for microwave cookers may be left inside the oven while it is operating.

Ordinary meat thermometers must not be used in the microwave but can be inserted into the centre of the joint when it has been taken out of the oven cavity. The following temperatures after the final standing time will help you to assess whether the meat is cooked. If your microwave cooker has the facility of a probe, set it to the temperatures given below, although it is advisable to check with the manufacturer's instructions before using.

Beef	
rare	60°C (140°F)
medium	70°C (160°F)
well done	80°C (175°F)
Lamb	80°C (175°F)
Pork	80°C (175°F)
Veal	80°C (175°F)
Poultry and game birds	80–85°C (175–185°F)

When braising, casseroling or stewing meat best results are obtained using a 50% setting or a lower 30% setting for the total cooking time. This will give a longer cooking period required for tenderising the meat and will also allow sufficient time for the food flavourings and seasonings to blend. The container should be covered with a lid for the entire cooking process to retain moisture and to prevent the liquid in the casserole from evaporating; and as the casserole is being cooked by microwave energy from all directions inside the oven – the top as well as the sides and base – it is best to ensure that the food is well covered with the cooking liquid so that the meat at the top does not overcook and toughen.

Defrosting

Defrosting can be carried out completely in the microwave cooker or by a combination of microwave defrosting and natural thawing, commencing the defrosting in the microwave and then leaving the meat to thaw thoroughly in the refrigerator, larder or at room temperature. Although thinner cuts of meat can be thawed and cooked in one heating operation, generally it is better to ensure that all meat is completely defrosted before cooking to obtain the most even results.

As when cooking by microwave, thinner ends of joints and small cuts can be protected with smooth pieces of aluminium foil during the defrosting process, to prevent the outer sections from beginning to cook while the centre parts are still thawing. It is acceptable if the outside of the meat does start cooking during defrosting, providing the meat is cooked immediately afterwards, although the partially cooked parts should be protected with aluminium foil during the cooking period.

The meat should be turned halfway through the defrosting process to ensure even defrosting. Smaller cuts, such as chops, steak, liver and sausages, should be separated and turned as soon as possible after defrosting begins. When defrosting minced meat or sausage meat, the thawed portions should be scraped away and removed leaving the still-frozen part to be returned to the microwave.

Most meats require standing time to allow the heat to equalise during defrosting so that the outer portions do not overheat. With a defrost setting on a variable power microwave, this is automatically given during the off cycles at these lower power levels, but more even defrosting will be achieved if additional standing times are allowed as recommended in the charts below. The defrosting standing times given are the total resting time required and a better result is obtained if this time is spread evenly throughout the defrosting period. Longer periods of defrosting without standing times will obtain a quicker defrost but may result in a less even thawing. If in doubt, remove the meat from the microwave when it feels warm to

Roast Turkey (page 81), Bread sauce (page 65), Cranberry Sauce (page 68), Christmas Pudding (page 114) and Custard Sauce (page 66)
Lamb Portugaise (page 84) and Rice Pudding (page 113)

the touch and allow to stand or complete thawing naturally.

Meat which is covered during defrosting – either with a lid on a casserole dish, with clingfilm or in a roasting bag – will retain more moisture and defrosting will be slightly faster. Casseroles should be placed in a dish large enough to take the thawed food and to allow room for stirring and breaking down the icy portions. During defrosting and reheating the casserole, allow approximately 2 min per 25g (1oz) using 30–50% setting or 1 min using 100% (full) setting.

The defrosting and cooking charts given here are based on meats which have been removed straight from the freezer for defrosting and are fully thawed before cooking. If meats are partially thawed before being placed in the microwave for defrosting or are not completely thawed before cooking then the times on the charts will require some adjustments to suit.

•GUIDELINES AT-A-GLANCE

- **Aluminium foil** in small, smooth pieces can be wrapped around drumsticks, wing tips and breastbones of poultry and narrow ends of legs of lamb etc for half the cooking time to prevent over-cooking.

- **Arrange** the thicker ends of foods such as chops and chicken portions towards the outside of the dish and the thinner parts towards the centre. Place cut or sliced meat in an even layer when defrosting, reheating and cooking. For joints of meat with fat on one side only see Fat (below). Large poultry birds are placed breast side down and turned over halfway through cooking.

- **Browning** does not occur due to the comparatively short cooking times, though large joints of meat and poultry will become lightly browned if the cooking time is about 15 min or longer. Alternatively, brown in a preheated oven or under a hot grill at the end of the microwave cooking time. A browning dish will help small cuts of meat and poultry to brown (page 14).

- **Casseroles** cooked in the microwave are often more tender if left to cool and then reheated before serving; otherwise cook at a low 30–50% setting to ensure greatest degree of tenderness. Stir casseroles occasionally during defrosting, reheating and cooking to obtain even results.

- **Containers** such as round or oval dishes with lids can be used for casseroles, and microwave roasting dishes with trivets or roasting bags for joints of meat and poultry. Slit the base of the roasting bag to allow the juices to run out. Browning dishes can be useful for smaller cuts (page 14).

- **Cooking** in the microwave will not tenderise meat in the same way as cooking conventionally, so prime cuts give the best results together with the choice of the correct cooking power level. When 'roasting' meat and poultry use a 50–80% setting and, when casseroling, the 30–50% setting, depending on the type of meat being cooked.

- **Cover** with a lid or pierced clingfilm when defrosting, reheating and when a moist result is required, eg for casseroles or gammon joints. Poultry and meat joints can also be covered, but a slightly 'boiled' result will be obtained unless a microwave roasting rack or trivet to keep the meat out of the juices is used. Instead, a light covering with kitchen paper towel will help absorb moisture and prevent splashes.

- **Crackling** on pork can be helped to crispness by scoring and rubbing the skin with salt; otherwise remove the skin from the joint and grill conventionally.

- **Cut** or slice meat evenly to ensure the best results when cooking, reheating or defrosting.

- **Defrost** frozen meats thoroughly before cooking in the microwave to obtain even cooking. Joints of meat and poultry will require a 30% setting; larger joints may need a standing period in addition to thaw evenly. Small cuts can be defrosted using a 30–50% setting and casseroles a 50–70% setting depending on the type and quantity of meat. Giblets should be removed from poultry as soon as possible during defrosting and smaller cuts separated into an even layer.

- **Fat** readily absorbs microwave energy and cooks quickly. Place joints of meat with fat on one side only fat side down and turn over halfway through cooking or protect with small, smooth pieces of aluminium foil.

- **Game** birds and venison which are young and tender are suitable for cooking in the same way as poultry and joints; meat from older, tougher birds and animals is better suited to casserole cooking at 30% setting.

- **Joints** of meat which are boned, rolled and tied into a regular shape give best results. Irregularities should be protected with foil for half the cooking time.

●**Marinade** cheaper cuts to help tenderise them before cooking in the microwave.

●**Mince** or cut cheaper meats into small pieces before cooking in the microwave to obtain tender results.

●**Overcooking** will produce hard, tough results. Always allow a little less time at first and cook for a few minutes longer if necessary.

●**Popping** of foods such as kidney and liver which may happen during cooking is caused by heat build-up inside small vessels or membranes which eventually burst. Ensure skin, piping and cores of kidneys are removed, and turn to a lower setting should popping occur.

●**Reheating** can be carried out at 70–100% setting depending on the quantity and type of meat. Arrange cooked, sliced meat in an even layer; take care not to overheat or further cooking will take place.

●**Salt** should not be sprinkled over meat and poultry for roasting as it can toughen the outside surface. The exception is pork crackling when salt rubbed into the scored skin can assist in achieving crispness.

●**Seasonings** (with the exception of salt), spices and herbs may be used to enhance flavour and appearance.

Defrosting and cooking joints

Meat	Defrosting time 30–50%	Cooking time 100% (full)	Cooking time 70% setting	Internal temperature	Special points
	½kg (1lb)	½kg (1lb)	½kg (1lb)		
Beef, joints on bone	10–12 min, stand 60–70 min	Rare 4–6 min Med 5–7 min Well 6–8 min stand 15–25 min	10–11 min 11–13 min 12–14 min stand 20 min	60°C (140°F) 70°C (160°F) 80°C (175°F)	Cover bone end with foil during defrosting and cooking
Beef, rolled boned	8–10 min, stand 50–60 min	Rare 4–6 min Med 5–7 min Well 6–8 min stand 15–25 min	10–11 min 11–13 min 12–14 min stand 10–15 min	60°C (140°F) 70°C (160°F) 80°C (175°F)	Turn joint on sides during defrosting
Lamb	6 min, stand 30–40 min	7–9 min, stand 15–30 min	11–13 min, stand 20 min	80°C (175°F)	Cover knuckle end of lamb with foil once thawed
Pork or ham	7–8 min, stand 60–70 min	7–9 min stand 15–30 min	12–14 min, stand 20 min	80°C (175°F)	Try to get an evenly shaped joint. Tie for roasting after thawing
Veal	5 min, stand 20–30 min	7–9 min stand 15–30 min	11–13 min stand 20 min	80°C (175°F)	Foreleg may need covering with foil during defrosting
POULTRY Chicken, duck or game birds whole unboned	6–7 min, stand 20–30 min	5–7 min, stand 5–10 min	9–10 min, stand 5 min	80–85°C (175–185°F)	Cover drumsticks and wings with foil during defrosting and half of the cooking period
Turkey, whole	5–7 min, stand 50–60 min	7–9 min stand 25–35 min	10–12 min, stand 10–15 min	80–85°C (175–185°F)	Cover drumsticks, wings and breastbone with foil for up to ¾ of the cooking period.

Defrosting and cooking smaller cuts

Type or cut of meat	Defrosting time 30–50%	Standing time	Special points	Cooking
Fillet steak 2 × 200g (7oz)	6–8 min	12 min	Cover any thin ends with foil. Turn over halfway through	Use as required See recipes or browning dish chart
Stewing or braising meat, eg beef or lamb 675g (1½lb)	11–12 min	10 min	Separate pieces of meat during defrosting	Simmer on 30% setting 1–1½ hr
Minced beef 450g (1lb)	10–11 min	11 min	Break up during defrosting. Remove thawed meat from oven	Cook on 50% setting 30–40 min
Belly pork strips 450g (1lb) (4 strips)	4–5 min	5 min	Separate strips during defrosting	Use as required or cook for 8–10 min, turning during cooking
Offal eg kidney, liver, hearts, tongues 450g (1lb)	9–10 min	4 min	Separate pieces during defrosting	Simmer on 30–50% setting for ½–1½ hr depending on type
Sausage meat 450g (1lb)	6–7 min	10 min	Break thawed sausage meat up and remove from oven during defrosting	Use as required
Sausages 450g (1lb)	6–7 min	10 min	Separate during defrosting	Prick skins and cook for 9–10 min
Bacon 225g (8oz)	4–5 min	5 min	Separate rashers during defrosting	5–6 min
Lamb chops 2 × 100g (4oz)	4–5 min	5 min	Separate chops during defrosting	5–6 min
Pork chops 2 × 225g (8oz)	6–8 min	10 min	Separate chops during defrosting	10–11 min
Chicken portions 1 × 275–365g (10–13oz)	7–8 min	10 min	If necessary protect with aluminium foil during cooking	5–7 min

- **Standing times** may be necessary when roasting large joints of meat and poultry depending on the power setting chosen. Generally, lower power settings will lessen the need for a standing period halfway through cooking. If the meat is cooked to the desired degree at the end of cooking time, standing is unnecessary.

- **Temperature probes** and thermometers are useful when cooking joints and reheating casseroles (page 19).

- **Turn** joints of meat and poultry and thick smaller cuts over halfway through cooking or defrosting to ensure even results.

Suet dumplings (serves 4–6)
POWER LEVEL: 100% (FULL)
colour photograph opposite

100g (4oz) self-raising flour
½ × 5ml tsp (½tsp) salt
50g (2oz) shredded suet
1–2 × 5ml (1–2 tsp) dried mixed herbs, optional
cold water to mix

1 Sift the flour and salt. Stir in the suet, herbs and sufficient cold water to form a soft manageable dough.
2 Knead lightly and form into walnut size balls, rolling between the palms of the hands with a little extra flour if necessary.
3 Drop the dumplings onto the top of a hot, simmering casserole or stew in a deep, large dish. Cover and cook until light and well risen – about 4½–5 min.

Suet Dumplings (page 82)

Steak and kidney suet crust pie *(serves 4)*
POWER LEVEL: 100% (FULL) AND 30%

An alternative to the traditional steak and kidney pudding, this dish has suet crust pastry over the top of the meat only.

25g (1oz) butter or margarine
1 medium onion, peeled and chopped
450g (1lb) chuck steak
3 lambs' kidneys
25g (1oz) flour
salt and freshly ground black pepper
425ml (¾pt) beef stock, boiling
100g (4oz) suet crust pastry (page 84)

1 Melt the butter or margarine in a bowl for 1 min on 100% (full) setting, add the onion and toss well in the butter. Cook for a further 2 min.
2 Trim any fat from the meat and cut into 1.25cm (½in) dice. Skin and core the kidneys, cut into small pieces and add to the meat.
3 Mix the flour and seasonings, add to the meat and toss in the flour. Add to the onion and mix well.
4 Cook on 100% (full) setting for 5–6 min until the meat is browned and add the boiling stock. Stir, cover and heat until boiling for approximately 3–4 min.
5 With the microwave on 30% setting, continue to cook the meat for a further 40–50 min.
6 Drain off most of the gravy and reserve. Place the meat into a 700–850ml (1¼–1½pt) oval pie dish and smooth the top.

7 Roll out the pastry into an oval to fit the inside of the dish. Cover the meat with the pastry and press into the side edges of the dish.

8 Cover loosely with clingfilm slit with the pointed end of a sharp knife and cook on 100% (full) setting for 4½–5 min, turning once half-way through.

9 Serve hot, serving the reserved gravy separately.

Suet crust pastry

225g (8oz) self-raising flour
pinch salt
100g (4oz) shredded suet
2–3 × 5ml tsp (2–3 tsp) dried mixed herbs, optional
150ml (¼pt) cold water approximately

1 Sift the flour and salt, stir in the suet and herbs if used.

2 Mix in sufficient cold water to form a soft, manageable dough.

3 Knead lightly and use as required.

Lamb portugaise (serves 4–6)
POWER LEVEL: 70%, 30% AND 100% (FULL)
colour page 79

1½kg (3lb) loin of lamb, boned
walnut stuffing (page 85)
25g (1oz) butter
25g (1oz) plain flour
275ml (½pt) stock
1 × 15ml tbsp (1tbsp) redcurrant jelly
juice ½ lemon
juice ½ orange
salt and pepper
1 × 15ml tbsp (1tbsp) mint, chopped

1 Wipe the lamb with a damp cloth. Spread the stuffing over the meat, roll up and tie securely with string.

2 Score the surface of the lamb with a sharp knife.

3 Place the lamb in a large shallow dish and 'open' roast on 70% setting for 15 min, giving the dish a half turn at the end of the cooking period.

4 Reduce to 30% setting and cook for a further 20–30 min until cooked through, leave to stand.

5 Melt the butter in a bowl for 1 min on 100% (full) setting and blend in the flour.

6 Add the stock, jelly, fruit juices and seasonings, gradually and stir until well blended.

7 Cook the sauce for 5 min on 100% (full) setting, stirring twice during the cooking time. Stir in the mint.

8 Slice the lamb, pour over a little of the sauce and serve the remainder separately.

Kidney and bacon casserole (serves 4)
POWER LEVEL: 100% (FULL) AND 60%

450g (1lb) lambs' kidneys
1 × 15ml tbsp (1tbsp) plain flour
2 × 5ml tsp (2tsp) gravy powder
1 × 5ml tsp (1tsp) mixed herbs
pinch garlic granules
salt and pepper
1 × 15ml tbsp (1tbsp) oil
1 onion, chopped
4 rashers streaky bacon, diced
1 carrot, thinly sliced
1 × 396g (14oz) can tomatoes
1 stock cube
boiling water
dash worcestershire sauce
100g (4oz) mushrooms, sliced
1 × 15ml tbsp (1tbsp) cornflour
For garnish:
1 × 15ml tbsp (1tbsp) chopped parsley
For serving:
suet dumplings (page 82), optional

1 Halve the kidneys and remove any skin and core. Season the flour with gravy powder, herbs, garlic, salt and pepper. Toss the kidneys in the flour.

2 Heat the oil in a large casserole dish for 1 min. Add the onion and bacon and cook for 2 min. Add the kidneys, cover and cook for 2 min.

3 Add the carrot. Drain the tomatoes, reserving the juice. Crumble the stock cube into the tomato juice and make the liquid up to 275ml (½pt) with boiling water.

4 Add the tomatoes, liquid and worcestershire sauce to the casserole. Cook, still covered, for 10–30 min, on 60% setting. Add the mushrooms, replace the lid and cook for 5 min.

5 Blend the cornflour with a little water, then stir into the casserole. Cover and cook on 100% (full) for 3 min, or until boiling. Sprinkle with parsley before serving. Alternatively serve topped with suet dumplings.

Mexican chicken (serves 4)
POWER LEVEL: 100% (FULL) AND 70%

25g (1oz) butter
1 green pepper, deseeded and sliced
1 red pepper, deseeded and sliced
2 medium-sized onions, chopped
2 cloves garlic, crushed
salt and pepper
1 × 396g (14oz) can tomatoes
2 × tbsp (2tbsp) tomato purée
4 chicken portions

100g (4oz) sweetcorn
100g (4oz) mushrooms, washed and sliced
4 × 15ml tbsp (4tbsp) single cream
For garnish:
2 × 15ml tbsp (2tbsp) chopped parsley

1 Melt the butter in a large casserole dish for 1 min.
2 Add the peppers, onions, garlic and seasoning, then cover with clingfilm and cook for 3 min. Mix the tomatoes and tomato purée into the pepper mixture.
3 Season the chicken joints lightly and add to the pepper mixture. Cover and cook for 25–35 min on 70% setting.
4 Add the sweetcorn and mushrooms and cook, still covered, for a further 15–20 min.
5 Remove the chicken joints from the casserole. Stir the cream into the sauce and return the chicken to the casserole dish. Sprinkle with parsley before serving.

Duck in orange and ginger sauce (serves 4)
POWER LEVEL: 100% (FULL) AND 50%

1 × 15ml tbsp (1tbsp) oil
1 onion, chopped
4 portions duckling
2 oranges
1 chicken stock cube
boiling water
3 × 15ml tbsp (3tbsp) clear honey
1½ × 5ml tsp (1½tsp) ground ginger
salt and pepper
1 bay leaf
1 × 15ml tbsp (1tbsp) cornflour

1 Heat the oil in a large casserole dish for 1 min. Add the onions, cover and cook for 3 min.
2 Add the duck portions, cover and cook for 5 min.
3 Grate the rind from the oranges. Squeeze the juice from 1½ of the oranges. Add the stock cube and make the juice up to 550ml (1pt) with boiling water.
4 Add the honey, ginger and seasoning to the liquid, then pour over the duck. Sprinkle the orange rind over the duck and add the bay leaf.
5 Cover and cook for 10 min, reduce to 50% and cook for a further 40–50 min.
6 Blend the cornflour with a little water. Remove the duck portions from the casserole. Stir the cornflour into the sauce after skimming off the surplus fat and removing the bay leaf. Cook for 3 min on 100% (full) or until boiling. Stir well.
7 Return the duck to the sauce and reheat for 2 min. Before serving, garnish with orange slices from the remaining ½ orange.

Pork with apricots and prunes (serves 4)
POWER LEVEL: 100% (FULL) AND 50%

2 × 15ml tbsp (2tbsp) oil
1 carrot, sliced
1 onion, chopped
450g (1lb) lean pork, diced
1 × 212g (7½oz) can apricots
1 × 212g (7½oz) can prunes
1 chicken stock cube
boiling water
1 × 15ml tbsp (1tbsp) sherry
salt and black pepper
1 × 15ml tbsp (1tbsp) cornflour

1 Heat the oil in a large, shallow casserole dish for 2 min. Add the prepared carrot and onion and cook for 3 min.
2 Add the pork, cook for 3 min, stir and cook for 2 min.
3 Drain the apricot and prune juices into a measuring jug. Add the stock cube and make the juices up to 550ml (1pt) with boiling water. Add the sherry.
4 Season the meat well, add the liquid and half the apricots and prunes. Cover and cook on 50% setting for 45–55 min until tender.
5 Blend the cornflour with a little water and stir into the casserole. Cook for 3 min on 100% (full), or until boiling.
6 Add the rest of the apricots and prunes. Cook for 2 min and adjust seasoning, if necessary, before serving.

Walnut stuffing
POWER LEVEL: 100% (FULL)

100g (4oz) walnuts
1 medium-sized onion
40g (1½oz) butter
40g (1½oz) breadcrumbs
1 × 15ml tbsp (1tbsp) chopped parsley
1 × 5ml tsp (1tsp) dried marjoram
½ lemon, grated rind and juice
1 egg, beaten
salt and pepper

1 Finely chop the walnuts and onion. Melt the butter in the microwave for 1 min. Add the onion and cook for 3 min.
2 Mix in the rest of the ingredients, using just enough beaten egg to bind the stuffing. Season well.
3 The stuffing can also be made by melting the butter for 1 min and then liquidising all the ingredients together. This gives a finely textured stuffing.

Moussaka (serves 4–6)
POWER LEVEL: 100% (FULL) AND 50%

25g (1oz) butter
225g (8oz) onions, finely chopped
450g (1lb) minced lamb or beef
225g (8oz) tomatoes, skinned and chopped
2 × 15ml tbsp (2tbsp) tomato purée
2 × 15ml tbsp (2tbsp) stock or water
1 × 5ml tsp (1tsp) salt
675g (1½lb) aubergines, thinly sliced
4 × 15ml tbsp (4 tbsp) white wine
1 egg, beaten
4 × 15ml tbsp (4tbsp) grated parmesan cheese
275ml (½pt) white sauce (page 65)

1 Melt the butter in a casserole dish for 1 min. Add the onions to the butter and cook uncovered, for 2 min. Add the meat, stir, and cook for 3–4 min.
2 Stir in the tomatoes, tomato purée, stock or water and salt. Cover and cook for 15–20 min on 50% setting.
3 Cook the aubergines (page 93).
4 Fill a large glass or pottery dish with alternate layers of meat mixture and the aubergines. Sprinkle the wine over the moussaka.
5 Add the beaten egg and half the cheese to the basic white sauce. Stir well and adjust seasoning to taste. Pour the sauce over the moussaka and sprinkle the rest of the cheese on top.
6 Cook, uncovered on 100% (full) for 20–25 min, turning the dish halfway through the cooking time.
7 Serve with a green or tomato and onion salad.

Note: *Cooked, sliced potatoes can be used instead of the aubergines if preferred.*

Veal with aubergine (serves 4)
POWER LEVEL: 100% (FULL)
colour photograph opposite

4 veal escalopes, about 100g (4oz) each
few drops lemon juice
4 slices ham, about 25g (1oz) each
25g (1oz) butter
freshly ground black pepper
1 onion, peeled and thinly sliced
2–3 cloves garlic, crushed
450g (1lb) aubergines, trimmed and thinly sliced
4 tomatoes, skinned and quartered
1 × 15ml tbsp (1tbsp) tomato purée
salt
1 glass white wine or stock
50g (2oz) cheddar cheese, grated
For garnish:
chopped parsley

1 Trim away any fat from the escalopes and beat into thin slices. Lay them out flat and sprinkle with a few drops of lemon juice.
2 Arrange a slice of ham on top of each escalope, then roll them up neatly and secure each one with a cocktail stick or tie with string.
3 Melt the butter in a large casserole for 1 min, arrange the veal rolls in the dish and turn or brush them with the butter. Sprinkle with black pepper.
4 Cover and cook for 8–10 min, turning the dish halfway through. Remove the veal rolls and keep warm.
5 Add the onion to the butter and juices in the dish, cover and cook for 2 min. Add the garlic and aubergines, toss over well, cover and cook for 6–8 min or until tender.
6 Add the tomatoes, tomato purée, salt to taste and the wine or stock. Cover and cook for 3–4 min.
7 Remove the cocktail sticks or ties from the veal and replace the rolls in the dish on top of the aubergine mixture; sprinkle with the grated cheese and reheat for 2–3 min until the cheese is melted.
8 Serve hot sprinkled with plenty of chopped parsley. Plain boiled potatoes in their jackets go well with this dish.

Quick poor man's cassoulet (serves 6–8)
POWER LEVEL: 100% (FULL)
colour page 30

40g (1½oz) lard
2 large cloves garlic, finely chopped
4 pork strips, boned, trimmed and diced
175–225g (6–8oz) stewing lamb, diced
150ml (¼pt) chicken stock
225g (8oz) garlic or pork sausage, cut into 1.5cm (½in) cubes
2 × 425g (15oz) cans baked beans
2 × 15ml tbsp (2tbsp) brandy, optional
salt and pepper
For garnish:
1 × 15ml tbsp (1 tbsp) chopped parsley
For serving:
fresh bread or garlic bread (page 141)

1 Melt the lard in a large casserole for 2–3 min. Add the garlic and pork strips. Cook for 2 min, then add the lamb and stock and cook for 2 min.
2 Add the sausage, beans and brandy, if used. Season and stir well.
3 Cook for 10 min, on 100% (full) and a further 20 min on 50%. Sprinkle with parsley before serving.
4 Serve hot with crusty fresh bread or garlic bread.

Baked Avocados with Walnut Cheese (page 56), Veal with Aubergine (opposite) and Creamed Potatoes (page 97)

Casserole of sausage *(serves 3–6)*
POWER LEVEL: 100% (FULL) AND 70%

6 large pork sausages with herbs
6 thick lean bacon rashers, rinds removed
25g (1oz) butter
2 × 15ml tbsp (2tbsp) oil
1 large onion, finely chopped
1½ × 5ml tsp (1½tsp) dried sage
2 × 15ml tbsp (2tbsp) flour
425ml (¾pt) hot stock
salt and freshly ground black pepper
150ml (¼pt) soured cream
For garnish:
chopped parsley

1 Roll up each sausage with a rasher of bacon and tie with fine string or secure with wooden cocktail sticks.
2 Melt the butter and oil in a casserole dish for 2 min, stir in the onion, cover and cook for 5 min. Add the dried sage and the sausages and continue to cook for 4 min.
3 Remove the sausages to a plate and stir the flour into the dish. Gradually add the stock, cover and bring to the boil about 3–4 min, stirring every minute.
4 Add seasoning to taste. Return the sausages to the casserole and reduce to 50% setting. Cover and cook for 15 min.
5 Stir the soured cream into the dish and allow to stand for 5 min. Reheat for 1–2 min if necessary before serving garnished with chopped parsley.

Carbonnade of beef (serves 4)
POWER LEVEL: 100% (FULL) AND 50%

50g (2oz) butter
3 large onions, thinly sliced
675g (1½lb) braising steak, cut into 2.5cm (1in) cubes
1 × 15ml tbsp (1tbsp) seasoned flour
50g (2oz) streaky bacon, diced
275ml (½pt) brown ale
boiling stock
salt and pepper
bouquet garni
1 × 5ml tsp (1tsp) french mustard
15g (½oz) cornflour
For serving:
crusty french bread

1 Melt the butter in a large casserole dish for 1½ min on 100% (full) setting. Add the onions and cook for 4 min.
2 Toss the meat in the seasoned flour.
3 Add the bacon to the onions, cook for 1 min on 100% (full) setting, add the meat, cook for a further 2 min.
4 Stir in the brown ale and sufficient stock to cover the meat. Add the seasonings, bouquet garni and mustard.
5 Cover and cook on 50% setting for 60–70 min, stirring occasionally.
6 Leave the casserole to cool slightly.
7 Remove the bouquet garni and adjust seasonings.
8 Blend the cornflour with a little of the cooking liquor and stir into the casserole.
9 Reheat on 100% (full) setting for 3–4 min, stirring every 2 min until heated through and thickened.
10 Serve with crusty french bread.

Hungarian goulash (serves 4)
POWER LEVEL: 100% (FULL) AND 50%

450g (1lb) stewing steak, cut into small cubes
3 × 15ml tbsp (3tbsp) seasoned flour
25ml (1fl oz) oil
2 medium-sized onions, chopped
1 green pepper, deseeded and chopped
2 × 5ml tsp (2tsp) paprika
3 × 5ml tsp (3tsp) tomato purée
pinch grated nutmeg
salt and pepper
50g (2oz) plain flour
275–425ml (½–¾pt) boiling stock
2 tomatoes, skinned and quartered
bouquet garni
For serving:
boiled rice or pasta (page 102)

1 Toss the meat in the seasoned flour. Heat the oil in a large dish for 1–2 min on 100% (full) setting.
2 Stir in the meat then add all the other ingredients, blending well.
3 Cover and cook for 10–14 min on 100% (full) setting, then cook for 30–40 min on 50% setting, stirring twice throughout.
4 Remove bouquet garni and serve hot with boiled rice or pasta.

Crown roast of lamb (serves 4)
POWER LEVEL: 100% (FULL) OR 70%

2 best ends of lamb (5–6 cutlets each)
Orange and herb stuffing:
50g (2oz) butter
50g (2oz) onion, chopped
100g (4oz) fresh white breadcrumbs
1 orange, grated rind and juice
2 × 15ml tbsp (2tbsp) fresh chopped herbs
or
1 × 15ml tbsp (1tbsp) dried mixed herbs
seasoning
1 egg, beaten
For garnish:
cutlet frills
For serving:
glazed onions (page 96)

1 If you give the butcher sufficient notice, he will prepare the best ends of lamb by trimming away any excess fat and forming the two joints into a round or crown. Tie the crown securely with string.
2 Melt the butter for 1½ min on 100% (full) setting, toss the onion in the butter, cover and cook for a further 3 min. Add all the remaining ingredients for the stuffing and mix well together.
3 Place the meat onto a suitable cooking container and spoon the stuffing into the centre cavity. Allow 9 min per 450g (1lb) if using 100% (full) power or 11 min per 450g (1lb) if using a 70% setting.
4 Protect the tips of the cutlet bones with small smooth pieces of aluminium foil during the cooking time. Allow the joint to stand for 15–20 min halfway through the cooking time and a further 5–10 min at the end.
5 Place cutlet frills over the bones before serving the crown roast garnished with glazed onions.

Note: *Guard of Honour is prepared and cooked in a similar way except instead of the joints being formed into a crown, the best ends are placed back to back with the tips of the bones crossed like swords.*

Spare ribs sweet and sour (serves 2–3)
POWER LEVEL: 100% (FULL) AND 70%

675g (1½lb) spare rib chops
25g (1oz) butter
25g (1oz) onion, chopped
25g (1oz) plain flour
275ml (½pt) chicken stock, boiling
25g (1oz) green pepper, deseeded and chopped
3 × 15ml tbsp (3 tbsp) crushed pineapple
1 × 15ml tbsp (1tbsp) wine vinegar
2 × 15ml tbsp (2tbsp) worcestershire sauce
25g (1oz) soft brown sugar
1 × 15ml tbsp (1tbsp) tomato purée
salt and pepper

1 Place the spare ribs in a large shallow dish. Cook for 3 min. Remove the chops from the dish and keep warm.
2 Melt the butter in the dish for 1 min. Add the onion and cook for 3 min. Stir in the flour, then add the stock gradually.
3 Stir in the remaining ingredients and mix well together.
4 Add the chops to the sauce. Cook, covered, for 5 min.
5 Turn the chops and stir the sauce, then return to the microwave and cook, uncovered, on 70% setting for 25–30 min, stirring and turning the meat once halfway through.

Chilli con carne (serve 4–6)
POWER LEVEL: 100% (FULL) AND 50%

2 × 15ml tbsp (2tbsp) oil
2 large onions, finely chopped
450g (1lb) minced beef
2 × 15ml tbsp (2tbsp) tomato purée
1–2 × 15ml tsp (1–2tsp) chilli powder
1 × 5ml tsp (1tsp) paprika
salt and pepper
1 × 397g (14oz) can kidney beans
For serving:
boiled rice (page 102)

1 Heat the oil in a large bowl for 2 min. Add the onions and cook for 3 min. Add the meat and mix well.
2 Cover and cook for 2 min, stir, cook for 2 min. Add the tomato purée and seasonings, mixing well.
3 Drain the kidney beans, reserving the juice and making up to 225ml (8fl oz) with water. Add the liquid to the meat.
4 Cover and cook on 50% setting for 20–30 min, stand for 5 min. Stir in the kidney beans, then cook for 5–10 min. Skim off the surplus fat and adjust the seasoning before serving.

Cottage pie (serves 4–6)
POWER LEVEL: 100% (FULL) AND 50%
colour page 70

25g (1oz) butter or margarine
1 small onion, finely chopped
450g (1lb) minced beef
25g (1oz) flour
150ml (¼pt) beef stock
1 × 5ml (1tsp) chopped parsley
salt and freshly ground black pepper
1 × 5ml tsp (1tsp) worcestershire sauce
450g (1lb) creamed potatoes (page 97)
knob butter
paprika for sprinkling

1 Melt the butter or margarine in a large round casserole for 1 min. Add the onion and cook for 2–3 min.
2 Add the minced beef, mix with the onion, cover and cook for 5–6 min until browned, stirring once or twice and breaking down any lumps with a fork.
3 Stir in the flour, stock, parsley, seasoning and worcestershire sauce. Cover and cook for 10 min on 100% (full) and a further 20–30 min on 50% setting, stirring every 5 min.
4 Wipe the sides of the dish and cover the meat with the potato, marking the surface with a fork. Alternatively, pipe the potato over the top using a large star nozzle fitted into a forcing bag.
5 Top with slivers of butter and cook on 100% (full) until hot through (1–2 min if the ingredients are still hot, 5–6 min if cool). Sprinkle with paprika or brown the top under a hot grill.

Stuffed hearts (serves 4)
POWER LEVEL: 100% (FULL) AND 30%

4 sheep's hearts
sage and onion stuffing (page 90, ½ quantity)
25g (1oz) butter
2 onions, finely sliced
275–425ml (½–¾pt) boiling beef stock
salt and pepper
bouquet garni
1 × 15ml tbsp (1tbsp) cornflour
For garnish:
chopped parsley

1 Soak the hearts in cold salt water for 30min, then clean thoroughly. Remove pipes and trim. Fill with the sage and onion stuffing and secure the tops with thread.
2 Melt the butter in a casserole dish for 1 min, add the onions, mix well and cook, covered, for 4 min.

3 Add the hearts and brush with the onion and butter juices. Cook, covered, for 2 min, turning the hearts halfway through.

4 Add sufficient stock to cover the hearts. Season to taste with salt and pepper and add the bouquet garni. Bring to the boil in the microwave, about 4 min.

5 Reduce to 30% setting and continue to cook, covered, for about 1½–1¾ hr until the hearts are tender. Leave to stand for 20 min.

6 Blend the cornflour with a little cold water and add to the dish. Cook until thickened, 1½–2 min, stirring halfway through.

7 Garnish with plenty of chopped parsley and serve hot.

Sage and onion stuffing

POWER LEVEL: 100% (FULL)

50g (2oz) butter
450g (1lb) onions, chopped
1 × 15ml tbsp (1tbsp) fresh chopped sage or
2 ×5ml tsp (2tsp) dried sage
100g (4oz) fresh white or brown breadcrumbs
salt and pepper
1 egg, beaten

1 Melt the butter in a bowl for 1½ min. Toss the onions in the butter and cook for 4–5 min until soft.

2 Stir in the sage, breadcrumbs and seasoning, mixing well. Allow to cool slightly before binding with the egg. Use for pork or chicken.

Turkey meat loaf

POWER LEVEL: 70%

450g (1lb) cooked turkey meat (or chicken or ham)
1 large onion
100g (4oz) breadcrumbs
3 × 15ml tbsp (3tbsp) tomato purée
4 eggs
½ × 5ml tsp (½tsp) allspice
pinch nutmeg
salt and pepper

1 Mince the meat and onion together and place in a large mixing bowl. Add all the other ingredients and mix thoroughly.

2 Press the mixture into a loaf dish and cook in the microwave for 20–25 min. Turn the dish every 5 min if necessary.

3 Serve hot with vegetables or cold with salad.

Chicken and sweetcorn oatie pie (serves 4)

POWER LEVEL: 100% (FULL)

1 × 5ml tsp (1tsp) cornflour
150ml (¼pt) chicken stock, approximately
225g (8oz) cooked chicken, roughly chopped
325g (11½oz) can sweetcorn
salt and freshly ground black pepper
100g (4oz) plain flour
pinch salt
50g (2oz) rolled oats
75g (3oz) butter or margarine

1 Lightly grease a large ovenware pie dish.

2 Blend the cornflour with a little of the stock, add the rest and cook for 1½–2 min, stirring every minute until thickened.

3 Add the chicken and the sweetcorn. Mix together, add seasoning to taste and a little extra stock if necessary to moisten. Place the mixture into the prepared pie dish.

4 Sift the flour and salt. Stir in the rolled oats and rub in the butter to form a coarse crumb mixture. Sprinkle over the chicken and sweetcorn.

5 Cook for 8–10 min until hot through and topping is cooked, giving a quarter turn every 2 min. Serve hot.

Armenian lamb (serves 4)

POWER LEVEL: 100% (FULL) AND 30%

1kg (2lb) fillet end leg of lamb
40g (1½oz) butter
2 medium-sized onions, chopped
1 clove garlic, chopped
25g (1oz) plain flour
1 × 5ml tsp (1tsp) ground cumin seed
½ × 5ml tsp (½tsp) ground allspice
2 × 15ml tbsp (2tbsp) tomato purée
275ml (½pt) stock
salt and pepper
For serving:
rice pilaf (page 103)

1 Remove the meat from the bone and cut into small cubes, about 2cm (¾in) square.

2 Melt the butter in a dish for 2 min, add the onion and garlic, cook for 3 min. Add the meat to the onion and garlic and cook, covered, for 2 min.

3 Add all the other ingredients. Cook, covered, for 5 min, reduce to 30% setting and cook for a further 45–55 min.

4 Serve with rice pilaf.

Vegetables

Fresh vegetables cooked in the microwave are delicious and retain their full flavour, colour and nutritional value as they are cooked in their own juices, requiring very little additional liquid. In fact some vegetables – spinach and spring greens, for example – are cooked using only the water which clings to the leaves after washing. Roasting bags and boiling bags are useful for cooking vegetables as they can be easily shaken or turned over to stir the contents during the cooking cycle. Remember, however, that the wire ties supplied with some makes must not be used; rubber bands or string ties make suitable alternatives and the

Green Beans Italian Style (page 98), Broad Beans with Ham (page 96) and French Bean Salad (page 96)

bag should be tied loosely to allow some steam to escape. Vegetables will remain hot for a considerable time after cooking if the bag is not opened so it is possible to cook several varieties of vegetable one after another and serve them together.

If preferred, vegetables may be cooked using more water in a casserole dish, covered with a lid or pierced clingfilm, but the cooking time should be increased to allow for the extra volume in the oven. It is not always quicker to cook vegetables by microwave than cooking conventionally, but the results are well worthwhile.

Blanching vegetables

It is possible to blanch vegetables for the freezer in the microwave oven but only attempt small quan-

tities at a time. Some vegetables are more successful and will keep a better colour than others.

The vegetables should be prepared for blanching in the normal way, placed in a large covered casserole with water allowing 75–100ml (3–4fl oz) per 450g (1lb) vegetables, depending on the type – for example, sliced runner beans would require slightly less water than cauliflower florets.

The vegetables should be cooked for half the recommended cooking time given on the vegetable cooking chart, but it is important to shake or stir them at least once during the blanching period. After blanching, cool the vegetables in iced water, then pack and freeze in the normal way.

Vegetables may be blanched in boiling bags for convenience, with very little water – about as much as recommended when cooking vegetables. To blanch them, cook in the microwave for half the recommended cooking time, shaking them frequently throughout. Chill them by plunging the whole package up to the opening in a bowl of iced water; this will reduce the temperature and expel the air at the same time, automatically creating a vacuum pack for the freezer. Seal the bag in the normal way and freeze.

Home-frozen vegetables when required for use should be cooked for the full time recommended for fresh vegetables but allow an extra 1–3 min if using them straight from the freezer, when no extra water will be required.

Frozen vegetables

Frozen vegetables are defrosted and cooked in one operation, using 100% (full) setting.

Vegetable	Cooking time	
	225g (½lb)	450g (1lb)
asparagus	6–7 min	10–11 min
beans, broad	7–8 min	10–11 min
beans, french or runner	7–8 min	10–11 min
broccoli	6–8 min	8–10 min
cabbage	6–7 min	10–11 min
carrots	6–8 min	9–10 min
cauliflower florets	4–6 min	7–9 min
corn kernel	3–4 min	7–8 min
corn-on-the-cob	4–5 min (1 cob)	7–8 min (2 cobs)
courgettes	4–5 min	6–8 min
peas	4–5 min	8–9 min
spinach, chopped or leaf	7–8 min	10–11 min
stewpack	6–8 min	9–11 min
swedes or turnips	7–8 min	10–12 min
vegetables mixed, diced	5–6 min	7–9 min

Commercial frozen products may cook quicker than home-frozen ones. This is due to the fact that commercial freezing takes place at very high speed and, as a result, the ice crystals are smaller and melt more quickly during cooking. The times given in the preceding chart are approximate, as the type and size of the container and the freezing method used will affect the cooking time required. Also the degree of cooking is a personal choice – some may prefer crisper vegetables, while others prefer them cooked a little longer. Adjust the cooking times to suit your own individual requirements.

Canned vegetables

Most canned vegetables are cooked during the processing and, therefore, only need reheating in the microwave. The food must be removed from the can and placed in a suitable covered container. Heat on 100% (full) setting for 3–4 min for the 400–425g (14–15oz) size and for 2–2½ min for the 200–225g (7–8oz) size. Stir the contents of the dish halfway through the cooking time to ensure even heating.

Drying herbs

Preserving herbs by drying in the microwave is very quick and easy compared with conventional methods and the microwave cooker dries small quantities very successfully. Many varieties of herbs are annual plants and, when near the end of their season, it is possible to dry them by microwave to last through the winter months. The method is simple and the results are excellent, retaining better colours and aromas than conventionally dried herbs.

It is preferable if the herbs are clean and dry when picked, otherwise wash them thoroughly and pat them dry between pieces of kitchen paper towel. Gently squeeze as much moisture as possible from them after washing as this will help to cut down the drying time and give better results. Remove the leaves from the stems and measure about 1 cupful (25g/1oz). Spread the herbs out evenly onto two thicknesses of kitchen paper towel placed on the microwave cooker shelf and cover with two more pieces of kitchen paper towel. This helps to absorb moisture during the heating process.

Heat on 100% (full) setting for 4–6 min checking every min and turning the kitchen paper towels with the herbs over once. Check after minimum time – when dry, the herbs will be brittle and break very easily. Leave to cool between the kitchen paper towels before crushing and storing in an airtight jar which should be kept in a cool, dry place.

Fresh vegetable cooking chart

Vegetable and quantity	Preparation	Amount of salted water to be added	Cooking time in mins 100% (full)
artichokes, jerusalem 450g (1lb)	peel and cut into even-sized pieces	4 × 15ml tbsp (4tbsp) or 25g (1oz) butter	8–10
asparagus 225g (8oz)	trim and leave whole	2 × 15ml tbsp (2tbsp)	thin spears 6–8 thick spears 8–10
aubergines 450g (1lb)	wash, slice, sprinkle with salt and leave for 30 min, rinse	2 × 15ml tbsp (2tbsp)	8–10
beans, broad 450g (1lb)	remove from pods	3 × 15ml tbsp (3tbsp)	8–10
beans, french 450g (1lb)	wash and cut	2 × 15ml tbsp (2tbsp)	8–10
beans, runner 450g (1lb)	string and slice	2 × 15ml tbsp (2tbsp)	8–10
beetroot 450g (1lb)	peel and slice	2 × 15ml tbsp (2tbsp)	7–8
225g (8oz) whole	prick skin, wrap in clingfilm		12–15
broccoli 450g (1lb)	trim, cut into spears	2 × 15ml tbsp (2tbsp)	8–12
brussels sprouts 450g (1lb)	wash, remove outer leaves and trim	2 × 15ml tbsp (2tbsp)	8–10
cabbage 450g (1lb)	wash and shred finely	2 × 15ml tbsp (2tbsp)	8–10
carrots 225g (8oz)	*new* wash, scrape and cut into strips or leave whole, depending on size	2 × 15ml tbsp (2tbsp)	7–10
	old scrape or peel and slice	,,	7–10
cauliflower 675g (1½lb)	wash and cut into florets	4 × 15ml tbsp (4tbsp)	10–11
450g (1lb) whole	trim outside leaves, wash	,,	10–11
celery 350g (12oz)	wash, trim and slice	3 × 15ml tbsp (3tbsp)	10–12
corn-on-the-cob 2 × 225g (8oz)	wash and trim	4 × 15ml tbsp (4tbsp) or 40g (1½oz) butter	6–8
courgettes 450g (1lb)	wash, trim and slice	—	8–10
leeks 450g (1lb)	wash, trim and slice	2 × 15ml tbsp (2tbsp)	7–10
marrow 450g (1lb)	peel, cut into 2cm (¾in) rings, remove seeds and quarter the rings	2 × 15ml tbsp (2tbsp)	8–10
mushrooms 225g (8oz)	peel or wipe or wash	2 × 15ml tbsp (2tbsp) of stock or 25g (1oz) butter	5–6
okra 450g (1lb)	wash, trim, sprinkle with salt, leave for 30 min, rinse	2 × 15ml tbsp (2tbsp) or 25g (1oz) butter or oil	8–10
onions 225g (8oz)	peel and slice	2 × 15ml tbsp (2tbsp) or 25g (1oz) butter or oil	5–6

Vegetable and quantity	Preparation	Amount of salted water to be added	Cooking time in mins 100% (full)
parsnips 450g (1lb)	peel and slice	2 × 15ml tbsp (2tbsp)	8–10
peas 225g (8oz)	remove from pods	2 × 15ml tbsp (2tbsp)	8–10
potatoes 450g (1lb)	wash and scrub thoroughly or peel, cut into even sized pieces	2 × 15ml tbsp (2tbsp)	10–12
potatoes, old in their jackets 450g (1lb)	wash and scrub thoroughly, dry and prick skins	—	10–12
spinach 450g (1lb)	break up the thicker stalks, wash thoroughly	—	6–8
spring greens 450g (1lb)	break up thicker stalks, wash and shred	—	8–10
swedes 450g (1lb)	peel and dice	2 × 15ml tbsp (2tbsp)	6–7
tomatoes 450g (1lb)	wash and halve, place in shallow dish	—	6–8
turnips 450g (1lb)	peel and dice	2 × 15ml tbsp (2tbsp)	8–10

•GUIDELINES AT-A-GLANCE

•**Additional liquid** is minimal when 'boiling' vegetables – just 2–3 × 15ml tbsp (2–3tbsp) is all that is required for most varieties.

•**Arrange** larger whole vegetables such as jacket potatoes or whole tomatoes in a circle on a plate or on the oven shelf for even cooking. Vegetables such as asparagus or broccoli spears should be arranged so that the thick stems are towards the outside of the dish and the more tender tips or curds are towards the centre.

•**Containers** such as boiling or roasting bags are useful as the contents can easily be shaken or stirred. However, they can be a little expensive and so microwave casserole dishes or bowls covered with lids or pierced clingfilm are ideal.

•**Cooking** times for fresh vegetables are approximately 8–12 min for 450g (1lb) depending on the variety (see cooking chart on page 93). The power setting is 100% (full) for most vegetables unless used as part of a composite dish in which case lower settings can be used.

•**Cover** dishes with a lid or pierced clingfilm when cooking, defrosting or reheating vegetables. The exception is when cooking large whole vegetables such as jacket potatoes or tomatoes.

•**Deep-fat frying** should not be attempted as the temperature of the fat or oil cannot be controlled. However, frozen chips can be quickly defrosted in the microwave which reduces the conventional frying time.

•**Defrosting** before cooking is not necessary for most frozen vegetables – cook them straight from the frozen state when no additional liquid is required. When defrosting a vegetable casserole or 'au gratin' dish, use a 30–50% power setting until evenly thawed before finally heating through.

•**Frozen oven chips** can be cooked in the microwave. Refer to page 15.

•**Lemon juice** squeezed over peeled potatoes will help prevent discoloration during cooking.

•**Oil or butter** can be kept to a minimum when lightly 'frying' vegetables and when preparing casseroles or stews. Stir the vegetables so that they are lightly coated in the fat before cooking.

•**Prick or score** larger whole vegetables such as jacket potatoes, tomatoes or aubergines to prevent the skin bursting during cooking.

Almondine Potatoes (page 97) and Creamed Mushrooms and Peas (page 97)

●**Reheating** precooked vegetables is carried out at 100% (full). Vegetable casseroles or 'au gratin' dishes will require a 50–70% setting to ensure the sauce does not overheat and bubble before the main ingredient is heated through.

●**Roast** potatoes are not particularly successful as they do not brown or become crisp. The use of a browning dish will help.

●**Salt** should not be sprinkled onto vegetables before cooking as it can have a toughening effect. Add a little salt to the cooking water and adjust the seasoning to taste after cooking.

●**Sauté** or lightly fry onions, peppers, carrots, mushrooms in a little butter or oil when preparing a casserole or serving them as a vegetable. Sautéeing vegetables such as tomatoes, aubergines and fennel is best done in a large shallow dish to keep stirring to a minimum if it is important that the pieces do not break.

●**Stir** vegetables once or twice during cooking, bringing the outer ones to the centre of the dish and the inside ones to the edge for even cooking results. If boiling bags are used, shake the bag once or twice during cooking.

●**Timings** will need to be increased by one-third to a half when doubling the amount of vegetables given in the cooking chart. One jacket potato weighing 100–150g (4–5oz) will take 5–6 min, 2 will take 7–9 min, 3 will take 10–11 min and so on. The age and thickness of vegetables will also effect cooking times so test regularly during cooking.

●**Turn** large whole vegetables over halfway through cooking – jacket potatoes, aubergines, beetroots, corn-on-the-cob for example – to ensure they cook evenly.

●**Undercook** rather than overcook, as vegetables will continue to cook by residual heat during their standing time at the end of cooking. This is particularly important if preparing in advance, to ensure that they do not overcook when reheated.

Broad beans with ham *(serves 4–6)*
POWER LEVEL: 100% (FULL) AND 50%
colour page 91

450g (1lb) shelled broad beans
2 × 15ml tbsp (2tbsp) salted water
275ml (½pt) béchamel sauce (page 65)
2 × 15ml tbsp (2tbsp) cream
225g (8oz) lean cooked ham, shredded
1 × 15ml tbsp (1tbsp) freshly chopped parsley

1 Cook the broad beans with the salted water in a suitable covered container for 8–10 min on 100% (full) setting. After cooking, if the beans are old remove the thin skins.
2 Add the beans to the sauce with the cream and ham. Reduce to 50% setting and cook for a further 4–5 min until heated through, but do not allow to boil.
3 Stir in the chopped parsley and serve.

Note: *225–350g (8–12oz) butter beans, soaked and cooked (page 102) or canned butter beans, can be used instead of broad beans for this dish.*

French bean salad *(serves 4–6)*
POWER LEVEL: 100% (FULL)
colour page 91

French beans, lightly cooked and served cold, make an excellent ingredient for a mixed salad, or are delicious served on their own with a plain dressing.

450g (1lb) french beans, trimmed and left whole
2 × 15ml tbsp (2tbsp) salted water
6 × 15ml tbsp (6tbsp) olive oil
2 × 15ml tbsp (2tbsp) lemon juice or wine vinegar
salt and freshly ground black pepper
pinch sugar
For garnish:
1 hardboiled egg

1 Wash the beans and place them with the salted water in a serving dish. Cover and cook for 6 min, shaking or stirring the beans twice throughout. Leave to stand for a few minutes. The beans should be crisp.
2 Whisk the olive oil, lemon juice or wine vinegar, seasoning and sugar together.
3 Drain the beans, add the dressing and allow to cool.
4 When cold, toss the beans in the dressing.
5 Separate the egg white from the yolk. Chop the white finely and rub the yolk through a sieve.
6 Garnish the beans attractively with the egg yolk and white and serve.

DO NOT FREEZE

Stuffed cabbage leaves *(serves 4)*
POWER LEVEL: 100% (FULL) AND 50%
colour page 62

This is a good way of using up left-over cold meats and makes a substantial main course.

8 large cabbage leaves, trimmed and washed
2 × 15ml tbsp (2tbsp) salted water
25g (1oz) butter
1 large onion, peeled and finely chopped
350g (12oz) cooked chicken or ham, minced
1 × 15ml tbsp (1tbsp) chopped parsley
4 × 15ml tbsp (4tbsp) fresh white breadcrumbs
200–225g (7–8oz) can tomatoes
salt and freshly ground black pepper
For serving:
tomato sauce (page 65)

1 Place the cabbage leaves with the salted water in a casserole dish or boiling bag and cook on 100% (full) setting for 4–5 min. Drain well.
2 Melt the butter for 1 min on 100% (full) setting, add the onion, toss well, cover and cook for a further 5–6 min until transparent and soft.
3 Stir in the minced cooked chicken or ham, parsley and breadcrumbs.
4 Drain the tomatoes and reserve the juice. Add the tomatoes to the meat mixture with sufficient of the juice to moisten. Add salt and pepper to taste.
5 Divide the mixture between the cabbage leaves then roll up each one into a parcel and secure with a cocktail stick or tie with string.
6 Place the stuffed cabbage leaves in a buttered serving dish, cover and cook on 50% setting for 8–10 min until heated through.
7 Serve hot with tomato sauce.

Glazed onions *(serves 4–5)*
POWER LEVEL: 100% (FULL)

450g (1lb) button onions or shallots
boiling water
25g (1oz) butter
2 × 15ml tbsp (2tbsp) caster sugar

1 Peel the onions and place in a large bowl or casserole dish. Cover with boiling water.
2 Cover the dish and bring the water up to the boil in the microwave, drain leaving the onions in the dish.
3 Add the butter to the onions, cover and cook for 5 min. Shake the dish to stir the onions and spinkle with the caster sugar.
4 Cook uncovered for 3–4 min until tender and glazed.
5 Serve hot.

Creamed potatoes *(serves 4)*
POWER LEVEL: 100% (FULL)
colour page 87

450g (1lb) potatoes, washed
2 × 15ml tbsp (2tbsp) salted water
75–125ml (3–4fl oz) milk
25g (1oz) butter
salt and pepper

1 Prick the skins of the potatoes with a fork. Place with the salted water in a casserole dish, cover and cook for 10–12 min or until tender. Test with a fork.
2 Drain the potatoes, remove the skins or cut in half and scoop out the potato from the skins.
3 Mash the potatoes with a fork or potato masher.
4 Heat the milk for 1 min and add to the potatoes with the butter and seasoning.
5 Beat well together and serve hot.

Almondine potatoes
colour page 95

Follow the method and ingredients for creamed potatoes, omitting the milk but stirring in the butter and seasonings to taste. Allow the mixture to cool then refrigerate until cold. Divide the mixture into 8 portions and roll into balls, shaped between the palms of the hands, using a little flour, if necessary, to prevent the potatoes from sticking. Roll the potato balls in finely chopped and toasted almonds. Place on the microwave cooker shelf or in a serving dish and heat through uncovered for about 3 min.

Mushrooms au gratin *(serves 4)*
POWER LEVEL: 100% (FULL)

25g (1oz) butter
450g (1lb) button mushrooms, washed and sliced
salt and pepper
275ml (½pt) béchamel sauce (page 65)
150ml (¼pt) single cream
3 × 15ml tbsp (3tbsp) browned breadcrumbs
3 × 15ml tbsp (3tbsp) grated cheddar and
    parmesan cheese, mixed

1 Melt the butter in a serving dish for 1 min. Add the mushrooms, season lightly, cover and cook for 5 min; leave to stand for a few minutes.
2 Heat the béchamel sauce, if necessary, then stir in the cream.
3 Drain the mushrooms and spoon the sauce over the mushrooms. Mix the breadcrumbs with the cheese and sprinkle over the top of the sauce. Heat in the microwave for 2–3 min until the cheese is melted, or brown under a hot grill.

Tomato and mushroom crumble *(serves 4–6)*
POWER LEVEL: 100% (FULL)
colour page 58

550ml (1pt) tomato sauce (page 65)
225g (8oz) mushrooms, washed and sliced
75g (3oz) wholewheat flour
75g (3oz) plain flour
½ × 5ml tsp (½tsp) salt
½ × 5ml tsp (½tsp) dry mustard
75g (3oz) butter or margarine
75g (3oz) cheese, finely grated
For garnish:
tomato slices

1 Lightly grease a large round ovenware dish.
2 Mix the tomato sauce with the sliced mushrooms and place in the greased dish.
3 Sift the flours with the salt and mustard and rub in the butter or margarine finely. Stir in the grated cheese.
4 Sprinkle the crumble topping lightly over the tomato and mushroom mixture and smooth the top.
5 Cook for 8–10 min, giving a quarter turn every 2 min until hot through and the crumble is cooked.
6 Serve hot garnished with tomato slices.

Creamed mushrooms and peas *(serves 4)*
POWER LEVEL: 100% (FULL)
colour page 95

4 large rashers bacon
225g (8oz) button mushrooms, washed and sliced
350g (12oz) frozen peas
salt and freshly ground black pepper
pinch mixed herbs
150ml (¼pt) double cream
For serving:
triangles of toasted or fried bread

1 Remove the rinds from the bacon and cut each rasher into strips.
2 Place the bacon strips into a serving dish, cover and cook for 2 min. Add the mushrooms, toss well in the fat from the bacon, cover and cook for 5–6 min.
3 Place the frozen peas in a bowl, cover and cook for 2½ min. Add salt, pepper and herbs, toss well, cover and cook for 2½–3½ min. Drain.
4 Add the peas to the mushrooms and bacon. Stir in the cream and adjust the seasoning.
5 Cook for 30–60 sec until just heated through without boiling.
6 Serve garnished with triangles of toasted or fried bread.

German red cabbage (serves 4–6)
POWER LEVEL: 100% (FULL) AND 70%
colour page 107

450g (1lb) red cabbage, very finely shredded
50g (2oz) butter, melted
1 large onion, peeled and sliced
2 cloves garlic, finely chopped
1 cooking apple, peeled and sliced
1 bay leaf
pinch each dried parsley and thyme
pinch each ground cinnamon and nutmeg
salt and freshly ground black pepper
1 orange, grated rind
2 × 15ml tbsp (2tbsp) brown sugar
1 × 5ml tsp (1tsp) caraway seeds
1 small wineglass red wine

1 Toss the shredded cabbage in the melted butter, cover and cook for 3–4 min.
2 Add all the other ingredients and stir well. Cover and cook on 70% setting for 35–40 min stirring 2–3 times throughout.
3 Remove the bay leaf and serve hot.

Green beans Italian style (serves 4)
POWER LEVEL: 100% (FULL)
colour page 91

Runner or french beans can be use for this dish – a good way of serving beans towards the end of their season.

450g (1lb) runner or french beans, prepared and sliced thickly
2 × 15ml tbsp (2tbsp) salted water
40g (1½oz) butter
1–2 × 15ml tbsp (1–2tbsp) olive oil
2 × 5ml tsp (2tsp) freshly chopped parsley or sage
1–2 cloves garlic, crushed
salt and freshly ground black pepper
2–3 × 5ml tsp (2–3tsp) parmesan cheese, grated
For garnish:
freshly chopped herbs

1 Wash the beans and place with the salted water in a serving dish, cover and cook for 8–10 min. Allow to stand for a few minutes.
2 Melt the butter for 1½min, add the olive oil, parsley or sage and the garlic and heat for 1 min.
3 Add the drained beans, salt and pepper to taste, toss well, cover and cook for 3 min. Stir in the parmesan cheese to taste.
4 Serve hot garnished with chopped herbs.

Note: *A 225g (8oz) can of tomatoes may be added with the beans before stirring in the parmesan cheese. Allow an extra 1½min cooking time.*

Asparagus flan (serves 6)
POWER LEVEL: 100% (FULL) AND 50%
colour page 103

175g (6oz) light wholemeal pastry (page 44)
25g (1oz) butter or margarine
1 small onion, peeled and finely chopped
290g (10½oz) can condensed asparagus soup
3 eggs, beaten
3 × 15ml tbsp (3tbsp) single cream or top of the milk
salt and pepper to taste
100g (4oz) cheese, grated
For decoration:
10–12 canned, frozen or fresh cooked aspargus spears

1 Roll out the pastry, line a 20cm (8in) flan dish and bake blind (page 44).
2 Melt the butter or margarine in a bowl for 1 min on 100% (full) setting, toss in the chopped onion and cook for a further 2–3 min until soft.
3 Beat together the soup, eggs, cream and seasoning until smooth and well blended. Stir in the cooked onion.
4 Cook the mixture on 50% setting for 6–8 min until heated through, whisking every 2 min. Stir in the cheese.
5 Pour into the cooked flan case and cook on 50% setting for 11–13 min, turning every 3 min. Allow to stand for a few minutes.
6 Heat the asparagus spears for 1–1½ min on 100% (full) setting and arrange on the top of the flan.
7 Serve on its own as a snack or with potatoes and salad as a main meal.

Fried onions (serves 3–4)
POWER LEVEL: 100% (FULL)

2 large onions, peeled and finely sliced
3 × 15ml tbsp (3tbsp) oil or dripping
caster sugar for dusting

1 Push the onion slices through to form rings.
2 Heat the oil or dripping for 2–3 min in a large bowl. Toss in the onion rings so that they are well coated in the oil.
3 Cover and cook for 5 min, stir well and dust with a little caster sugar. Cover and cook for 3–4 min until tender.
4 Serve hot with sausages or steaks.

Note: *Alternatively, the onions may be cooked in a browning dish which has been preheated for 5 min. Add the onion rings which have been tossed in the oil or dripping, cover and cook for 6–7 min, tossing the onions over once halfway through.*

Pissaladière with Garlic Bread (below)

Pissaladière *(serves 6)*
POWER LEVEL: 100% (FULL) AND 70%
colour photograph above

This strongly flavoured tart is characteristic of dishes from southern France and is similar to the Italian pizza but with a lighter pastry base. It makes a substantial lunch or supper dish.

175g (6oz) rich shortcrust pastry (page 43)
3 × 15ml tbsp (3tbsp) olive oil
2 large onions, peeled and finely sliced
1–2 cloves garlic, crushed or finely chopped
225g (8oz) can tomatoes
1 × 15ml tbsp (1tbsp) tomato purée
2 × 5ml tsp (2tsp) mixed chopped herbs, eg basil, oregano, thyme
salt and freshly ground black pepper
1 × 5ml tsp (1tsp) caster sugar
50g (2oz) can anchovy fillets
50–75g (2–3oz) black olives
For serving:
crusty french bread or garlic bread (page 141)

1 Roll out the pastry, line a 20cm (8in) flan dish and bake blind (page 44).
2 Place the oil, onions and garlic into a large bowl and toss well. Cover and cook on 100% (full) setting for 5–6 min until the onions are soft and transparent. Shake or stir twice throughout. Drain off the liquid.
3 Roughly chop the tomatoes and place in a bowl with the tomato purée, herbs, seasoning and sugar. Stir and boil in the microwave on 100% (full) setting until the liquid quantity is reduced and the mixture is fairly thick.
4 Add the tomato mixture to the drained onions and pour into the pastry case.
5 Drain the anchovy fillets and cut in half lengthwise. Arrange over the top of the flan in a lattice design. Garnish with the olives.
6 Cook on 70% setting for 12–15 min until heated through thoroughly. Alternatively, heat through on 100% (full) setting for 3 min, allow to stand for 3 min, repeat until hot through.
7 Serve hot with crusty french or garlic bread.

99

Mediterranean stuffed aubergines *(serves 4–6)*
POWER LEVEL: 100% (FULL) AND 50%

2 medium-sized aubergines
salt for sprinkling
2 × 15ml tbsp (2tbsp) oil
1 onion, finely chopped
½ green pepper, finely chopped
2 cloves garlic, finely chopped
225g (8oz) minced beef or lamb
4 tomatoes, skinned and chopped
1 courgette, trimmed, halved and thinly sliced
2 × 15ml tbsp (2tbsp) tomato purée
1 × 5ml tsp (1tsp) oregano
salt and black pepper to taste
For garnish:
grated parmesan cheese

1 Trim the aubergines. Cut into 8 thick slices, sprinkle with salt and heat in the microwave for 3 min. Leave to stand for 10–15 min. Wash thoroughly in cold water.
2 Remove the centre of the aubergines and reserve. Place the aubergine rings in an oven-ware serving dish.
3 Heat the oil in a mixing bowl for 2 min. Add the onion, pepper and garlic and cook for 3 min. Add the meat and cook for 4 min.
4 Chop the reserved aubergine centres and stir into the meat mixture along with the rest of the ingredients. Cover the bowl with clingfilm and cook on 50% setting for 15 min, stand for 5 min.
5 Cover and cook the aubergine rings, in the serving dish, for 4–5 min on 100% (full). Stuff the rings with the filling. Cover and cook for 3 min. Sprinkle with parmesan cheese before serving.

Stuffed baked marrow *(serves 4)*
POWER LEVEL: 100% (FULL)

1 medium marrow, peeled, cut lengthwise and deseeded
1 large onion, chopped
1 clove garlic, crushed
1 green pepper, deseeded and chopped
450g (1lb) tomatoes, skinned and chopped
1 × 15ml tbsp (1tbsp) fresh chopped basil or 1 × 5ml tsp (1tsp) dried basil
1 × 15ml tbsp (1tbsp) tomato purée
salt and pepper
50g (2oz) mushrooms, chopped
175g (6oz) cooked chicken or ham, diced
25g (1oz) breadcrumbs
50g (2oz) cheddar cheese, grated
2 × 15ml tbsp (2tbsp) chopped parsley.

1 Place the marrow shells side by side in a large oval dish. Cover with a lid or pierced clingfilm and cook for 5–8 min until the marrow is just tender, if necessary turning the dish or re-arranging the marrow halfway through.
2 Place the onion, garlic and green pepper in a bowl, cover and cook for 8 min, stirring once. Add the tomatoes, basil, tomato paste and seasoning, and continue to cook for a further 4 min.
3 Add the mushrooms and diced meat and cook for 6–8 min, uncovered, until the sauce has thickened slightly.
4 Pour any liquid that has collected in the marrow shells into the bottom of the dish. Pile the stuffing into the marrow shells. Cover and cook for 15–18 min until the marrow is tender. Drain the liquid from the dish.
5 Mix together the breadcrumbs, cheese and parsley and sprinkle over the stuffed marrows. Heat, uncovered, for 3–4 min, until the cheese is melted.

DO NOT FREEZE

Rice, pasta and pulses

Rice, pasta and pulses cook extremely well in the microwave – probably better than by most conventional menthods – and this is true also for defrosting and reheating after freezing. The main advantage, though, is that little or no attention is required during the cooking time and the kitchen remains relatively free of steam.

Rice
Long-grain rice may be boiled using lots of salted water and draining afterwards, or by carefully measuring the quantity of salted water so that the rice absorbs all the liquid during cooking, thereby retaining more B vitamins. If the latter method is used, the ratio of rice to water is 1:2, ie 1 cup of rice to 2 cups of water, allowing about 1 × 5ml tsp (1tsp) salt for this quantity.

Easy-cook rice absorbs more water than the normal long-grain rice and takes about 1–2 min longer to cook. Brown rice has a 'nuttier' texture and a delicious flavour which compensates for the fact that it takes approximately double the amount of cooking time for white rice.

Pasta
Pasta should be cooked in a large, covered container with plenty of boiling salted water and a little oil to provide sticking. When cooking quantities larger than 450g (1lb), you may find that conventional cooking methods are more convenient. When cooking pasta in the microwave, ensure that it is completely covered with water – any pieces that protrude above will become hard and brittle. To help prevent this, hold the pasta under the boiling water with a spoon or fork until it softens, before covering and placing in the microwave to cook. It may be boiled until it is completely cooked in the microwave, or it can be cooked for half the recommended time and then allowed to stand for 10 min to soften before draining.

Pulses
With the exception of lentils, all pulses require soaking before cooking conventionally or by microwave. They should be soaked for at least 5 hr, or overnight, in cold water. Alternatively, cover them with boiling water, cover the dish with a lid or pierced clingfilm, and heat in the microwave on 100% (full) for 5 min. Allow them to stand for 1½ hr to swell and soften before draining and rinsing well.

To cook, place the pulses in a large container, ensuring that there is sufficient room for the water to boil during the cooking time. Cover with boiling water from the kettle and bring the dish to the boil in the microwave. Do not add any salt to the water as this prevents the pulses from softening and therefore lengthens the cooking time. The pulses are cooked on 100% (full) setting for the first 10 min, then reduced to 50% setting for the remainder of the cooking time. All pulses should be covered during the cooking period, and be prepared to top up the cooking liquid with extra boiling water from the kettle if necessary.

Defrosting and heating

To defrost 450g (1lb) of cooked rice, pasta or pulses, use a 30% or 50% setting, cover the dish, and place in the microwave for 4–5 min. Stir gently halfway through, carefully breaking down the thawed food and removing from the dish if necessary. Any unthawed portion may be returned to the microwave for another minute or two or rinsed in a sieve or colander under cold running water which will help to separate pieces before reheating if required. Alternatively, after the defrosting time, allow to stand for 2–3 min until completely thawed. Reheat on a 80–100% (full) setting for 3–4 min, again stirring halfway through; allow to stand for 1–2 min before serving. When reheating a made-up dish such as a risotto, lasagne or cannelloni – particularly when a sauce is included – a lower 50% setting is preferable for reheating. This ensures that the sauce and other ingredients are heated evenly throughout.

•GUIDELINES AT-A-GLANCE

- •**Boiling** liquid added to rice, pasta or pulses will cut down on cooking times. Ensure that pasta and pulses are well covered with boiling water and be prepared to top up from the kettle if necessary during cooking.

Rice, pasta and pulses cooking chart

Rice/pasta/ pulses	Preparation	Cooking time 100% (full)
Easy cook rice (american) 225g (8oz)	add 550ml (1pt) boiling salted water	12 min stand 5 min
Long-grain rice (patna) 225g (8oz)	add 550ml (1pt) boiling salted water and 1 × 15ml tbsp (1tbsp) oil	10 min, stand 5 min
Brown rice 225g (8oz)	add 550ml (1pt) boiling salted water	5 min on 100% (full) then 20–25 min on 50%
Egg noodles and tagliatelle 225g (8oz)	add 550ml (1pt) boiling salted water and 1 × 15ml tbsp (1tbsp) oil	5–6 min, stand 3 min
Macaroni 225g (8oz)	add 550ml (1pt) boiled salted water and 1 × 15ml tbsp (1tbsp) oil	8 min, stand 3 min
Pasta shells and pasta whirls 225g (8oz)	add 850ml (1½pt) boiling salted water and 1 × 15ml tbsp (1tbsp) oil	7–8 min, stand 2 min
Spaghetti 225g (8oz)	break spaghetti in half if necessary; add 850ml (1½pt) boiling salted water and 1 × 15ml tbsp (1tbsp) oil	12 min stand 2 min
Lasagne 225g (8oz)	add 1l (1¾pt) boiling salted water and 1 × 15ml tbsp (1tbsp) oil	10 min, stand 2 min
Red lentils 225g (8oz)	cover with boiling water	15–20 min
Large pulses eg butter beans flageolets, pinto, soya and kidney beans 225g (8oz), soaked	cover with boiling water	10 min on 100% (full) then 20–25 min on 50%
Small pulses eg aduki, brown or green lentils, black-eye beans 225g (8oz), soaked	cover with boiling water	10 min on 100% (full) then 10–15 min on 50%
Split peas 225g (8oz), soaked	cover with boiling water	10 min

●**Boil-overs** can occur if the container is not large enough to allow for the water to boil and the expansion of the food during cooking.

●**Containers** such as large bowls, jugs or casseroles are ideal for cooking rice, pasta or pulses.

●**Cooking** is normally carried out at 100% (full) setting for white rice and pasta. Pulses should be boiled initially on 100% (full) for 10–15 min then reduced to 50% for the remaining time. Brown rice also requires a 50% setting after intially boiling on 100% (full) setting (see chart).

●**Cover** the dish with a lid or pierced clingfilm always when cooking, defrosting or reheating.

●**Defrosting** should be carried out at 30–50% setting until thawed, breaking off the defrosted portions from the edges 2–3 times throughout. Any remaining ice crystals can be quickly thawed by rinsing in a sieve or colander under cold running water. This also helps to separate the pieces before reheating.

●**Hardening** of grains can occur if they are not covered sufficiently with boiling water. Any pasta protruding above the water level should be pushed down with a spoon and held until softened.

●**Oil** added with the boiling water will help prevent pasta sticking during cooking.

●**Refresh** plainly boiled pasta and rice in either fresh hot or cold water as appropriate, when it is important to prevent grains sticking after cooking.

●**Reheating** plainly boiled pasta and rice can be carried out at 80–100% (full) setting. If other ingredients are added to form a composite dish – a lasagne or risotto for example – a lower 50–70% setting is preferable to achieve more even results.

●**Salt** may be added to the water when cooking rice and pasta but do not add to pulses as it prevents them softening, therefore extending the cooking time.

●**Standing** times given for rice and pasta (see cooking chart) are only necessary if the food is not quite tender at the end of the cooking time. If it is cooked to the desired degree, it should not be allowed to stand. Alternatively, pasta may be cooked for half the time given on the chart and then allowed to stand for 10 min to swell and soften.

●**Test** pasta towards the end of cooking to obtain the ideal *al dente* result.

Layered noodle pudding *(serves 4–6)*
POWER LEVEL: 100% (FULL)
colour photograph below

This dish may be served as a substantial snack or with a meat dish as part of a main course.

225g (8oz) flat noodles eg tagliatelle
2 × 5ml tsp (2tsp) oil
1 × 5ml tsp (2tsp) salt
550ml (1pt) boiling water, approximately
75g (3oz) butter or margarine, melted
350g (12oz) cooked spinach, fresh or frozen
2 × 15ml tbsp (2tbsp) single cream or top of the milk
salt and freshly ground black pepper
25g (1oz) parmesan cheese, grated
For serving:
275ml (½pt) cheese sauce (page 65)

1 Well butter a 850ml (1½pt) pudding basin.
2 Place the noodles in a bowl with the oil and salt and pour on sufficient boiling water to cover. Stir, cover and cook for 7–9 min until tender; stir twice.

Layered Noodle Pudding with Cheese sauce (above) and Asparagus Flan (page 98)

3 Drain and rinse in hot running water. Drain well and stir in half the butter or margarine.
4 Mix well together the spinach, cream, seasonings, parmesan cheese and remaining butter or margarine.
5 Layer the butter noodles and spinach mixture in the greased pudding basin, beginning and ending with a layer of noodles.
6 Cover with clingfilm, making a slit with a sharp knife. Cook for 5 min, turning every 2 min. Leave to stand for a few minutes.
7 Remove clingfilm, invert onto a hot serving plate or dish and serve with cheese sauce.

Rice pilaf *(serves 4)*
POWER LEVEL: 100% (FULL)

Serve with meats, fish, casseroles or curries.

40g (1½oz) butter
1 small onion, chopped
225g (8oz) long-grain rice
425ml (¾pt) chicken stock
salt and pepper
75g (3oz) currants
75g (3oz) pistachio nuts or almonds, blanched and shredded

1 Melt the butter in a large shallow dish for 2 min. Add the onion and rice and cook for 3 min.

2 Add the stock and seasoning and cook, uncovered, for 12–15 min, adding extra stock if necessary.

3 Carefully stir in the currants and nuts before serving.

Aubergine macaroni pie (serves 4–6)
POWER LEVEL: 100% (FULL) AND 50%

225g (8oz) aubergine, thinly sliced
salt
3 × 15ml tbsp (3tbsp) olive oil, approximately
1 large onion, peeled and finely sliced
450g (1lb) minced beef
1–2 cloves garlic, crushed or finely chopped
salt and freshly ground black pepper
1 × 15ml tbsp (1tbsp) tomato purée
400g (14oz) can tomatoes
1 × 5ml tsp (1tsp) dried oregano or basil
275ml (½pt) natural yoghurt
2 eggs, beaten
100g (4oz) cheese, grated
225g (8oz) short-cut macaroni, cooked (page 102)

1 Place the aubergine slices on a plate, sprinkle with salt and leave for 30 min. Rinse in cold water and dry.

2 Place in a large round casserole dish, sprinkle on the oil, cover and cook on 100% (full) setting for 4–5 min until soft. Remove the slices onto a plate.

3 Add the onion to the casserole dish with a little more oil if necessary and cook for about 4 min until soft and transparent.

4 Add the minced beef, mix with the onion, cover and cook for 5–6 min until browned, stirring once or twice and breaking down any lumps with a fork.

5 Add the garlic, seasoning, tomato purée, tomatoes and herbs. Cover and cook for a further 10–15 min until tender, stirring twice throughout.

6 Wipe the sides of the dish and arrange the aubergine slices on the meat.

7 Mix together the yoghurt, beaten eggs, three-quarters of the cheese and the cooked macaroni in a large bowl.

8 Cook on 50% setting for 4–5 min until hot. Pour the mixture over the aubergine.

9 Continue to cook for 12–15 min until heated through and the topping is set.

10 Sprinkle with the remaining cheese and cook on 100% (full) setting for 1–2 min until melted or brown the top under a hot grill.

Pasta salad (serves 6–8)
POWER LEVEL: 100% (FULL)

550ml (1pt) boiling water
1 × 5ml tsp (1tsp) salt
1 × 15ml tbsp (1tbsp) oil
100g (4oz) shell pasta
50g (2oz) walnuts, chopped
50g (2oz) raisins
2 carrots
1 green eating apple
1 × 425g (15oz) can kidney beans
oil and vinegar salad dressing

1 Place water, salt and oil in a large bowl. Add the pasta and cook for 8 min until tender. Stir well, then drain and rinse with cold water.

2 Return the pasta to a serving bowl and stir in the walnuts and raisins.

3 Peel and dice the carrot; chop the apple, removing the core. Add carrot and apple to salad.

4 Drain the kidney beans and rinse if necessary. Finally add the beans and the dressing to the salad and toss lightly before serving.

Kedgeree (serves 6–8)
POWER LEVEL: 100% (FULL)

Kedgeree is traditionally a breakfast dish but also makes a substantial supper dish

500ml (18fl oz) boiling water
pinch salt
175g (6oz) long-grain rice
350g (12oz) smoked haddock
2 hard-boiled eggs
50g (2oz) butter
1 small onion, chopped
salt and pepper
1 × 15ml tbsp (1tbsp) chopped parsley

1 Place the boiling water in a large casserole dish. Add the salt and stir in the rice. Cover and cook for 15 min. Leave to stand for 10 min when all the water should be absorbed; if not, drain the rice.

2 Wash and trim the fish, place in an ovenware dish, cover and cook for 4 min. Flake the fish discarding the skin and the bones.

3 Chop one hard-boiled egg and slice the other. Melt the butter in a large dish for 2 min. Toss the onion in the butter. Cook for 4 min.

4 Add the rice, fish, chopped hard-boiled egg and seasoning. Mix well and warm through for 3–4 min.

5 Garnish with the sliced hard-boiled egg and chopped parsley before serving.

Tagliatelle and spinach gratinée *(serves 4)*
POWER LEVEL: 100% (FULL)

225g (8oz) tagliatelle
25g (1oz) butter or margarine
1 small onion, peeled and finely chopped
450g (1lb) frozen spinach, thawed
150ml (¼pt) single cream
salt and freshly ground black pepper
100g (4oz) cheddar cheese, finely grated
25g (1oz) fresh white breadcrumbs
15g (½oz) butter
grated parmesan cheese for sprinkling, optional
grated nutmeg for sprinkling

1 Cook the tagliatelle in boiling, salted water (see chart page 102) and drain well.
2 Melt 25g (1oz) butter in a large bowl for 1 min, add the onion, cover and cook for 2 min.
3 Add the spinach and heat through for 3 min. Stir in the cream and salt and pepper to taste.
4 Arrange layers of the tagliatelle, spinach and finely grated cheddar cheese in a serving dish.
5 Cover and heat through for 5–6 min. Scatter on the fresh white breadcrumbs, dot with the 15g (½oz) butter and sprinkle with the parmesan cheese if using.
6 Cook uncovered for 2–3 min until the butter is melted or, alternatively, brown under a hot grill.
7 Serve hot, sprinkled with grated nutmeg.

Lasagne *(serves 6)*
POWER LEVEL: 100% (FULL) AND 70%

850ml (1½pt) approx bolognaise sauce, using 450g (1lb) minced beef (page 68)
550ml (1pt) cheese sauce (page 65)
175g (6oz) lasagne
50g (2oz) cheese, grated
paprika, for sprinkling

1 Make up and cook the bolognaise and cheese sauces. Cook the lasagne according to the chart on page 102.
2 When the lasagne is cooked, drain off the water and pat the leaves dry with kitchen paper towel.
3 Fill a large oblong or oval dish with alternate layers of cheese sauce, bolognaise sauce and lasagne, beginning and ending with cheese sauce.
4 Sprinkle with the grated cheese and paprika. Cover and cook on 70% setting for 10–12 min, turning the dish once halfway through.
5 Serve hot.

Chicken pasta pie *(serves 4–6)*
POWER LEVEL: 100% (FULL) AND 50%

225g (8oz) short-cut macaroni
2 × 5ml tsp (2tsp) oil
1 × 5ml tsp (1tsp) salt
550ml (1pt) boiling water, approximately
350g (12oz) cooked chicken, minced
100g (4oz) ham, minced
150ml (¼pt) top of the milk, or milk and single cream
2 × 5ml tsp (2tsp) dried sage, thyme or basil
3 eggs, separated
1½ × 15ml tbsp (1½tbsp) tomato purée
salt and freshly ground black pepper
For garnish:
50g (2oz) cheddar cheese, grated
1 × 15ml tbsp (1tbsp) parmesan cheese

1 Well butter a 22.5cm (9in) round ovenware dish.
2 Place the macaroni in a bowl with the oil and salt and pour on sufficient boiling water to cover. Stir, cover and cook on 100% (full) setting for 8–10 min until plump and tender and most of the water has been absorbed. Stir twice.
3 Mix together the chicken, ham, milk, herbs, egg yolks, tomato purée and seasoning.
4 Whisk the egg whites until stiff and, with a metal spoon, fold into the meat mixture.
5 Rinse and drain the macaroni, place half in the bottom of the greased dish. Spread with the meat mixture and cover with the remaining macaroni.
6 Cover with clingfilm or a lid and cook on 50% setting for 15–18 min until cooked. Test the centre with a knife – the filling should be soft but set.
7 When cooked, leave to stand for 10–15 min. Garnish with the grated cheese and the parmesan cheese and serve hot.

Mushroom-stuffed cannelloni *(serves 4)*
POWER LEVEL: 100% (FULL)

Serve as a main dish or as a starter course.

3 × 15ml tbsp (3tbsp) oil
1 onion, peeled and finely chopped
2 cloves garlic, finely chopped
100g (4oz) mushrooms, chopped
1 × 5ml tsp (1tsp) dried sweet basil
salt and freshly ground black pepper
4 tomatoes, skinned and chopped
8 cannelloni tubes
275ml (½pt) béchamel sauce (page 65)
25g (1oz) grated parmesan cheese
paprika for sprinkling

1 Place 2 × 15ml tbsp (2tbsp) of the oil in a large bowl, add the onions and garlic, toss well, cover and cook for 2½ min.
2 Add the mushrooms, herbs and seasoning, cover and cook for 3 min. Stir in the tomatoes.
3 Cook the cannelloni in a large, covered bowl of boiling, salted water with the remaining 1 × 15ml tbsp (1tbsp) oil for 5–6 min. Drain the pasta and rinse in cold water.
4 Fill the cannelloni with the mushroom mixture and place in a serving dish.
5 Heat the béchamel sauce, if necessary, and stir in half the cheese. Spoon the sauce over the cannelloni. Sprinkle with the rest of the cheese and paprika.
6 Cook for 3–4 min until heated through and serve, handing more parmesan cheese separately.

Mixed bean casserole (serves 4–6)
POWER LEVEL: 100% (FULL) and 50%

350g (12oz) mixed beans, soaked
boiling water
2 large onions, chopped
2 cloves garlic, crushed
2 stalks celery, finely sliced
1 green pepper, deseeded and chopped
1 red pepper, deseeded and chopped
1 parsnip, peeled and diced
2 bay leaves
salt and freshly ground black pepper
2 × 5ml tsp (2tsp) dried mixed herbs
450g (1lb) tomatoes, skinned and chopped
2 × 15ml tbsp (2tbsp) tomato purée
425ml (¾pt) boiling vegetable stock
75–100g (3–4oz) cheddar cheese, grated

1 Drain and rinse the beans. Cover with boiling water and cook, covered, for 10 min. Leave to stand.
2 Place the onion, garlic, celery, green and red peppers and parsnip in a large serving dish. Cover and cook for 6–8 min, stirring once during cooking.
3 Drain the beans and add to the vegetables with the bay leaves, seasoning, mixed herbs, tomatoes, tomato purée and boiling stock. Cover and cook on 100% (full) for 10 min, then for a further 15 min on 50% until the larger beans are tender.
4 Cook for a further 10 min on 100% (full), uncovered, to reduce the sauce. Adjust the seasoning, sprinkle with the grated cheese, and heat for 2–3 min until melted, or brown under a grill.

Lentil and walnut rissoles (serves 4)
POWER LEVEL: 50% AND 100% (FULL)

175g (6oz) lentils
1 small onion, chopped
350ml (12fl oz) boiling water
50g (2oz) fresh breadcrumbs, approximately
2 × 15ml tbsp (2tbsp) chopped parsley
100g (4oz) curd cheese
salt and pepper
100g (4oz) walnuts, finely chopped

1 Place the lentils in a large bowl with the onion. Add the boiling water, cover and cook for 10 min on 50% setting. Stir and cook for a further 3 min or until the lentils are soft. Beat the lentils until smooth, then allow to cool.
2 Add the breadcrumbs, parsley, curd cheese and seasoning. Beat the mixture well together. It should be stiff enough to handle easily but, if not, add a little more breadcrumbs.
3 Divide the mixture into 8 and shape each piece into a round. Roll in the nuts, using them to prevent the rissoles from sticking to your hands.
4 Preheat a large browning dish for 6 min on 100% (full). Cook the rissoles for 2–3 min, turn them over and cook for a further 2–3 min. Serve hot or cold.

Aduki and orange casserole (serves 4–6)
POWER LEVEL: 100% (FULL) AND 50%

This mixture also makes a delicious stuffing for baked marrow.

450g (1lb) aduki beans, soaked
boiling water
2 large onions, chopped
1 clove garlic, crushed
450g (1lb) tomatoes, skinned and chopped
2 oranges, grated rind and flesh thinly sliced
salt and pepper
1 × 5ml tsp (tsp) dried marjoram

1 Drain and rinse the beans. Cover with boiling water and cook, covered, for 10 min on 100% (full) and a further 10 min on 50%. Leave to stand.
2 In a large covered dish cook the onions and garlic on 100% (full) for 4–5 min, stirring once throughout. Add the tomatoes, orange rind, orange slices, seasoning and marjoram. Cover and cook for 10 min, stirring once.
3 Drain the aduki beans and add them to the sauce, mixing well. Heat, uncovered, for 3–4 min until hot through. Correct the seasoning and serve immediately.

Stuffed Peppers (below) and German Red Cabbage (page 98)

Stuffed peppers *(serves 2)*
POWER LEVEL: 100% (FULL)
colour photograph above

2 medium green peppers
50g (2oz) long-grain rice
165ml (⅓pt) boiling chicken stock
1 onion, peeled and finely chopped
salt and pepper
1 bay leaf
50g (2oz) cooked ham or chicken, chopped
40g (1½oz) sultanas
For serving:
plain boiled rice

1 Cut a slice from the top of each pepper. Remove the core and seeds. Reserve the slice as a lid.
2 Cover and cook the peppers for 2 min, turn them over, cook for 2 min.
3 Place the rice in a bowl, stir in the boiling chicken stock, onion, seasoning and bay leaf.
4 Cover and cook for 5 min, stir and cook for a further 3–5 min or until all the stock is absorbed. Remove the bay leaf.
5 Add the ham or chicken and sultanas to the rice. Fill the peppers with the rice mixture and replace the lids.
6 Stand the peppers in the serving dish, cover and cook for 3 min. Serve with a little extra boiled rice.

Ham and split pea risotto *(serves 4–6)*
POWER LEVEL: 100% (FULL)

100g (4oz) green or yellow split peas, soaked
boiling water
225g (8oz) long-grain brown rice
550ml (1pt) boiling vegetable stock
4 large spring onions, trimmed and sliced
100g (4oz) lean cooked ham, cut into small strips
40g (1½oz) flaked almonds
salt and pepper
For garnish:
sliced tomato

1 Drain and rinse the peas. Place them in a bowl and cover with boiling water. Cover with a lid or pierced clingfilm and cook for 8–10 min until the peas are soft but not mushy. Allow to stand for a few minutes, then drain.
2 Cook the rice in the boiling stock in a covered dish for 20–25 min. Allow to stand for 5 min.
3 Cook the onions in a large serving dish, covered, for 3 min, stirring once during cooking. Add the ham, almonds, split peas and rice. Season with salt and pepper and stir well.
4 Heat, uncovered, for 3–4 min until piping hot. Garnish with sliced tomato before serving.

Fruits and puddings

Those favourite jam and syrup puddings that are almost a thing of the past because of the extent of the steaming period necessary, are available again with microwave cooking in just a fraction of the time. Jellies for trifles and gelatine for mousses can be melted in seconds and fresh fruit in wine or liqueur can be quickly prepared for a really delicious simple sweet. The range of desserts which may be prepared or cooked by microwave is almost never ending; the advantage being that they can be made in advance and served cold or reheated when required, in individual portions if necessary, according to your family's preference. Although traditional pies are not as successful because the fillings tend to boil out before the pastry tops are cooked, a selection of puddings, crumbles, flans and fruit dishes are all here ready for you to try.

When cooking steamed puddings in the micro-wave, they should be covered with clingfilm to keep in the moisture; however, they should be removed from the cooker while still slightly moist as cooking will continue and the puddings will set during the standing time.

Fresh fruit can be prepared in the normal way, sprinkled with sugar and cooked in a roasting bag or boiling bag in a similar manner to fresh vegetables. The fruit should be checked and stirred or turned regularly to make sure it does not over-cook. When it is important that the fruit pieces do not break, cook them in a covered casserole when a little more liquid should be used and the cooking time increased accordingly to account for the extra volume in the oven. Fruits cooked in their skins, such as baked apples, should first be pricked or scored to prevent the fruits from bursting during the cooking process. As most fruits may be cooked with no additional liquid, they

Fruit cooking chart

Fruit and quantity	Preparation	Cooking time	
		100% (full)	50%
cooking apples 450g (1lb)	Peel, core and slice. Sprinkle with sugar to taste	6–8 min	11–15 min
apricots 450g (1lb)	Stone and wash. Sprinkle with sugar to taste	6–8 min	11–15 min
peaches 4 medium-sized	Stone and wash. Sprinkle with sugar to taste	4–5 min	7–8 min
pears 6 medium-sized	Peel, halve and core. Dissolve 75g (3oz) sugar and a pinch of cinnamon in a little hot water. Pour over the pears.	8–10 min	15–20 min
plums, cherries, damsons, greengages 450g (1lb)	Stone and wash. Sprinkle with sugar to taste and add grated rind of ½ lemon.	4–5 min	7–8 min
rhubarb 450g (1lb)	Trim, wash and cut into short lengths. Add 100g (4oz) sugar and grated rind of 1 lemon	7–10 min	14–20 min
soft fruits 450g (1lb)	Top and tail currants, hull the berries. Wash well and add sugar to taste.	3–5 min	6–10 min

can soon be sieved or puréed to make sauces to pour over ice-cream, natural yoghurt or puddings.

Frozen fruits

Frozen fruits to be served cold are partially defrosted by microwave and then allowed to stand at room temperature until completely thawed: see chart below.

Frozen fruit cooking chart

Fruit and quantity	30–50%
in dry sugar 450g (1lb)	4–8 min, stand until thawed
in sugar syrup 450g (1lb)	8–12 min stand until thawed
in dry pack (free flow or open frozen) 450g (1lb)	4–8 min, stand until thawed

Dried fruits

Although dried fruits can be cooked without soaking, it is preferable to soak them before cooking, to ensure plump and tender fruits. The exceptions are dates, figs, sultanas, raisins etc, which do not require soaking before use in cake and pudding recipes unless specified.

The fruits can either be soaked for 6–8 hr or overnight, or heated in a covered dish with water in the microwave for 6–10 min on 100% (full) setting, then allowed to stand for up to 1 hr to plump and soften. After soaking 225g (8oz) dried fruits, drain them and place in a suitable container. Add fruit juice, water, or water and wine mixed, some lemon rind or juice and demerara sugar or honey to taste. Cover and cook on 100% (full) setting for about 10 min, stirring halfway through. Leave to stand for a few minutes before serving.

•GUIDELINES AT-A-GLANCE

•**Additional liquid** is unneccessary when cooking fruits unless required as part of the recipe or for enhancing flavours.

•**Arrange** large whole fruits such as baked apples or pears in a circle on a plate or dish to ensure even cooking.

•**Browning** of microwave baked puddings such as crumbles and charlottes will not occur unless partly baked conventionally, combined with a convection system, or finished separately under a hot grill.

•**Containers** such as casserole dishes, plates or bowls are all suitable shapes for cooking, and boiling bags may be used when defrosting and cooking fruits.

•**Cooking** may be carried out on 100% (full) setting unless cooking a rich pudding or a heavier mixture when a lower 30–50% power setting will enable it to cook through more evenly. In addition, cook fruits at 30–50% when it is important that the pieces do not break.

•**Cover** the dish with a lid or pierced clingfilm when defrosting, cooking or reheating. This is particularly important for 'steamed' sponge or suet puddings and when cooking fruits to retain moisture. The exception is when 'baking' foods such as crumbles and charlottes and when reheating pastry items.

•**Cut** or slice fruits into even sized pieces when appropriate to ensure even cooking results.

•**Defrost** fruits and puddings using 30 or 50% setting although individual servings can be defrosted and reheated in one operation at 90–100% (full) setting.

•**Heat** citrus fruits for 1–2 min or until warm before cutting and squeezing, for maximum yield of juice. Heat fruits such as peaches for 1–2 min until just hot, to enable the skins to be peeled off easily, although if skinning several fruits the conventional method may be more convenient.

•**Overheating** when defrosting, reheating or cooking will cause dry, hard results – particularly of puddings, pies and other farinaceous desserts – which cannot be rectified. Give less time at first and heat for a few seconds longer if necessary.

●**Pastry** dishes such as pies are not recommended for cooking by microwave energy alone as the filling tends to boil out before the pastry is cooked, although they can be reheated successfully. Shortcrust pastry flans are successful providing the flan case is cooked before the filling is added. Cover pastry dishes with kitchen paper towel to help absorb moisture when defrosting and reheating.

●**Reheat** using a 90–100% (full) setting for small individual servings and when it is possible to stir a dish. Otherwise use a lower 50–70% setting to ensure even results.

●**Skins** of large, whole fruit should be pricked or scored to prevent them bursting when cooking by microwave.

●**Soak** dried fruit quickly by cooking in juice or water for 6–10 min on 100% (full) and leaving for up to 1 hr to swell and soften.

●**Stir** fruits gently during defrosting, cooking or reheating to ensure even results.

Crisp gooseberry pie *(serves 4–6)*
POWER LEVEL: 100% (FULL)

675g (1½lb) gooseberries
75–100g (3–4oz) sugar
25g (1oz) butter
½ × 5ml tsp (½tsp) cinnamon
100g (4oz) plain flour
pinch salt
50g (2oz) rolled oats
75g (3oz) butter or margarine
100g (4oz) demerara sugar
For serving:
custard sauce (page 66)

1 Top and tail and wash the gooseberries. Cover and cook them with the sugar, butter and cinnamon for 5–6 min until just soft. Drain off some of the juice and reserve. Place the fruit in a 20–22.5cm (8–9in) dish and leave to cool.
2 Sift the flour with the salt, stir in the rolled oats, and rub in the butter or margarine. Stir in the demerara sugar. This will make a coarse crumb mixture.
3 Sprinkle the mixture over the gooseberries and cook for 8–10 min until hot through and the topping is cooked. Turn 2 or 3 times throughout.
4 Serve hot or cold with custard sauce and hand the rest of the juice separately.

Chocolate pudding *(serves 6–8)*
POWER LEVEL: 100% (FULL)

75g (3oz) plain chocolate
50g (2oz) butter or margarine
275ml (½pt) milk
75g (3oz) soft brown sugar
1 × 5ml tsp (1tsp) vanilla essence
2 eggs, separated
150g (5oz) brown breadcrumbs
For serving:
chocolate sauce (page 66)

1 Lightly grease a 1¼l (2pt) pudding basin.
2 Break up the chocolate and place in a bowl with the butter or margarine, milk, brown sugar and vanilla essence. Heat for about 2½ min then stir until blended.
3 Beat the egg yolks and stir into the chocolate mixture with the breadcrumbs.
4 Whisk the egg whites until stiff and fold into the mixture.
5 Pour into the prepared pudding basin and cover with clingfilm, slit with the pointed end of a sharp knife.
6 Cook for 6½–7½ min, turning once halfway through.
7 Leave to stand for 5 min before turning out.
8 Serve with a little chocolate sauce poured over the pudding and hand the rest of the sauce separately.

Oranges in caramel *(serves 4–6)*
POWER LEVEL: 100% (FULL)
colour page 123

8 oranges
225g (8oz) granulated sugar
150ml (¼pt) cold water
1 × 5ml tsp (1tsp) grand marnier, optional
150ml (¼pt) warm water

1 Finely grate the rind of 3 of the oranges. Remove the peel and outer membrane for each fruit.
2 Hold the oranges over a serving dish. Slice the oranges, holding each one together with a wooden cocktail stick.
3 Stir the sugar into the cold water with the liqueur, if used. Bring to the boil in the microwave, without stirring, and cook until a light golden brown, approximately 10–12 min.
4 Quickly add the warm water to the caramel, protecting your hand from the steam with a towel. Return to the microwave for 30 sec. Stir well and leave to cool.
5 Pour the cooled caramel over the oranges in the serving dish and sprinkle with the grated orange rind. Chill well before serving.

Cherry and praline flan (serves 6–8)

POWER LEVEL: 100% (FULL)
colour photograph below

1 × 20cm (8in) baked flan case using rich short-crust pastry (page 43)
1 × 15ml tbsp (1tbsp) custard powder
2 × 5ml tsp (2tsp) caster sugar
150ml (¼pt) milk
150ml (¼pt) double cream, whipped
100g (4oz) praline, crushed
2 × 450g (1lb) cans black cherries
2 × 5ml tsp (2tsp) arrowroot
4 × 15ml tbsp (4tbsp) redcurrant jelly
For serving:
whipped cream

1 Place the flan case on a large serving plate or in its flan dish.
2 Make a custard with the custard powder, caster sugar and milk, cook for 2–3 min, stirring every minute until thick. Beat well then leave to cool.
3 When cold, whisk the custard and fold in the whipped cream and praline. Place the mixture in the bottom of the flan case and smooth the top.

4 Drain the cherries; reserve 150ml (¼pt) of the juice and blend this with the arrowroot,
5 Melt the redcurrant jelly for about 1 min and add to the cherry juice and arrowroot. Stir well then heat for 2–3 min until thick, stirring frequently.
6 Stone the cherries if necessary and arrange over the praline cream. Glaze with the thickened juice and leave to cool and set.
7 Serve cold with whipped cream.

Variation
Substitute finely chopped hazelnuts for the crushed praline.

DO NOT FREEZE

Praline

This is not really successful in the microwave so is best made conventionally. Place equal weight quantities of unblanched almonds and caster sugar into a heavy-based saucepan and heat slowly over a low heat until the sugar is melted and turned to a nut brown colour. Stir with a metal spoon as soon as the sugar starts to colour. Turn the mixture onto an oiled tin or plate to cool. When cold, crush with a rolling pin or grind it in a blender or liquidiser. Store in an airtight container.

Cherry and Praline Flan (above)

Apple bread pudding (cuts into 8 wedges)
POWER LEVEL: 100% (FULL) AND 50%

225g (8oz) bread
225ml (8fl oz) milk
50g (2oz) butter or margarine
50g (2oz) demerara sugar
2 × 5ml tsp (2tsp) mixed spice
1 egg, beaten
50g (2oz) mixed chopped peel
175g (6oz) mixed dried fruit (sultanas, raisins, currants, glacé cherries)
1 medium cooking apple
few drops lemon juice
demerara sugar for sprinkling

1 Lightly grease a 20cm (8in) flan dish.
2 Break the bread into small pieces and place in a bowl. Soak with milk, break down the bread with a fork. Beat thoroughly until smooth.
3 Melt the butter or margarine for 1½ min on 100% (full) setting; add to the bread with the sugar, spice, egg, peel and dried fruit. Mix together thoroughly.
4 Turn the mixture into the prepared dish and cook on 50% setting for 10 min. Leave to stand for 5 min.
5 Peel, core and slice the apple and arrange over the top of the pudding. Sprinkle the apple with a few drops of lemon juice.
6 Cook for a further 10 min on 50% setting.
7 Serve hot or cold sprinkled with demerara sugar.

Linzer torte (serves 6)
POWER LEVEL: 100% (FULL)
colour page 123

225g (8oz) almond pastry (page 113)
450g (1lb) raspberries, fresh or frozen, thawed
75–100g (3–4oz) caster sugar
2 × 15ml tbsp (2tbsp) redcurrant jelly
For serving:
whipped cream

1 Prepare the almond pastry, roll out on a lightly floured surface and line a 20cm (8in) flan dish. Reserve the trimmings. Chill the flan case for about 20 min in the refrigerator.
2 Bake the flan case blind (page 44).
3 Fill the flan case with the raspberries and sugar. Roll out the reserved pastry, cut into strips and make a lattice design across the top of the flan.
4 Cook the flan for 7–8 min or until the lattice is cooked through. Allow to cool.
5 Warm the redcurrant jelly for 15–30 sec and brush over the lattice to make a thick glaze.
6 Serve cold with whipped cream.

Summer pudding (serves 6)
POWER LEVEL: 100% (FULL)
colour page 119

This pudding is 'uncooked' – packed full of blackcurrants, loganberries, raspberries and strawberries – and delicious when served with whipped cream.

675g (1½lb) blackcurrants, loganberries, raspberries, strawberries, mixed
100g (4oz) caster sugar
6–8 slices white bread, crusts removed
For serving:
whipped double cream

1 Pick over the fruits and wash. Place in a large bowl with the sugar, cover with a lid or cling-film.
2 Cook for about 5 min, gently shaking or turning 2–3 times throughout to stir the contents without breaking the fruit. Leave to cool slightly, drain off and reserve some of the juice.
3 Line a 850ml (1½pt) pudding basin with the bread, starting by cutting to fit the base, then the sides. Cut the slices so that they fit closely together. Reserve some for the top.
4 Spoon the fruit into the basin and cover with the remaining bread. Place a plate that fits inside the basin over the pudding and press down with a weight.
5 Chill for about 8 hr or overnight. Remove the weight and unmould the pudding onto a serving dish or plate.
6 Use the reserved juice to coat any parts of the bread which have not been soaked by the fruit juice during the chilling.
7 Serve with whipped cream.

Fruit crumble (serves 4)
POWER LEVEL: 100% (FULL)

675g (1½lb) fresh or canned fruit (use 900g (2lb) if the fruit has to be stoned)
100g (4oz) caster sugar
175g (6oz) plain flour
75g (3oz) butter
50g (2oz) demerara sugar
For serving:
custard sauce (page 66) or cream

1 Prepare the fruit, then place it in the bottom of a pie dish with the caster sugar.
2 Sift the flour into a bowl and rub in the butter. Stir in most of the demerara sugar.
3 Sprinkle the mixture over the fruit and top with the remaining demerara sugar.
4 Cook for 10–12 min, turning the dish halfway through the cooking time.

Blackcurrant cobbler *(serves 4–6)*
POWER LEVEL: 100% (FULL)

Cobbler is a scone mix topping – delicious with blackcurrants but amost any stewed fruit can be used.

675g (1½lb) blackcurrants, fresh or frozen, thawed
75–100g (3–4oz) sugar
100g (4oz) self-raising flour
100g (4oz) wholewheat flour
pinch salt
½ × 5ml tsp (½tsp) baking powder
50g (2oz) butter or margarine
25g (1oz) caster sugar
milk for mixing
demerara or soft brown sugar for sprinkling
For serving:
cream

1 Pick over and wash the fresh blackcurrants if used. Cover and cook the blackcurrants with the sugar for 4–5 min until just soft. Drain off some of the juice and reserve. Place the fruit in a 17.5–20cm (7–8in) dish.
2 Sift the self-raising flour, add the wholewheat flour, and stir in the salt and baking powder. Rub in the butter or margarine finely, stir in the caster sugar. Mix to a soft scone dough with the milk.
3 Knead lightly on a floured surface and roll out to 1.25cm (½in) thick. Cut into rounds with a 5cm (2in) cutter.
4 Arrange the scone rounds over the top of the fruit and brush with milk. Sprinkle with the sugar.
5 Cook for 5–6 min, turning twice throughout.
6 Serve hot or cold with cream and hand the reserved fruit juice separately.

Almond pastry

225g (8oz) plain flour
pinch salt
pinch cinnamon
100g (4oz) butter
100g (4oz) caster sugar
1 lemon, grated rind
65g (2½oz) ground almonds
1 egg beaten
1 egg yolk

1 Sift flour, salt and cinnamon together. Rub in the butter finely, stir in the sugar, lemon rind and ground almonds, mixing well together.
2 Beat the egg and egg yolk together and add to the dry ingredients. Mix well to form a soft dough.
3 Chill before rolling out.

Rice pudding *(serves 3–4)*
POWER LEVEL: 100% (FULL) AND 60%
colour page 79

50g (2oz) pudding rice
25g (1oz) caster sugar
25g (1oz) butter
550ml (1pt) milk
1 × 5ml tsp (1tsp) ground nutmeg, optional
For decoration:
1 × 312g (11oz) can mandarin oranges, optional

1 Place all the ingredients except nutmeg in a 1¼l (2pt) dish or bowl and stir.
2 Leave the dish uncovered and bring to boiling point, 7–10 minutes on 100% (full) setting, stirring every 5 min.
3 Reduce to 60% setting and cook for 20–25 minutes stirring every 5 min.
4 Sprinkle with ground nutmeg or, when cold, decorate with mandarin oranges.

Chocolate semolina pudding *(serves 4)*
POWER LEVEL: 100% (FULL)

550ml (1pt) milk
40g (1½oz) semolina or ground rice
50g (2oz) caster sugar
15g (½oz) butter
50g (2oz) chocolate, broken into squares

1 Bring the milk to the boil in a 1¼l (2pt) pie dish. This will take approximately 5 min.
2 Add the semolina, sugar and butter; stir.
3 Cook for 5 min until thick, stirring frequently.
4 Add the chocolate and stir until melted.
5 Serve hot or cold.

Banana and apricot compôte *(serves 4–6)*
POWER LEVEL: 100% (FULL)

3 firm bananas
3 × 5ml tsp (3tsp) lemon juice
100g (4oz) dried apricots, soaked overnight
25–50g (1–2oz) demerara sugar
50g (2oz) raisins
grated nutmeg for sprinkling
For serving:
whipped cream

1 Peel and slice the bananas and sprinkle with the lemon juice.
2 Place the apricots in a bowl with 150ml (¼pt) of the soaking liquid, add the sugar and raisins.
3 Cover and cook for 5 min until hot.
4 Pour the apricots and raisins over the bananas and allow to cool. Sprinkle with grated nutmeg.
5 Serve chilled with whipped cream.

DO NOT FREEZE

Honey baked apples *(serves 4)*
POWER LEVEL: 100% (FULL)

4 medium-sized cooking apples
40g (1½oz) butter
50g (2oz) soft brown sugar
25g (1oz) sultanas
2 × 15ml tbsp (2tbsp) chopped walnuts
2 × 15ml tbsp (2tbsp) water
1 × 15ml tbsp (1tbsp) lemon juice
1½ × 15ml tbsp (1½tbsp) clear honey
For serving:
cream
custard sauce (page 66)

1 Cores the apples but do not peel. Score them around the middle and place in a suitable serving dish.
2 Mix together the butter, sugar, sultanas and nuts. Fill the centre of each apple with the mixture.
3 Blend the water, lemon juice and honey together and spoon over the apples.
4 Cover the apples with lightly greased greaseproof paper and cook for 6–8 min.
5 Serve hot or cold with cream.

Note: *Cook 1 apple for 2–3 min; cook 2 apples for 4–5 min.*

Orange macaroni pudding *(serves 4–6)*
POWER LEVEL: 100% (FULL)

175g (6oz) macaroni
550ml (1pt) boiling water
1 × 15ml tbsp (1tbsp) oil
1 × 15ml tbsp (1tbsp) butter or margarine
25g (1oz) flour
275ml (½pt) milk
2 oranges, grated rind and juice
2 × 15ml tbsp (2tbsp) demerara sugar
75g (3oz) sultanas
½ × 5ml tsp (½tsp) grated nutmeg

1 Place the macaroni in a covered dish with the boiling water and the oil. Cover and cook for 6 min. Allow to stand, covered, for 5 min while preparing the sauce.
2 Melt the butter or margarine in a bowl for 1 min, then stir in the flour. Gradually add the milk, stirring well between each addition.
3 Cook the sauce for 4–5 min, stirring every minute until thickened. Add the orange rind and juice, the sugar, sultanas and nutmeg and stir well together.
4 Drain the macaroni and fold into the sauce. Reheat the pudding for 2–3 min if necessary and serve immediately.

Grapefruit in brandy *(serves 4)*
POWER LEVEL: 100% (FULL)

A refreshing sweet course after a rich meal.

3 large grapefruit, peeled
75g (3oz) demerara sugar
150ml (¼pt) water
1 × 5ml tsp (1tsp) cinnamon
1 × 15ml tbsp (3tbsp) brandy

1 Remove all the pith from the peeled grapefruit and carefully take out the core from the centre with skewer. Cut into 1.25cm (½in) thick slices.
2 Add the sugar to the water with the cinnamon in a large, shallow dish.
3 Heat for 2 min, then stir until the sugar has dissolved in the water. Cook for a further 2 min, then lay the grapefruit slices in the syrup.
4 Cover and cook for 2–3 min, turning the slices over in the syrup halfway through.
5 Place the slices of grapefruit in a serving dish. Mix 3 × 15ml tbsp (3tbsp) of the syrup with the brandy and pour over the fruit.
6 Serve hot or chilled on their own.

Christmas pudding *(makes about 3.5 litres/6pt)*
POWER LEVEL: 50%
colour page 79

225g (8oz) plain flour
450g (1lb) fresh breadcrumbs
1 × 5ml tsp (1tsp) salt
2 × 5ml tsp (2tsp) mixed spice
1 orange, juice and grated rind
1 lemon, juice and grated rind
675g (1½lb) shredded suet
450g (1lb) brown sugar
450g (1lb) currants
450g (1lb) sultanas
225g (8oz) glacé cherries, quartered
50g (2oz) almonds, chopped
450g (1lb) raisins, stoned
100g (4oz) mixed peel
50g (2oz) ground almonds
675g (1½lb) cooking apples, chopped
1 medium carrot, grated
8 eggs, beaten
1 wineglass brandy or milk, beer, stout or barley wine to mix
For serving:
cornflour sauce (page 66) and/or rum or brandy butter (page 64)

1 Place the flour, breadcrumbs, salt, mixed spice, grated rinds of the orange and lemon, suet and sugar in a large bowl. Mix thoroughly together.
2 Add all the fruit, nuts and grated carrot and mix well. Stir in the eggs, orange and lemon

juice. Stir in the brandy and/or sufficient milk or beer to mix to a soft dropping consistency. If time allows, leave the mixture to stand for 12–24 hr in a cool place.

3 Lightly grease or line with clingfilm 850ml (1½pt) and/or 1.1 litre (2pt) pudding basins to the total capacity of 3.5 litres (6pt). Fill the pudding basins to within about 1.25–2.5cm (½–1in) of the top. Cover each basin with clingfilm and slit with the pointed end of a sharp knife.
4 Cook the smaller puddings for 17–20 min and the larger ones for 26–30 min. Allow them to stand for 15–20 min before removing the clingfilm and inverting onto a plate.
5 Serve hot with cornflour sauce and/or rum or brandy butter.

Note: *The puddings may be cooked and then left to mature wrapped in greaseproof paper and then in aluminum foil. On the day, they can be reheated in the microwave for 2½–3½ min, depending on the size, using 100% (full) setting, or in individual portions for about 1 min each.*

Pear and Chocolate Crumble (above) with Chocolate Sauce (page 66)

Pear and chocolate crumble *(serves 4–6)*
POWER LEVEL: 100% (FULL)
colour photograph below

675g (1½lb) dessert pears
sugar to taste
75g (3oz) plain flour
75g (3oz) wholewheat flour
pinch salt
75g (3oz) butter or margarine
50g (2oz) demerara sugar
50g (2oz) polka dots or chocolate chips
For serving:
chocolate sauce (page 66)

1 Lightly grease a 20–22.5cm (8–9in) round dish.
2 Peel, quarter and core the pears, and place in the base of the prepared dish. Sprinkle with sugar to taste.
3 Sift the plain flour, stir in the wholewheat flour and salt. Rub in the butter or margarine finely, stir in the demerara sugar and the polka dots or chocolate chips.
4 Sprinkle the mixture over the pears and cook for 10–12 min, giving a quarter turn every 3 min.
5 Serve with chocolate sauce.

Dutch apple tart (serves 4–6)

POWER LEVEL: 100% (FULL)
OVEN TEMPERATURE: 200°C (400°F), MARK 6

450g (1lb) cooking apples, sliced
1 lemon, juice and grated rind
50g (2oz) almonds, roughly chopped
50g (2oz) sultanas
sugar to taste
225g (8oz) rich shortcrust pastry (page 43)
raspberry jam
icing sugar, optional
For serving:
cream

1 Place the cooking apples and lemon juice in a covered large dish or bowl or in a boiling or roasting bag.
2 Cook in the microwave for about 6 min, stirring the contents of the dish or shaking the bag 2–3 times throughout. The apples should be softened but not overcooked.
3 Pulp down the apples with a wooden spoon or fork and stir in the lemon rind, almonds, sultanas and a little sugar to taste. Leave to cool.
4 Roll out the pastry and line a 17.5cm (7in) flan dish. Roll out the trimmings and cut into thin strips.
5 Spread a little raspberry jam over the base of the flan and add the cooled apple mixture. Make a lattice design over the flan with the strips of pastry.
6 Bake in a preheated oven for 30–40 min until golden brown. Sprinkle with a little sieved icing sugar if preferred before serving hot or cold with cream.

Pear and orange cheese flan (serves 6)

POWER LEVEL: 100% (FULL) AND 50%

175g (6oz) wholewheat flour
pinch salt
75g (3oz) butter or margarine
tepid water to mix
3 large pears
½ × 5ml tsp (½tsp) ground cinnamon
25g (1oz) demerara sugar
1 orange, juice and grated rind
225g (8oz) curd cheese
2 eggs
5 × 15ml tbsp (5tbsp) clear honey

1 Place the flour and salt in a bowl and rub in the butter or margarine until the mixture resembles breadcrumbs. Mix to a firm dough with the tepid water. Turn out onto a lightly floured surface and roll out to line a 17.5–20cm (7–8in)

flan ring.
2 Place thin strips of aluminium foil around the upright edges of the pastry flan case. Prick the base of the case, line with pieces of kitchen paper towel then fill with baking beans.
3 Cook the flan 'blind' for 4 min on 100% (full) setting. Remove the beans, paper and foil and cook for a further 1½–2 min.
4 Peel the pears, cut in half lengthways and remove the cores. Place the pears, cinnamon, sugar and orange juice in a covered dish and cook for 5–6 min on 100% (full) until just soft. Carefully drain the pears and reserve the juice.
5 Cream the cheese and beat in the eggs, 3 × 15ml tbsp (3tbsp) of the honey and the juice from the pears. Pour the mixture into the flan case and cook for 15 min on 50% or until set. Allow to stand for 5 min.
6 Arrange the pears on top of the filling. Heat 2 × 15ml tbsp (2tbsp) honey in a small bowl and stir in the grated orange rind. Brush the glaze over the flan and serve warm or cold.

Sponge pudding (serves 4)

POWER LEVEL: 100% (FULL)
colour page 123

100g (4oz) butter
100g (4oz) caster sugar
2 eggs
100g (4oz) self-raising flour
few drops vanilla essence
For serving:
custard sauce (page 66)

1 Grease a 1¼l (2pt) pudding basin. Cream the butter and sugar in a mixing bowl, until light and fluffy.
2 Gradually beat in the eggs. Stir in the flour and vanilla essence then turn the mixture into the prepared basin.
3 Cook in the microwave for 5 min, or for 6 min if making one of the variations.

Variations
Syrup Place 3 × 15ml tbsp (3tbsp) of golden syrup in the bottom of the basin. Add the pudding mixture and cook as above.
Sultana Stir 50–75g (2–3oz) of sultanas into the pudding mixture. Cook as above.
Jam Place 3 × 15ml tbsp (3tbsp) of jam in the bottom of the basin. Add the pudding mixture and cook as above.
Pineapple Arrange 5 small pineapple rings in the prepared basin. Put a glacé cherry in the centre of each ring, then add the pudding mixture and cook as above.

Cakes, biscuits and scones

Home-made cakes can be cooked in the micro-wave most successfully, giving a good light texture. They do not brown as when baking in a conventional oven, but chocolate or coffee cakes or gingerbreads are 'self-coloured' anyway and there is much to be said for them being cooked so quickly. Prepared and frozen icing for decoration can be quickly thawed in the microwave and chocolate for a topping can be melted in 1–2 min, so it really is possible to bake a home-made cake or gâteau in next to no time for that unexpected guest.

Any suitable container including paper may be used for cooking cakes, but straight-sided ones give good results and a better shape. The container may be lined with lightly greased grease-proof paper but do not sprinkle with flour as this will only result in a doughy crust being formed on the outside of the finished cake. Make sure that the container is sufficiently large to allow for the mixture to rise; as a general guide, only half fill the dish with mixture. Generally, the wetter the mixture, the better the result. Cakes with a high proportion of fruit require lower settings for best results.

If during the cooking process, the mixture should appear to rise unevenly, it will normally level out towards the end of the cooking period; if in doubt, just turn the container approximately every 2 min. Overcooking causes dry, hard cakes, so remove from the oven when they seem slightly moist on top. As a general rule, when the cake has risen completely give 1 min more cooking time then remove from the microwave. Although it is not usually necessary, should the outside of the cake be set before the centre, it is possible to protect these outside edges by covering with smooth pieces of aluminium foil for the last few minutes of the cooking period (see 'Aluminium Foil', page 13). After cooking, allow the cake to stand for 10–15 min before removing it on to a cooling tray.

Not all biscuit recipes are successful in the microwave; better results are from those mixtures which are cut into pieces after cooking. However, the few recipes included in this section are well worth trying and good results can be obtained.

I have included some scone recipes as they are very quickly cooked and can almost be made while the rest of the tea is being prepared.

Defrosting

When thawing a large, frozen, cream cake, give it only 1–1½ min on 30–50% setting and then let it stand until completely thawed, otherwise the cream may melt before the cake is completely thawed; it is better to allow individual cream cakes to thaw naturally. Other large cakes may be given 4–5 min in the microwave and then allowed to stand for 9–12 min before serving. An individual cake, scone or slice of cake requires only 30–45 sec in the microwave depending on size and type and is then allowed to stand for 2 min before serving. Do not allow frozen cakes to get hot when thawing as this may result in a dry cake. As soon as it feels warm, remove the cake from the cooker and allow it to stand and heat equalise. It is not then completely thawed, put it back into the microwave for another minute.

Most biscuits will thaw out very quickly at room temperature; one or two should be heated in the microwave for no longer than 10–25 sec and a plate of biscuits for no longer than 1 min. Leave them to stand for a few minutes before serving.

●GUIDELINES AT-A-GLANCE

- **Arrange** individual cakes, biscuits or scones in a circle on the microwave shelf to obtain even cooking results. If some should be cooked before others, remove them from the oven before leaving the remainder to carry on cooking.

- **Biscuits** which are cut into pieces after cooking and 'cookie' types are the most successful. If large quantities are required, it is probably better to batch bake in a conventional oven.

- **Browning** does not occur when baking by microwave unless combined with a convection system.

117

●**Cakes** cooked by microwave have good flavours, although light mixtures and sponges are inclined to have a slightly 'steamed' taste and, of course, are pale in appearance. Both of these points can be overcome by decorating attractively.

●**Containers** such as soufflé dishes, microwave cake dishes or ring moulds are good shapes for large cakes. Individual cakes cooked in paper cases can be placed in muffin/tart trays or small cups to help retain a neat shape. Biscuits and scones may be cooked direct on the oven shelf or placed on plates or trays. Microwave 'girdle' scones can be cooked in a browning dish.

●**Cooking** is carried out on 100% (full) for most cakes, biscuits and scones although richer cake mixtures require 30–50% setting to ensure even results. Always remove from the oven when still slightly moist on top to prevent overcooking.

●**Coverings** over dishes are not required when cooking or defrosting cakes, biscuits or scones.

●**Decorate** with toppings such as icings, red jams, redcurrant jelly, sugar or apricot glaze, chopped nuts, grated or melted chocolate, coloured sugar strands or simply a sprinkling of sugar. Melted toffees and chocolate sweets such as Mars bars also make good toppings for children (see Cooking Hints and Tips page 31).

●**Line** the base of the dish with baking parchment or lightly greased greaseproof paper or just brush lightly with oil when necessary, although microwave cakes do not stick to the container as when baked conventionally. Do not flour the container as this will give a doughy finish to the outside of the cake.

●**Meringues** can be cooked to the recipe included in this section but they are not the same texture as conventional meringues.

●**Mixtures** such as whisked sponges and genoese or melted and batter mixtures are inclined to give best results due to the extra moisture content. Rich fruit cakes are also very good when cooked on a low 30% setting. Minimal beating of creamed mixtures is necessary to ensure the cake does not sink back after removal from the microwave.

●**Overheating** in the microwave when defrosting, heating or cooking will cause dry, hard results. Always give a little less time at first and cook for a little longer if necessary. Remove cakes from the oven when still slightly moist on top. If a micro-wave cake seems to go stale quickly, this is an indication of overcooking. Wrap or decorate as soon as possible after cooking to retain moisture.

●**Roll** the cake around in the container after cooking to bring it away from the side edges. This will give a neat result and make removal from the container much easier.

●**Scones** can be quickly baked by microwave. The use of wholewheat flour will give a better colour and the browning dish can be used for 'girdle' scones. Cooked scones may be warmed in the microwave before serving.

●**Standing** times should be allowed to ensure biscuits and cakes set before transferring onto a cooling rack.

●**Turn** the container regularly throughout the cooking time if necessary should the cake seem to rise unevenly.

Chocolate honey cake *(cuts into 8)*
POWER LEVEL: 100% (FULL)

175g (6oz) butter
75g (3oz) demerara sugar
2 × 15ml tbsp (2tbsp) clear honey
3 eggs, beaten
125g (4½oz) self-raising flour
40g (1½oz) cocoa
1 × 5ml tsp (1tsp) instant coffee
4 × 15ml tbsp (4tbsp) hot water
few drops vanilla essence
chocolate fudge icing (page 119)

1 Lightly grease an 18.75cm (7½in) cake dish and line the base with a circle of greaseproof paper.
2 Cream the butter, add the sugar and honey and beat well together until light and fluffy.
3 Add the eggs gradually, beating well after each addition.
4 Sift the flour and cocoa together and fold into the creamed mixture with a metal spoon.
5 Dissolve the coffee in the hot water and fold into the mixture with the vanilla essence.
6 Place mixture into the prepared container and cook for 5½–6½ min.
7 Leave until cool before turning out onto a wire rack.
8 When cold, cut in half horizontally. Sandwich the two halves together with half the fudge icing and pour the remainder over the top.

Summer Pudding (page 112)

Chocolate fudge icing

POWER LEVEL: 100% (FULL)

25g (1oz) butter
50g (2oz) soft brown or demerara sugar
2 × 15ml tbsp (2tbsp) cocoa
3 × 15ml tbsp (3tbsp) cold water
2 × 5ml tsp (2tsp) milk
225g (8oz) icing sugar, sifted
2 × 15ml tbsp (2tbsp) warm water
few drops vanilla essence

1 Place the butter and sugar into a large bowl.
  Blend the cocoa with the cold water and add to
  the bowl with the milk.
2 Heat for 1–2 min, stir until the sugar is dissolved.
3 Heat until boiling, then allow to boil for 2–2½
  min.
4 Add icing sugar, warm water and vanilla
  essence. Mix together then beat well for 5 min.
5 Pour over the cake whilst still warm as this icing
  sets when cold.

Walnut and chocolate brownies *(makes 12–16)*

POWER LEVEL: 100% (FULL)

50g (2oz) butter or margarine
50g (2oz) plain chocolate
150g (5oz) dark soft brown sugar
50g (2oz) self-raising flour
pinch salt
2 eggs, beaten
½ × 5ml tsp (½tsp) vanilla essence
50g (2oz) walnuts, chopped
demerara sugar for sprinkling

1 Line a 17.5cm (7in) square dish or an equivalent-
  size oblong dish.
2 Melt the butter and chocolate for about 3 min,
  mix well together and add the sugar.
3 Sift the flour and salt into a bowl and add the
  chocolate mixture, eggs, vanilla essence and
  walnuts. Beat until smooth and pour into the
  prepared container.
4 Cook for 4–5 min, turning every minute.
5 Leave for 1–2 min to cool slightly before
  sprinkling with demerara sugar.
6 Mark into squares and leave to cool before cutting and serving.

119

Rich fruit cake *(cuts into 8 or 12)*
POWER LEVEL: 30%
colour page 47

2 eggs, beaten
2 × 15ml tbsp (2tbsp) black treacle
175 g (6oz) dark soft brown sugar
2½ × 15ml tbsp (2½tbsp) oil
175g (6oz) self-raising flour
½ × 5ml tsp (½tsp) salt
1 × 5ml tsp (1tsp) mixed spice
150ml (¼pt) milk
450g (1lb) mixed dried fruit
50g (2oz) glacé cherries, quartered
50g (2oz) mixed chopped peel
50g (2oz) chopped nuts

1 Lightly grease a 18.75cm (7½in) round cake dish and line the base with a circle of grease-proof paper.
2 Mix together the eggs, treacle, sugar and oil. Sift the flour, salt and mixed spice.
3 Gradually stir in the flour mixture alternately with the milk. Mix thoroughly.
4 Add the fruit, peel and nuts and place the mixture into the prepared container; smooth the top.
5 Cook on 30% setting for 40–50 min or until a skewer leaves the centre of the cake clean.
6 Leave for 30–40 min before turning out onto a cooling rack.

Rich sultana and cherry cake *(cuts into 8)*
POWER LEVEL: 30%

175g (6oz) glacé cherries
350g (12oz) sultanas
100g (4oz) plain flour
pinch salt
75g (3oz) butter
1 lemon, grated rind
75g (3oz) caster sugar
2 eggs, beaten

1 Lightly grease an 18.75cm (7½in) round cake dish and line the base with a circle of grease-proof paper.
2 Wash and dry the cherries thoroughly. Cut in half and mix with the sultanas.
3 Sift the flour with the salt and add about a third to the cherries and sultanas. Toss so that the fruit is lightly coated with the flour.
4 Cream the butter, add the lemon rind and sugar and beat together until light and fluffy.
5 Add the eggs gradually, beating well after each addition.
6 Fold in the flour alternately with the fruit.
7 Place into the prepared container and smooth

the top.
8 Cook for 35–45 min turning if necessary 2–3 times, or until a skewer leaves the centre of the cake clean.
9 Cool for 20–30 min, turn out onto a rack.

Flapjacks *(cuts into 8 wedges)*
POWER LEVEL: 100% (FULL) AND 60%

3 × 15ml tbsp (3tbsp) golden syrup
100g (4oz) demerara sugar
100g (4oz) butter or margarine
225g (8oz) rolled oats
1 × 5ml tsp (1tsp) baking powder
½ × 5ml tsp (½tsp) salt
1 egg, beaten

1 Line a 20cm (8in) round dish with clingfilm.
2 Place the syrup, sugar and butter into a bowl and heat on 100% (full) for 2–2½ min. Stir until well blended and the sugar is dissolved.
3 Stir in the remaining ingredients and place in the prepared container.
4 Cook on 60% setting for 6–8 min, turning every 1¼ min.
5 Leave for a few minutes to set and then mark into wedges.
6 When cool, remove from the dish and serve cut into wedges.

Queen cakes *(makes about 24)*
POWER LEVEL: 100% (FULL)

175g (6oz) butter or margarine
175 (6oz) caster sugar
3 eggs
175g (6oz) self-raising flour
pinch salt
75g (3oz) currants
milk for mixing
24 paper cases, approximately

1 Place 6 paper cake cases into a 6-ring microwave muffin pan, or individual dishes or cups.
2 Cream the butter or margarine, add the sugar and beat well together until light and fluffy.
3 Add the eggs gradually, beating well after each addition.
4 Sift the flour and salt and toss in the currants. Fold into the creamed mixture with a metal spoon.
5 Mix in sufficient milk to give a soft dropping consistency.
6 Place spoonfuls of the mixture into the paper cases until no more than two-thirds full.
7 Cook for 2–2½ min, turning or rearranging once halfway through.
8 Remove onto a cooling rack and cook the remainder in batches of 6.

Chocolate cup cakes *(makes 12–16)*
POWER LEVEL: 100% (FULL)

75g (3oz) self-raising flour
25g (1oz) cocoa
pinch salt
50g (2oz) butter or margarine
50g (2oz) soft brown sugar
1 egg, beaten
120ml (4fl oz) milk, approximately
chocolate fudge icing (page 119) or melted chocolate
hazelnuts, optional
16 paper cases, approximately

1 Place 6 paper cases into a 6-ring microwave muffin pan, or individual small dishes or cups.
2 Sift the flour, cocoa and salt into a bowl. Rub in the butter or margarine finely, stir in the sugar.
3 Mix in the egg and the milk to form a very soft, almost runny mixture.
4 Half fill the paper cases with the mixture and cook for 2 min, turning or rearranging after 1 min.
5 Remove the cakes onto a cooling rack and cook the remainder in batches of 6 and 4.
6 When cold, coat the top of each cake with chocolate fudge icing or melted chocolate. Decorate with a hazelnut on the top of each cake.

DO NOT ICE BEFORE FREEZING

'One stage' victoria sandwich *(cuts into 8)*
POWER LEVEL: 100% (FULL)

175g (6oz) soft margarine
175g (6oz) caster sugar
3 eggs, beaten
175g (6oz) self-raising flour
pinch salt
2 × 15ml tbsp (2tbsp) hot water
jam, or buttercream
icing sugar for dusting

1 Lightly grease a 18.75–20cm (7½–8in) cake dish and line the base with greaseproof paper.
2 Place all the ingredients except the jam and icing sugar into a bowl and mix until combined, then beat well until smooth.
3 Place the mixture into the prepared dish, smooth the top and cook for 6½–7½ min. Leave for 5–10 min before placing on a cooling rack.
4 When cold, cut in half horizontally and sandwich together with jam or buttercream. Dust the top with icing sugar.

Banana and walnut cake *(serves 8–12)*
POWER LEVEL: 60% AND 100% (FULL)

oil
100g (4oz) butter or margarine
100g (4oz) light brown sugar
2 eggs, beaten
100g (4oz) wholewheat flour
2 × 5ml tsp (2tsp) baking powder
2 bananas, mashed
100g (4oz) walnuts, chopped
milk for mixing, optional

1 Lightly oil a deep 17.5cm (7in) round cake dish and line the base with greaseproof paper or baking parchment.
2 Cream together the butter or margarine and sugar until light and fluffy, gradually add the eggs. Fold in the flour and baking powder, then the mashed bananas and walnuts. Add a little milk if necessary to give a soft consistency.
3 Turn the mixture into the prepared dish and cook, uncovered, for 8–10 min on 60% then a further 1–2 min on 100% (full) setting.
4 Allow to cool slightly before turning out onto a rack, then leave until cold. Serve cut into slices.

Whisked sponge *(cuts into 8)*
POWER LEVEL: 100% (FULL)

A light sponge cake which relies on the whisking of air into the eggs as the raising agent, best eaten on the day it is made.

4 eggs
100g (4oz) caster sugar
100g (4oz) plain flour
pinch salt
jam
whipped cream
icing sugar for dusting

1 Lightly grease a 18.75–20cm (7½–8in) cake dish and line the base with greaseproof paper.
2 Whisk the eggs and sugar together until trebled in volume and really thick and creamy.
3 Sift the flour and salt and sprinkle over the mixture, very carefully folding in with a metal spoon and turning the mixture over from the base of the bowl to ensure that all the flour is mixed in.
4 Pour into the prepared container and cook for 4½–5 min. Leave for 5–10 min before placing on a cooling rack.
5 When cold, cut in half horizontally and sandwich the two halves together with jam and cream. Dust the top with icing sugar.

Genoese sponge sandwich *(cuts into 8)*
colour photograph opposite

This cake has better keeping qualities than the whisked sponge and makes a good base for various fillings and toppings for richer gâteaux.

Follow the ingredients and method for the previous recipe. Melt 50g (2oz) butter for 1–1½ min and add to the thickened mixture with the flour by pouring the melted butter in a thin stream down the side of the bowl whilst folding in the flour and butter with a metal spoon. Fold in very carefully, ensuring that the spoon cuts across the base of the bowl so that all the flour and butter are well mixed in. Cook and decorate as for the whisked sponge, or fill and coat with buttercream and decorate with toasted almonds or fruit.

Buttercream
Soften 75g (3oz) butter and gradually add 175g (6oz) sifted icing sugar. Beat well after each addition and then beat until light and fluffy. Flavour and colour as required.

Peanut butter cookies *(makes about 36)*
POWER LEVEL: 100% (FULL)
colour photograph opposite

100g (4oz) butter
225g (8oz) soft brown sugar
100g (4oz) peanut butter
1 egg, beaten
175g (6oz) plain flour
¼ × 5ml tsp (¼tsp) baking powder
¼ × 5ml tsp (¼tsp) salt
1 × 5ml tsp (1tsp) vanilla essence

1 Cream the butter, add the sugar and beat well until soft. Beat in the peanut butter and the egg.
2 Sift the flour, baking powder and salt. Fold into the creamed mixture and add the vanilla essence.
3 Form the mixture into small balls, allowing 2 × 5ml tsp (2tsp) mixture for each. Flatten the balls of dough with a fork dipped in sugar.
4 Place 6 at a time on a microwave baking tray or on lightly greased greaseproof paper on the cooker shelf and cook for 1¾–2½ min depending on size. Turn once halfway through.
5 Leave to cool on a wire rack.

Shortbread *(makes 8 wedges)*
POWER LEVEL: 100% (FULL)
colour photograph opposite

75g (3oz) plain flour
75g (3oz) wholewheat flour
50g (2oz) ground rice
pinch salt
150g (5oz) butter
25g (1oz) caster sugar
caster sugar for dusting

1 Line a 17.5cm (7in) flan dish with clingfilm.
2 Sift the flours, rice and salt into a mixing bowl.
3 Rub in the butter finely.
4 Stir in the sugar and bring the mixture together with the palm of the hand and knead lightly.
5 Press the mixture into the prepared dish and smooth the top with a palette knife.
6 Mark into 8 and prick well with a fork.
7 Cook for 3–4 min, giving a quarter turn every minute.
8 Cool slightly, sprinkle with sugar then cut into pieces. Turn out and leave to cool on a cooling rack.

Note: *The wholewheat flour gives a nutty texture to the shortbread but, if preferred use all plain white flour.*

Caramel shortbread *(makes 8 wedges)*
POWER LEVEL: 100% (FULL)

Shortbread mixture (as above)

For the topping:
50g (2oz) butter
50g (2oz) caster sugar
1 × 15ml tbsp (1tbsp) golden syrup
200g (7oz) condensed milk
75g (3oz) plain chocolate

1 Follow the ingredients and method for shortbread using all plain flour. When cooked, leave in the dish and prepare the topping.
2 Place all the ingredients except the chocolate into a bowl and heat for about 3 min. Stir until well blended and the sugar is dissolved.
3 Heat until boiling and, stirring every ½ min, boil until thickened.
4 Leave to cool for 1 min before pouring over the shortbread base. Leave to cool and set.
5 Melt the chocolate for 2–2½ min and spread over the topping.
6 Mark into serving portions and leave until quite cold before cutting into wedges and removing from the dish.

Oranges in Caramel (page 110), Sponge Pudding (page 116) and Linzer Torte (page 112)

Peanut Butter Cookies (above), Shortbread (above), Genoese Sponge (above) and Sultana Cake (page 127)

Spicy scone round *(cuts into 6)*
POWER LEVEL: 100% (FULL)

175g (6oz) self-raising flour
pinch salt
1 × 5ml tsp (1tsp) mixed spice
½ × 5ml tsp (½tsp) baking powder
40g (1½oz) butter or margarine
2 × 5ml tsp (2tsp) sugar
milk for mixing

1 Lightly grease a 17.5cm (7in) round flan dish and line the base with greaseproof paper.
2 Sift the flour, salt, mixed spice and baking powder, rub in the butter or margarine finely.
3 Stir in sugar and enough milk to make a soft dough; knead lightly on a floured surface.
4 Roll out to about 1.25cm (½in) thick. Using a 6.25cm (2½in) cutter, cut into 6 rounds.
5 Place 5 shapes round the outside edge of the container and 1 in the centre.
6 Cook for 2 min, turn, cook for 1–2 min.
7 Serve hot or cold, split and spread with butter.

Iced scone round

Follow the recipe for spicy scone round. When cooked and cool, decorate with glacé icing (page 127), quartered glacé cherries and chopped nuts.

DO NOT FREEZE WHEN ICED AND DECORATED

Wholewheat scones *(cuts into 6 or 8 wedges)*
POWER LEVEL: 100% (FULL)

100g (4oz) plain flour
pinch salt
1 × 5ml tsp (1tsp) bicarbonate of soda
1 × 5ml tsp (1tsp) cream of tartar
100g (4oz) wholewheat flour
2 × 5ml tsp (2tsp) sugar
50g (2oz) butter or margarine
150ml (¼pt) buttermilk or fresh milk with 1½ × 5ml tsp (1½tsp) baking powder

1 Lightly grease a 17.5cm (7in) round flan dish and line the base with greaseproof paper.
2 Sift the flour, salt, bicarbonate of soda and cream of tartar into a bowl, stir in the wholewheat flour and sugar. Rub in the butter finely.
3 Stir in the buttermilk or fresh milk with baking powder and mix to a soft dough. Knead lightly on a floured surface.
4 Roll out or shape into a round about 17.5cm (7in) in diameter and place in the prepared container. Score to half the depth into 6 or 8 wedges. Dust with wholewheat flour.
5 Cook for 4½–5 min. Serve hot or cold split into wedges, with butter.

Girdle scones *(makes 8–10)*
POWER LEVEL: 100% (FULL)

Traditionally cooked on a girdle, these microwave 'girdle' scones are cooked in a browning dish.

225g (8oz) plain flour
pinch salt
1 × 15ml tbsp (1tbsp) baking powder
50g (2oz) butter or margarine
1 × 5ml tsp (1tsp) sugar
150ml (¼pt) milk or milk and water mixed
oil

1 Sift the flour, salt and baking powder into a bowl. Rub in the butter or margarine finely. Stir in the sugar and mix to a soft manageable dough with the milk.
2 Knead lightly on a floured surface and roll into a round approximately 6mm (¼in) thick. Cut into rounds with a 5cm (2in) cutter or cut the large round into 8 triangles.
3 Preheat the browning dish for 4–5 min, depending on size. Lightly brush the base with oil.
4 Quickly place the scones in the browning dish, arranging the triangles with the pointed ends towards the centre.
5 Cook for 1 min, turn the scones over and the dish around, cook for 1½–2 min.
6 Leave to cool on a wire rack. Serve hot or cold, split and buttered.

Sultana girdle scones (makes 8–10)

Follow the ingredients and method for girdle scones, adding 2 × 15ml heaped tbsp (2 heaped tbsp) sultanas to the dry ingredients.

Cheesy girdle scones (makes 8–10)

Follow the ingredients and method for girdle scones, omitting the sugar and adding 50g (2oz) grated cheddar cheese to the dry ingredients.

Fruited ginger biscuits *(makes 20–24)*
POWER LEVEL: 100% (FULL)

100g (4oz) wholewheat flour
½ × 5ml tsp (½tsp) bicarbonate of soda
1 × 5ml tsp (1tsp) ground ginger
½ × 5ml tsp (½tsp) ground cinnamon
50g (2oz) currants
50g (2oz) butter or margarine
3 × 15ml tbsp (3tbsp) clear honey

1 Place together the dry ingredients and make a well in the centre.
2 Place the butter or margarine and honey in a small bowl and heat for 1½–2 min until the margarine is melted. Beat well.

3 Pour the syrup into the bowl with the dry ingredients and mix together thoroughly.

4 Divide the mixture into 20–24 balls, the size of walnuts, by rolling between your hands. Place on a piece of greaseproof paper or baking parchment, and flatten each one slightly by pressing with the back of a fork.

5 Cook the biscuits, 8 at a time, for 1½–2 min. Allow to cool slightly before transferring to a cooling rack. Store in an airtight tin.

Microwave meringues (makes 40)
POWER LEVEL: 100% (FULL)

These fondant meringues are most successful although they do not have the slightly soft centres associated with conventional ones. Timing is important to ensure the mixture is fully risen and set before removal from the oven otherwise, it will sink. If overcooked, the centres will caramelise.

1 egg white
250–350g (9–12oz) icing sugar, sieved

1 Break up the egg white lightly with a fork and then work in as much icing sugar as possible. The amount of sugar will depend on the size of the egg.

2 Work the mixture together with your hands until it is dry and can be kneaded. If the mixture is too sticky, add a little more icing sugar; if too dry, add just a drop or two of cold water. Knead well together.

3 Divide the mixture and mould into 40 even pieces about the size of marbles. Arrange 6 in a circle on baking parchment or greaseproof paper on the microwave oven shelf, leaving plenty of room for the meringues to spread.

4 Cook, uncovered, for about 1 min until risen and firm. Remove to a wire rack to cool and cook the remaining mixture, 6 at a time, as above.

Note: *If preferred, the meringues can be placed into paper cases and cooked 8 at a time for about 1¼ min.*

Pavlova base (makes 3)

Follow the recipe above and divide the mixture into 3. Roll out each piece as thinly as possible on baking parchment or greaseproof paper using a little icing sugar to prevent the rolling pin sticking. Trim into rounds using a 15cm (6in) plate as a guide and cut the paper around each circle to fit the microwave shelf or turntable. Cook one at a time for 1¾–2 min until risen and firm. Peel off the paper and leave the meringue to cool on a wire rack.

Muesli cake (serves 8–12)
POWER LEVEL: 100% (FULL) AND 50%

175g (6oz) muesli
100g (4oz) dark brown sugar
2 × 15ml tbsp (2tbsp) malt extract
175g (6oz) sultanas
225ml (8fl oz) apple juice, approximately
2 cooking apples, peeled and grated
175g (6oz) wholewheat flour
3 × 5ml tsp (3tsp) baking powder
1 × 5ml tsp (1tsp) mixed spice
For decoration:
walnut halves

1 Lightly oil a deep 15–17.5cm (6–7in) round cake dish.

2 Place the muesli, sugar, malt extract, sultanas and apple juice in a bowl, cover and heat for 3 min on 100% (full) setting. Stir and allow to stand, covered, for 5 min.

3 Add the apple, flour, baking powder and spice to the muesli and mix well to a soft dropping consistency, adding a little more apple juice if necessary.

4 Turn the mixture into the prepared dish and cook, uncovered, for 20–25 min on 50%.

5 Allow to stand for a few minutes before turning out onto a cooling rack. Decorate with walnut halves.

Note: *This cake is quite rich and you will only require a small slice at a time.*

Almond slices (makes about 12 slices)
POWER LEVEL: 70%

3 egg whites
100g (4oz) ground almonds
175g (6oz) caster sugar
50g (2oz) self-raising flour
few drops almond essence
25–50g (1–2oz) almonds, blanched and chopped

1 Lightly grease a dish approximately 15 × 15cm (6 × 6in) square or an equivalent-size oblong size.

2 Whisk the egg whites until stiff and holding shape, then using a metal spoon carefully fold in the ground almonds, caster sugar, sifted flour and almond essence.

3 Place the mixture into the prepared dish, smooth the top and scatter with the chopped almonds.

4 Cook on 70% setting for 5–6 min, turning every 1½ min.

5 Leave to cool for a few minutes before cutting into slices and removing to a wire rack to cool.

Cherry and walnut ring cake *(cuts into 8–10)*
POWER LEVEL: 100% (FULL)

100 g (4oz) butter or margarine
100g (4oz) caster sugar
2 eggs, beaten
175g (6oz) self-raising flour
pinch salt
50g (2oz) walnuts, chopped
1–2 × 15ml tbsp (1–2tbsp) milk
100g (4oz) glacé cherries, halved
icing sugar for dusting

1 Lightly grease a 20cm (8in) microwave ring mould and line base with greaseproof paper.
2 Cream the butter or margarine until soft, add the sugar and beat well until light and fluffy.
3 Add the eggs gradually, beating well after each addition.
4 Sift the flour and salt and fold into the creamed mixture with a metal spoon. Add the walnuts and milk, mix well to form a soft mixture.
5 Place the cherries over the base of the container and spoon in the mixture.

Cherry and Coconut Ring Cake (below), Fruit Gingerbread (page 127) and Coconut Cake (page 127)

6 Cook for 5–6 min, turning once halfway through if necessary. Leave for 10–15 min before turning onto a cooling tray.
7 When cool, dust heavily with icing sugar.

Cherry and coconut ring cake
colour photograph above

Follow the ingredients and method for cherry and walnut ring cake, substituting 50g (2oz) desiccated coconut for the walnuts. More milk will be necessary to make a soft mixture. Decorate with toasted coconut.

Toasted desiccated coconut
POWER LEVEL: 100% (FULL)

Place the coconut onto a flat dish or plate or in a roasting bag and cook in the microwave, stirring or shaking frequently, for about 5 min or until the required toasted colour has been obtained.

Sticky gingerbread *(cuts into 12–16 wedges)*
POWER LEVEL: 100% (FULL) AND 70%

100g (4oz) butter or margarine
225g (8oz) black treacle
75g (3oz) soft brown sugar
2 × 15ml tbsp (2tbsp) orange marmalade
150ml (¼pt) milk
½ × 5ml tsp (½tsp) bicarbonate of soda
100g (4oz) self-raising flour
2 × 5ml tsp (2tsp) ground ginger
1 × 5ml tsp (1tsp) mixed spice
100g (4oz) wholewheat flour
2 eggs, beaten
apricot glaze (page 140)

1 Lightly grease a 22.5cm (9in) cake dish and line the base with greaseproof paper.
2 Place the butter or margarine, treacle, sugar and orange marmalade into a bowl, heat on 100% (full) setting for 2–3 min then stir until blended.
3 Warm the milk for 30 sec on 100% (full) setting and stir in the bicarbonate of soda.
4 Sift the self-raising flour and spices, stir in the wholewheat flour.
5 Add the treacle mixture, milk and eggs to the dry ingredients and mix thoroughly until smooth.
6 Pour the mixture into the prepared dish and cook on 70% setting for 12–14 min, turning every 3 min.
7 Place on a cooling rack and, when cool, brush with apricot glaze. Serve cut into wedges.

Fruit gingerbread (colour page 126)

Follow the ingredients and method for sticky gingerbread, adding 50g (2oz) sultanas or raisins or chopped crystallised ginger or pineapple to the dry ingredients. When cool, brush with apricot glaze and decorate with flaked almonds.

Note: *If your microwave cooker has no variable power control setting, either divide the mixture into two and cook each separately, or make up half quantity. Place in a 15cm (6in) cake dish and cook for 3½–4½ min at 100% (full) setting.*

Basic cake mixture *(cuts into 8)*
POWER LEVEL: 100% (FULL)

225g (8oz) self-raising flour
pinch salt
100g (4oz) butter or margarine
100g (4oz) soft brown sugar
2 eggs, beaten
few drops lemon juice
milk for mixing
apricot glaze, optional (page 140)

1 Lightly grease a 18.75–20cm (7½–8in) cake dish and line the base with greaseproof paper.
2 Sift the flour and the salt, rub in the butter or margarine finely, stir in the sugar.
3 Mix in the eggs, lemon juice and sufficient milk to form a soft dropping consistency.
4 Turn the mixture into the prepared dish and cook for 5½–7 min. Allow to cool slightly before removing from the dish onto a cooling rack.
5 When cold, brush with apricot glaze.

Fruit cake

Follow the ingredients and method for the basic cake mixture adding 150g (5oz) mixed dried fruit to the dry ingredients after the sugar.

Sultana cake (colour page 123)

Follow the ingredients and method for the basic cake mixture, adding 150g (5oz) sultanas to the dry ingredients after the sugar.

Coconut cake (colour page 126)

Follow the ingredients and method for the basic cake mixture, adding 175g (6oz) desiccated coconut to the dry ingredients after the sugar; a little more milk for mixing may be required. When cold, decorate with glacé icing (see below) and toasted coconut (page 126).

Glacé icing

Mix 175g (6oz) sifted icing sugar with sufficient hot water to make a soft paste, thick enough to coat the back of the spoon. Mix well and use immediately.

DO NOT FREEZE.

Preserves

The advantages of cooking preserves in the micro-wave are that they can be made quickly with little fuss and bother, the flavours are enhanced, and particularly important with jams and marmalades, a very good colour is retained. In addition, the kitchen remains cooler and free of smells and it really is possible to make small quantities without the worry of the food sticking or burning onto the base of the cooking container.

Fresh fruit with a high pectin content – citrus fruits, gooseberries and blackcurrants – give best results. Fruit which is low in pectin – straw-berries and apricots – should have citric acid, lemon juice or commercial pectin added.

For some jams, blackcurrant for example, the liquid quantity is reduced compared with con-ventional recipes, as there is very little evapora-tion from the surface during cooking in the micro-wave oven. At the same time, however, it is important to soften the fruit and release the pectin during the initial cooking stage, therefore the balance of water to fruit needs to be correct. As a general rule, cut the quantity of water by one-third when converting your own jam recipes. On the other hand, in marmalade making, about the same quantity of water to fruit is required as for conventional methods to ensure that the peel is softened sufficiently before adding the sugar and boiling for the final set.

•GUIDELINES AT-A-GLANCE

•**Boil-overs** will occur when making jams and marmalades if the container is not large enough to allow for the expansion of the mixture when boil-ing to reach setting point.

•**Containers** should be heatproof and wide-necked to allow maximum surface area for boiling and re-duction of the liquids. A 3l (6pt) ovenproof glass mixing bowl is ideal.

•**Cooking** is carried out at 100% (full) setting for most preserves unless the fruits or vegetables re-quire a lower power setting at the initial cooking stage to tenderise them.

•**Cover** preserves with a lid or pierced clingfilm during the initial cooking stage, but leave un-covered when boiling the mixture to reach setting point or to thicken.

•**Heat** citrus fruits for 1–2 min until warm for maximum juiciness before cutting and squeezing.

•**Peel** for marmalade will soften more if left to soak overnight in the liquid and juices. Alternatively cook at a lower 50% setting until the peel is softened sufficiently.

•**Quantities** of fruits or vegetables to yield up to 2½kg (5½lb) of preserves only should be at-tempted. If larger quantities are required, cook in two lots in the microwave, otherwise conven-tional methods may be more convenient.

•**Setting point** can be measured with a sugar thermometer when the temperature should be 105°C (220°F), although some jams and mar-malades may require a degree or two higher to ob-tain a good set. It is always a good idea to check setting point in the normal way, by pouring a little preserve onto a saucer and leaving it to cool for a few minutes. Setting point is reached if the skin formed on top of the preserve wrinkles when touched. If difficulty is found in obtaining setting point:
1 The water to fruit ratio may be too high, or the fruit has yielded more juice in which case boil at 100% (full) for a longer time.
2 Check the power output of your microwave. If it is a 500 or 600 watt model, the preserve may take 5–10 min longer to reach setting point.
3 The quantity of preserve is too large, divide into two and bring each to setting point separately.

•**Standing** or cooling time is required after cooking some preserves to ensure the fruit or peel is evenly distributed when potting.

●**Sterilize** the glass jars in the microwave by adding water to each and heating until the water is boiling rapidly. Drain and dry before pouring in the preserve. Top with waxed discs and, when completely cold, cover the jars with cellophane tops and label clearly.

●**Sugar** can be warmed for a few minutes in the microwave before adding to the preserve. This will cut down on the length of time required to dissolve the sugar.

●**Sugar thermometers** can be used to check the setting point (see above) but should not be left in the preserve during cooking unless specially designed for use in the microwave.

●**Temperature probes** are not usually suitable for use when preserve making as they are not calibrated to the high temperatures required for reaching setting point. Check with the manufacturer's instructions.

Apricot jam *makes about 2½kg (5lb)*
POWER LEVEL: 100% (FULL)

1½kg (3½lb) apricots
225ml (8fl oz) water
6g (¼oz) citric acid
1¾kg (4lb) preserving sugar

1 Wash, halve and stone the apricots. Place in a large glass bowl with the water and citric acid.
2 Cover with a lid or clingfilm slit with the pointed end of a sharp knife. Cook for 15–20 min, stirring 2–3 times throughout.
3 Add the sugar and stir well. Cook uncovered for 45–50 min, or until setting point is reached, stirring every 5–10 min.
4 Allow to stand for 20–30 min. Warm jars, then pot the jam, seal and label.

Plum jam *(makes about 2½kg/5lb)*
POWER LEVEL: 100% (FULL)

1½kg (3lb) plums, washed and stoned
150ml (¼pt) boiling water
1½kg (3lb) sugar, granulated or preserving

1 Place the prepared plums in a large bowl with the boiling water. Cover with a lid or pierced clingfilm, then cook for 10 min. Stir the plums, recover, and cook for a further 5 min.
2 Add the sugar and stir well. Cook, uncovered, for 25 min or until setting point is reached, stirring every 5 min.
3 Pot, seal and label.

Lemon curd *makes about 1kg (2lb)*
POWER LEVEL: 100% (FULL)

175g (6oz) butter
4 eggs
2 egg yolks
275g (10oz) caster sugar
4 large lemons, grated rind and juice

1 Cut the butter into pieces and place in a large bowl. Heat for 4–5 min until melted.
2 Beat together the rest of the ingredients and stir into the butter.
3 Cook uncovered for 6–7 min, stirring every minute until thick enough to coat the back of a wooden spoon.
4 Pour the curd into small jars then seal and label.

Note: *Lemon curd does not keep well so is best made in small quantities and stored in a cool place for about 1 month.*

Diabetic marmalade *(makes about 2½kg/5lb)*
POWER LEVEL: 100% (FULL)

4 large oranges
550ml (1pt) boiling water
1½kg (3lb) sorbitol
1 × 225ml (8fl oz) bottle of commercial pectin

1 Wash and dry the fruit, place in the microwave and heat for 2 min. Squeeze the juice and place in a large bowl. Remove and discard the pith and pips.
2 Shred the orange peel finely and add to the juice with the boiling water. Cover and cook for 15–20 min, stirring once.
3 Add the sorbitol and stir well. Cook, uncovered, for 25 min, stirring every 5 min.
4 Remove the marmalade from the microwave and add the pectin. Allow to stand for 10 min then pour into small warmed jars and seal immediately.
5 Diabetic marmalade is best if sterilized. This may be done conventionally on a trivet in a saucepan on the hob, or in the microwave using a temperature probe. If no temperature probe is fitted to your model, a thermometer may be used instead, but this should not be left in the microwave during the heating process unless specially designed. For sterilizing by microwave, stand the jars in a deep bowl so that they do not touch and cover the jars with cold water. Heat for approximately 1 hr on 50% (defrost) setting, to a temperature of 72°C (164°F). Hold at this temperature for 10 min.

Note: *Use small jars with metal screw-tops for the diabetic marmalade.*

Hot 'n' spicy chutney *makes about 900g (2lb)*
POWER LEVEL: 100% (FULL)
colour photograph opposite

450g (1lb) cooking apples, peeled, cored and
  sliced
1 large onion, chopped
1 clove garlic, finely chopped
25g (1oz) salt
225g (8oz) brown sugar
325ml (13fl oz) malt vinegar
225g (8oz) raisins
25g (1oz) ground ginger and dried mustard, mixed
½ × 5ml tsp (½tsp) cayenne papper

1 Place the apples, onion, garlic, salt and sugar in
  a large bowl with the malt vinegar.
2 Cover and cook for approximately 10 min or
  until soft.
3 Purée the mixture in a blender or pass through
  a sieve. Add the raisins.
4 Mix the spices with a little of the purée and add
  to the chutney. Leave to stand overnight, then
  pot, seal and label.

Note: *If preferred, all the ingredients may be
cooked together and potted without puréeing.*

Three fruit marmalade *makes about 2½kg (5½lb)*
POWER LEVEL: 100% (FULL)
colour photograph opposite

2 grapefruit
2 large lemons
2 oranges
850ml (1½pt) boiling water
1.8kg (4lb) preserving sugar

1 Wash, dry and halve the fruit. Squeeze out the
  juice and place it in a large glass bowl.
2 Remove the pith and pips from the fruit skins
  and tie them in a piece of muslin or fine cloth.
  Shred the peel according to your preference –
  fine, medium or coarse.
3 Place the peel in the bowl with the juice and the
  bag of pith and pips. Add 275ml (½pt) boiling
  water and leave to stand for 1 hr. Remove the
  bag.
4 Add the rest of the boiling water. Cover with
  clingfilm and cook for 20–30 min, depending
  on the thickness of the peel.
5 Add the sugar and stir until dissolved. Cook,
  uncovered, for 25–30 min, stirring every 5 min
  until setting point is reached.
6 Allow the marmalade to stand for 30 min, then
  pot, seal and label.

Apple and ginger preserve *makes about 675g (1½lb)*
POWER LEVEL: 100% (FULL)

450g (1lb) cooking apples, washed
1 × 15ml tbsp (1tbsp) lemon juice
6g (¼oz) root ginger
275ml (½pt) water
450g (1lb) preserving sugar
100g (4oz) preserved ginger, finely chopped

1 Slice the apples without peeling and place in a
  large glass bowl with the lemon juice.
2 Bruise the ginger by hitting it with a rolling
  pin, then add it to the apples.
3 Add the water, cover with clingfilm and cook
  for 10 min. Remove the ginger.
4 Press the apples through a jelly cloth to extract
  all the juice. This should produce 550ml (1pt)
  of extract.
5 Add the sugar and preserved ginger to the
  extract. Stir until the sugar is dissolved. Cook
  uncovered for 25 min or until setting point is
  reached, stirring every 5 min.
6 Cool for 20–30 min, stir then pot, seal and label.

Sweetcorn relish *makes about 1½kg (3lb)*
POWER LEVEL: 100% (FULL)
colour photograph opposite

1 × 5ml tsp (1tsp) turmeric, or a few strands of
  saffron
225ml (8fl oz) distilled malt vinegar
1 red pepper, deseeded and diced
1 green pepper, deseeded and diced
1 stick celery, finely chopped
1 onion, peeled and finely chopped
1 clove garlic, finely chopped
675g (1½lb) sweetcorn kernels, fresh, frozen or
  canned
225g (8oz) caster sugar
pinch each mustard, mace, tarragon
2 × 15ml tbsp (2tbsp) arrowroot, blended with a
  little water

1 Add the turmeric or saffron to the vinegar and
  leave to turn yellow while preparing the vegetables.
2 Strain the vinegar into a large bowl and add all
  the vegetables except the sweetcorn. Cover and
  cook for 5 min.
3 Add the sweetcorn, sugar and seasonings. Stir
  well and cook for 5 min.
4 Add the arrowroot blended with water to the
  mixture. Stir well and cook for 5 min, stir, then
  cook for 3 min or until thickened.
5 Leave to cool slightly then pot, seal and label.

Selection of preserves

Date chutney *makes about 1¼kg (2½lb)*
POWER LEVEL: 100% (FULL)

450g (1lb) dates, roughly chopped
450g (1lb) raisins
1 medium onion, peeled and finely chopped
350g (12oz) brown sugar
2 cloves garlic, crushed
2 × 5ml tsp (2tsp) salt
4–6 chillies, finely chopped
550ml (1pt) vinegar

1 Place all the ingredients in a large bowl and cover with a lid or clingfilm, slit with the pointed end of a sharp knife.
2 Bring the mixture to the boil and cook until tender and the desired consistency is reached, about 30 min.
3 Leave to cool slightly then pot, seal and label.

Sweet damson pickle *makes about 1kg (2lb)*
POWER LEVEL: 50% AND 100% (FULL)

900g (2lb) damsons, washed
rind ½ lemon
6 cloves
6 allspice seeds
small piece each root ginger and cinnamon stick
450g (1lb) brown sugar
275ml (½pt) vinegar

1 Place the whole damsons in a large bowl. Tie the lemon rind and spices in a muslin bag.
2 Dissolve the sugar in the vinegar and pour over the damsons.
3 Cover with a lid or clingfilm slit with the pointed end of a knife and cook on 50% setting for 12–15 min until the damsons are tender.
4 Drain and reserve the vinegar; pack the fruit neatly into warmed jars.
5 Boil the vinegar in the microwave on 100% (full) setting until it is reduced to a thin syrup.
6 Pour over the fruit in the jars and seal and label immediately.

Rhubarb chutney *makes about 1½–2kg (3–4lb)*
POWER LEVEL: 100% (FULL)

1¼kg (2½lb) rhubarb, washed and cut into small
   pieces
225g (8oz) onions, peeled and finely chopped or
   minced
450g (1lb) sugar
6g (¼oz) ground ginger
25g (1oz) ground mixed spice
6g (¼oz) salt
425ml (¾pt) vinegar

1 Place the rhubarb, onions, sugar, spices and
salt in a large bowl. Stir in 150ml (¼pt) of the
vinegar.
2 Cover and cook for about 15 min, stirring every
5 min, until the rhubarb is tender.
3 Stir in the rest of the vinegar and cook uncovered until thick.
4 Pot, seal and label.

Strawberry jam *makes about 1½ kg (3lb)*
POWER LEVEL: 100% (FULL)
colour page 131

1¾kg (3½lb) strawberries, hulled and washed
15g (½oz) citric acid
1¼kg (2¾lb) preserving sugar

1 Place the strawberries in a large bowl. Sprinkle
with the citric acid and cook for about 15 min
until soft.
2 Add the sugar and stir well. Cook the jam,
uncovered, for 40 min or until setting point is
reached. Stir the jam every 10 min at the beginning of cooking and every 5 min towards the
end of the time.
3 Allow the jam to stand for 20–30 min. Pour into
warmed jars, seal and label.

Red tomato chutney *(makes about 1¼kg/ 2½lb)*
POWER LEVEL: 100% (FULL)

225g (8oz) onions, finely chopped
1½kg (3lb) ripe tomatoes, skinned and chopped
15g (½oz) salt
1 × 5ml tsp (1tsp) paprika
good pinch of cayenne pepper
150ml (¼pt) distilled malt vinegar
175g (6oz) granulated sugar

1 Place the onions in a large bowl, cover and
cook for 5 min, stirring once.
2 Add the tomatoes and cook for a further 8 min,
uncovered, until the vegetables are soft and
pulpy. Stir once during cooking.
3 Add the salt, spices and vinegar. Cook for 5
min, stir; continue to cook for a further 5 min.
4 Add the sugar and stir well. Cook, uncovered,
for 35–40 min until thick, stirring occasionally.
5 Pour into warmed jars. seal and label.

Blackcurrant jam *makes about 1kg (2lb)*
POWER LEVEL: 100% (FULL)

450g (1lb) blackcurrants
425ml (¾pt) boiling water
675g (1½lb) preserving sugar

1 Remove stalks, wash the fruit, drain well and
place in a large bowl with the boiling water.
2 Bring to the boil in the microwave then cook
for about 5 min until the fruit is tender.
3 Stir in the sugar until dissolved.
4 Cook uncovered for 25–30 min or until setting
point is reached, stirring every 5 min.
5 Allow to stand for 20 min and then pour into
warmed jars. Seal and label.

Breads

The advantage of proving dough in the microwave is that it is so fast – 450g (1lb) of white or brown bread dough can be proved in half the normal time required. The covered dough is given combinations of short bursts of microwave energy for 15 sec with standing or resting periods of 5–15 min, which allows an even distribution of warmth through the dough, ensuring a steady rise. After proving and shaping, the dough can be cooked by microwave in 6–7 min. This will produce a good-textured loaf with a soft crust. Of course it will not be browned as when baking conventionally, but if a crisper crust is preferred the dough can be partly cooked for 3–4 min in the microwave and then finished in a conventional oven preheated to a high temperature, for 8–10 min. Alternatively, the dough can be prepared and proved by microwave and afterwards completely cooked conventionally.

Loaves of bread and rolls which are to be proved and cooked in the microwave cooker must, of course, be placed in suitable microwave containers. The dough may be sprinkled with nibbed wheat, poppy seeds or sesame seeds for a more decorative finish.

Included in this section are some sweet yeast mixtures and a few breads which are leavened with soda rather than yeast.

Defrosting

Remember the textures of food affect thawing times and so a light vienna or french bread will thaw more quickly than the heavier-textured varieties. One roll or a slice of bread may be thawed in 10–25 sec, 2 would take 15–30 sec, and 3 would take 20–35 sec. Crumpets and slices of bread to be toasted may be cooked from the frozen state, whereas muffins and teacakes need to be thawed in the microwave for 10–20 sec before being cut and toasted or, if not toasted, leave them to stand for 2 min before serving. Loaves of bread should be defrosted on 30–50% setting for 4–8 min, depending on size and then allowed to stand for up to 12 min.

Sliced bread or rolls may be placed in cotton, linen or paper serviettes inside a wicker or straw basket, heated in the microwave and served direct to the luncheon or dining table.

●GUIDELINES AT-A-GLANCE

●**Arrange** individual rolls in a circle on the microwave cooker shelf when proving and cooking by microwave to ensure even results.

●**Browning** will not occur when baking by microwave unless combining with a convection system or part baking in a conventional oven. Alternatively, the top of a microwave loaf may be 'toasted' under a medium-hot grill to give a browned appearance.

●**Containers** must be suitable for use in the microwave when proving and cooking yeast doughs by microwave only, and they should also be heatproof if baking conventionally after proving by microwave or when using a combination system. If a metal tin is preferred, the final proving must be carried out by leaving in a warm place to rise before baking conventionally.

●**Conventional baking** after proving by microwave is recommended if a crisp crust is preferred. Alternative conventional baking methods are given in this section when appropriate, otherwise the dough can be part-baked by microwave for 3–4 min and finished in a conventional oven preheated to a high temperature for 8–10 min.

●**Cook** in the microwave if a soft crust is acceptable. Most yeast doughs are cooked using 100% (full) setting. Alternatively, after proving by microwave, cook in a conventional oven to achieve traditional browning as detailed above.

●**Cover** yeast doughs with clingfilm when proving. Leave the container uncovered when cooking.

●**Crusts** on a microwave baked loaf will be soft, similar in texture to traditional baps.

● **Defrost** using a 30–50% setting for most even results although individual rolls and slices of bread may be defrosted on 100% (full) then left to stand for a minute or two before serving.

● **Doughy bases** may occur, particularly on larger loaves, and can sometimes be caused by over-greasing of the container. Cooking on a raised level, ie using a microwave baking rack or an up-turned saucer, or ensuring there is a small gap between the base of the dish and the oven shelf should help – some microwave dishes available have rims on the bases. Otherwise, invert the loaf on the microwave shelf and cook for a further 1–2 min, then leave to stand on a cooling rack.

● **Heat** wicker baskets of rolls or sliced breads for lunch or dinner parties and serve straight to the table. Line the basket with a linen or paper napkin to absorb moisture.

● **Kitchen paper** towels are useful for absorbing moisture when reheating bread and rolls to retain crispness. Wrap it around the bread or place the loaf on top of the towels on the oven shelf.

● **Line** the base of the container with baking parchment or *lightly* greased greaseproof paper if preferred. When necessary, the container may be just lightly greased with oil but do not flour as this will result in a doughy crust forming when baking by microwave.

● **Overheating** in the microwave when defrosting, warming or cooking yeast doughs will cause dry, hard results. Always give less time at first and heat for a little longer if necessary. If a microwave loaf seems to go stale quickly, this is an indication of overcooking. Wrap as soon as possible after cooking to retain moisture.

● **Prove** yeast doughs by giving 15 sec on 100% (full) and then allow to stand. White and light yeast mixtures will require 5–10 min standing periods whereas wholewheat and richer doughs take longer to rise and may require 10–15 min standing periods. Repeat this combination of microwave energy and standing times until the dough is risen to about twice its size. After proving, the dough should be soft and light in texture; if it has hardened at the edges, overheating has occurred. Cut away the hard parts before re-kneading and shaping.

● **Toppings** such as poppy seeds, sesame seeds, knibbed wheat or chopped herbs may be used to decorate. Lightly oil the dough after proving and sprinkle with the topping before cooking in the microwave to produce a more attractive result.

● **Turn** the container if necessary during cooking to produce an even result. When defrosting, large loaves of bread should also be turned over half-way through.

● **Warm** the liquids and the flours in the microwave prior to mixing, kneading and proving. This ensures that the dough is evenly warm throughout at the beginning which assists the proving process.

White bread *(makes 1 loaf)*
POWER LEVEL: 100% (FULL)
colour page 135

This is a basic white bread dough which can also be used for pizzas or white rolls.

1 × 5ml tsp (1tsp) sugar
275ml (½pt) water
1 × 5ml tsp (1tsp) dried yeast
450g (1lb) plain flour
1 × 5ml tsp (1tsp) salt
40g (1½oz) butter or margarine
poppy seeds or sesame seeds for sprinkling

1 Lightly grease a 15cm (6in) soufflé dish or 900g (2lb) loaf dish and line the base with grease-proof paper.
2 Add the sugar to half the water and warm for 30 sec. Stir in the yeast and leave for 8–12 min to activate.
3 Sift the flour and salt into a bowl and warm for 30 sec. Rub in the butter or margarine finely.
4 Warm the rest of the water for 30 sec and add with the yeast to the flour, adding a little extra water if necessary to make a fairly soft dough. Knead thoroughly until the dough is smooth.
5 Place the dough in a bowl covered with cling-film and prove by heating for 15 sec and leaving to stand for 5–10 min. Repeat this 3–4 times until the dough had doubled in size.
6 Turn the dough onto a lightly floured surface and knead well until smooth. Shape the dough and place in the prepared container and prove as described previously until double in size.
7 Lightly oil the top of the dough and sprinkle with poppy seeds or sesame seeds.
8 Cook for 5 min, turning once if necessary. Leave to stand for 10 min, then turn out and cool on a wire rack.

Alternative conventional bake
Place the dough in a greased loaf dish or tin. If a

metal loaf tin is used, the second proving must be carried out conventionally in a warm place. Cook in a preheated oven at 220°C (425°F) Mark 7 for 20–30 min.

White rolls *(makes 16)*
POWER LEVEL: 100% (FULL)
colour photograph below

450g (1lb) white bread dough (page 134)
poppy seeds or sesame seeds for sprinkling

1 Follow the instructions for white bread until the end of the first proving at stage 5.
2 Turn the dough onto a lightly floured surface and knead well until smooth.
3 Divide the dough into 16 pieces, shape the rolls and place in a circle on a lightly greased microwave baking tray or oven shelf.
4 Heat for 15 sec and leave to stand for 5–10 min. Repeat until the rolls have well risen.
5 Lightly brush the rolls with oil and sprinkle with poppy seeds or sesame seeds.
6 Cook 8 at a time for 2 min, rearranging the rolls

if necessary halfway through. Leave to cool on a wire rack.

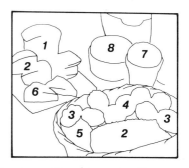

Selection of breads and rolls:
1 *Dark Rye Bread (page 136)*
2 *Light Wholewheat Bread (page 136)*
3 *White Rolls (above)*
4 *Light Wholewheat Rolls (page 136)*
5 *Baps (page 136)*
6 *Oatmeal Bread (page 137)*
7 *Cheese Bread (page 140)*
8 *White Bread (page 134)*

Alternative conventional bake
After the second proving on the microwave shelf, place the rolls on a lightly greased baking tray. Alternatively, prove on a baking tray in a warm place. Cook in a preheated oven at 220°C (425°F) Mark 7 for 15–20 min. For a more glossy finish, the rolls may brushed with beaten egg before baking.

Alternative shapes for rolls
Plait: Divide dough into three, shape each piece into a long roll and plait together securing ends firmly.
Twist:Divide dough into two, shape each piece into a long roll and twist together, securing ends firmly.
Knot: Shape dough into a long roll and tie into a knot.
Rings: Shape dough into a long roll and bend it round to form a ring, dampen the ends and secure by moulding them together.

Prove and bake as described in the recipe.

Light wholewheat bread (makes 1 loaf) and rolls (makes 16)
colour page 135

Follow the ingredients and method for white bread and rolls, substituting 225g (8oz) of wholewheat flour for white flour and using sesame seeds or nibbed wheat instead of poppy seeds for sprinkling.

Note: *Wholewheat flours tend to absorb slightly less liquid than the finer flours which fact should be taken into account when mixing the dough, and the proving times may be slightly longer.*

Light rye bread *(makes 1 loaf)*
POWER LEVEL: 100% (FULL)

This closer-textured bread has good keeping qualities and is delicious with smoked fish and cheese.

$1\frac{1}{2}$ × 5ml tsp ($1\frac{1}{2}$tsp) brown sugar
425ml (¾pt) water, approximately
1 × 5ml tsp (1tsp) dried yeast
450g (1lb) strong plain flour
100g (4oz) rye flour
$1\frac{1}{2}$ × 5ml tsp ($1\frac{1}{2}$tsp) salt
caraway seeds or cumin seeds for sprinkling, optional

1 Lightly grease a 22cm (9in) round dish or a 900g (2lb) loaf dish and line the base with greaseproof paper.
2 Add the sugar to a third of the water and warm

for 30 sec. Stir in the yeast and leave for 8–12 min to activate.
3 Mix the flours and salt well and warm for 30 sec. Warm the remaining liquid for 45 sec.
4 Add the yeast and sufficient of the remaining water to the flours to form a soft dough. Mix well, knead lightly and form into a ball.
5 Place the dough into a bowl cover with clingfilm and prove by heating for 15 sec and leaving to stand for 10–15 min. Repeat this process 3–4 times until the dough has doubled in size. If you have the time, knead and prove again.
6 Turn the dough onto a floured surface, knead well until smooth. Shape the dough and place into the prepared container.
7 With a sharp knife, make a cut across the top and widen this by pressing into it with the blade of the knife. Brush the top with oil, sprinkle with rye flour and a few caraway seeds or cumin seeds.
8 Prove as described previously until double in size. Cook for $5\frac{1}{2}$–$6\frac{1}{2}$ min, turning once halfway through if necessary. Leave for 10 min before turning out onto a wire rack to cool.

Note: $1\frac{1}{2}$ × 5ml tsp ($1\frac{1}{2}$tsp) *caraway or cumin seeds may be added to the flours before mixing for the characteristic flavour of rye bread.*

Alternative conventional bake
Place the dough in a greased round ovenware dish or loaf tin. If a metal tin is used, the second proving must be carried out conventionally in a warm place. Cook in a preheated oven at 230°C (450°F) Mark 8 for 15 min, reduce to 190°C (375°F) Mark 5 for 15 min, reduce to 160°C (325°F) Mark 3 for a further 10 min or until cooked through.

Dark rye bread (colour page 135)

Follow the ingredients and method for light rye bread using all rye flour.

Baps *(makes 6)*
POWER LEVEL: 100% (FULL)
colour page 135

These are light rolls suitable as hamburger buns and make good alternatives to bread slices when making sandwiches.

450g (1lb) white bread dough (page 134)

1 Follow the instructions for white bread until the end of the first proving at stage 5.
2 Turn the dough onto a lightly floured surface and knead well until smooth.
3 Divide the dough into 6, knead each piece and roll into an oval shape.

4 Place 3 baps on the floured microwave baking tray or shelf, dust with flour. Heat for 15 sec and leave to stand for 5–10 min. Repeat until well risen.

5 Cook for 2 min, rearranging the baps if necessary halfway through. Leave to cool on a wire rack.

6 Repeat stages **4** and **5** with the remaining 3 baps.

Alternative conventional bake
Prove the 6 baps in the microwave then place on lightly floured baking trays. Alternatively, prove on a baking tray in a warm place. Cook in a pre-heated oven at 220°C (425°F) Mark 7 for 5 min, then reduce to 200°C (400°F) Mark 6 for a further 15–20 min. The baps should be pale brown when cooked.

Soda bread *(makes 1 loaf)*
POWER LEVEL: 100% (FULL)

450g (1lb) plain flour
1 × 5ml tsp (1tsp) salt
1 × 5ml tsp (1tsp) bicarbonate of soda
1 × 5ml tsp (1tsp) cream of tartar
50g (2oz) butter or margarine
350ml (12fl oz) buttermilk or soured milk

1 Lightly grease and flour a 22cm (9in) round dish and line the base with floured, greaseproof paper.

2 Sift the flour, salt and raising agents into a bowl. Rub in the butter finely.

3 Add the milk and mix to a soft dough. Knead lightly on a floured surface and shape or roll into a large round about 2.5cm (1in) thick.

4 Place the dough into the prepared dish and sprinkle the top with flour. Score or cut into 8 wedges.

5 Cook for 5 min, turn the dish, cook for 1–2 min. Leave for 10–15 min before turning out to cool on a wire rack.

Alternative conventional bake
Cook in a round ovenware dish or tin in a pre-heated oven at 200°C (400°F) Mark 6 for 25–30 min.

Brown soda bread

Follow the ingredients and method for soda bread substituting 225g (8oz) of wholemeal flour for white flour.

Fly bread

Follow the ingredients and method for soda bread adding 50g (2oz) currants and 25g (1oz) caster sugar to the dry ingredients.

Oatmeal bread *(makes 1 loaf)*
POWER LEVEL: 100% (FULL)
colour page 135

275g (10oz) plain flour
175g (6oz) rolled oats
1 × 5ml tsp (1tsp) salt
1 × 5ml tsp (1tsp) bicarbonate of soda
1 × 5ml tsp (1tsp) cream of tartar
100g (4oz) butter or margarine
1 × 15ml tbsp (1tbsp) caster sugar
275ml (½pt) buttermilk or soured milk, approximately
rolled oats for sprinkling

1 Lightly grease a 22cm (9in) round dish and line the base with greaseproof paper; sprinkle with oats.

2 Sift the flour, mix in the oats, salt and raising agents. Rub in the butter finely, mix in the sugar.

3 Add sufficient of the milk to mix to a light scone dough. Knead lightly on a floured surface and shape into a round about 2.5cm (1in) thick.

4 Place into the prepared container. Score or cut into 8 wedges and sprinkle the top with oats.

5 Cook for 5 min, turning once halfway through. If necessary, test with a skewer and give an extra minute if not quite cooked.

6 Leave for 10–15 min before turning onto a wire rack to cool.

Alternative conventional bake
Cook in a round ovenware dish or tin in a preheated oven at 200°C (400°F) Mark 6 for 30–25 min.

Pizza napolitana
POWER LEVEL: 100% (FULL)

450g (1lb) pizza dough (see below)
550ml (1pt) tomato sauce (page 65)
350g (12oz) mozzarella cheese
50g (2oz) can anchovy fillets
75–100g (3–4oz) black olives
1–2 × 5ml tsp (1–2tsp) dried herbs, eg oregano, basil or marjoram
2 × 15ml tsp (2tsp) olive oil, approximately

1 Follow the method for the pizza dough. When the dough has been shaped and proved for the second time, add the topping as follows.

2 Spread each round of dough liberally with the tomato sauce. Cover with the cheese which has been thinly sliced, the drained anchovy fillets which have been split in two lengthways, and the black olives.

3 Sprinkle with the herbs and the olive oil (about 1–2 × 5ml tsp/1–2tsp for each pizza).

4 Cook the smaller pizzas for 5–6 min each, the larger ones for 7–8 min each, giving a quarter turn every 1½ min.

Variations
Pizza alla romana Omit the tomato sauce and anchovies and replace with extra mozzarella cheese and sprinkle liberally with grated parmesan cheese and fresh basil.
Pizza aglioe olio Omit the tomato sauce and cheese and replace with liberal amounts of crushed or finely chopped garlic, olive oil and chopped marjoram.
Onion pizza Follow the ingredients for pizza napolitana but add some lightly sautéed onion rings to the top with the anchovies and olives.
Mushroom pizza Omit the anchovies and olives and replace with lightly sautéed sliced mushrooms.
Seafood pizza Omit the cheese and replace with shelled mussels or prawns; sprinkle with oregano and chopped parsley (*colour photograph opposite*).
Ham pizza Follow the ingredients for pizza napolitana adding some sliced ham and mortadella sausage which have been thinly shredded (*colour photograph opposite*).

Pizza dough *(makes 3 large or 4 smaller pizzas)*
POWER LEVEL: 100% (FULL)

1 × 5ml tsp (1tsp) sugar
275ml (½pt) water, approximately
2 × 5ml tsp (2tsp) dried yeast
450g (1lb) plain flour
1½ × 5ml tsp (1½tsp) salt
3 × 15ml tbsp (3tbsp) olive oil

1 Lightly grease 3–4 × 20–25cm (8–10in) plates.
2 Add the sugar to half the water and heat for 30 sec. Stir in the yeast and leave for 8–12 min to activate.
3 Sift the flour and salt and warm for 30 sec, warm the rest of the water for 30 sec.
4 Add the yeast mixture to the flour and mix to a soft dough with the rest of the water, adjusting the quantity if necessary. When the mixture is smooth, turn onto a floured surface and knead well.
5 Place the dough in a bowl, cover with clingfilm and prove by heating for 15 sec, then letting it rest for 5–10 min. Repeat 3–4 times until dough is double in size.
6 Knead the dough again, this time working in the oil, a little at a time until all the oil is absorbed and the dough is pliable and smooth.
7 Shape the dough by rolling or pressing into 3 larger or 4 smaller rounds to fit the prepared

plates. Prove each round separately in rotation in the microwave as described above until well risen.

Savarin *(serves 8)*
POWER LEVEL: 100% (FULL)
colour photograph opposite

1 × 5ml tsp (1tsp) sugar
150ml (¼pt) water, approximately
2 × 5ml tsp (2tsp) dried yeast
225g (8oz) plain flour
½ × 5ml tsp (½tsp) salt
50g (2oz) butter or margarine
2 eggs, beaten
25g (1oz) flaked almonds
For serving:
syrup (page 140)
apricot glaze (page 140)
whipped cream
fruit salad

1 Lightly grease a 20cm (8in) microwave ring mould.
2 Add the sugar to the water and warm for 30 sec. Stir in the yeast and leave for 8–12 min to activate.
3 Sift the flour and salt and warm for 15 sec. Add the yeast mixture and a little more water if necessary. Mix and knead well; the dough should be fairly soft.
4 Cover and prove by heating for 10 sec and leaving to stand for 5 min. Repeat until the dough has doubled in size.
5 Melt the butter for 1½ min. Beat the butter and eggs into the dough until it resembles a thick batter. Beat well.
6 Arrange the flaked almonds in the base of the container and carefully pour in the batter.
7 Cover with clingfilm and prove as described earlier until the mixture is well risen in the mould.
8 Remove the clingfilm and cook for 6½–7 min, turning once halfway through..
9 Leave to cool for a few minutes before turning onto a cooling rack.
10 While still warm, pour the syrup over the savarin and when cool, brush with apricot glaze.
11 To serve, fill the centre with mixed fruit salad and decorate with swirls of whipped cream.

DO NOT FREEZE WITH THE FRUIT SALAD. FILL AND DECORATE JUST BEFORE SERVING

Savarin (above)

Seafood Pizza (above) and Ham Pizza (above)

Syrup
POWER LEVEL: 100% (FULL)

100g (4oz) caster sugar
150ml (¼pt) water
1 × 5ml tsp (1tsp) lemon juice
2 × 15ml tbsp (2tbsp) kirsch

1 Add the sugar to the water and heat for 1 min. Stir until the sugar is dissolved. Bring to the boil in the microwave and cook until a thick syrup is formed,
2 Stir in the lemon juice and kirsch and pour over the savarin while warm.

Apricot glaze
POWER LEVEL: 100% (FULL)

450g (1lb) apricot jam
2 × 15ml tbsp (2tbsp) lemon juice
4 × 15ml tbsp (4tbsp) water

Place all the ingredients in a bowl. Mix well together and then bring to the boil in the microwave. Allow to boil for 2–3 min, stirring frequently. Sieve and allow to cool and thicken slightly before use. This keeps very well in a covered jar so can be made in large quantities.

Cheese bread (makes 1 loaf)
POWER LEVEL: 100% (FULL)
colour page 135

175g (6oz) cheddar cheese, finely grated
1 × 5ml tsp (1tsp) sugar
275ml (½pt) water
1 × 5ml tsp (1tsp) dried yeast
450g (1lb) plain flour
1 × 5ml tsp (1tsp) salt
½ × 5ml tsp (½tsp) dried mustard
½ × 5ml tsp (½tsp) pepper
1 × 5ml tsp (1tsp) celery salt, optional

1 Dampen the inside of a 15cm (6in) soufflé dish and sprinkle with 1 × 15ml tbsp (1tbsp) of the finely grated cheese. There is no need to grease the dish.
2 Add the sugar to half the water and warm for 30 sec. Stir in the yeast and leave to activate for 8–12 min.
3 Sift the flour and seasonings and warm for 30 sec. Warm the rest of the water for 30 sec.
4 Reserving 1 × 15ml tbsp (1tbsp), stir the rest of the cheese into the flour. Add the yeast and warm water. Mix well and knead until the dough is smooth.
5 Place the dough in a bowl, cover with clingfilm and prove by heating for 15 sec and leaving to stand for 5–10 min. Repeat until the dough has doubled in size.
6 Knead on a floured surface, shape the dough and place in the prepared container. Prove as described previously until doubled in size. Sprinkle the top with the remaining cheese and celery salt, if using.
7 Cook for 5–6 min, turning once halfway through if necessary.
8 Leave for 10–15 min before turning out onto a wire rack to cool.

Alternative conventional bake
Place the dough in a greased, ovenproof dish or 450g (1lb) loaf tin. If a metal tin is used, the second proving must be carried out conventionally in a warm place. Cook in a preheated oven at 200°C (400°F) Mark 6 for approximately 45 min.

Chelsea buns (makes 8)
POWER LEVEL: 100% (FULL)

450g (1lb) white bread dough (page 134)
25g (1oz) butter
150g (5oz) currants
50g (2oz) soft brown sugar
soft brown sugar for sprinkling
pinch cinnamon or mixed spice
apricot glaze for top (above)

1 Lightly grease a large shallow dish.
2 Follow the instructions and method for the basic white bread dough until the end of the first proving.
3 Knead the dough on a floured surface. Roll out to a rectangle approximately 30 × 22.5cm (12 × 9in).
4 Melt the butter for 1 min and brush over the dough. Sprinkle over the currants and 50g (2oz) sugar. Roll up from one of the long sides like a swiss roll.
5 Cut into 8 slices and place side by side around the edge and middle of the prepared container. Prove as before until double in size. Sprinkle with the sugar and cinnamon or mixed spice.
6 Cook for 6–8 min, turning once halfway through if necessary. Leave to stand for 5–10 min before removing to a cooling rack.
7 Brush with hot apricot glaze.

Alternative conventional bake
Place the slices into a large greased shallow dish or tin. If a metal tin is used, the second proving must be carried out conventionally in a warm place. Cook in a preheated oven at 220°C (425°F) Mark 7 for 20–25 min.

Wholewheat hot cross buns *(makes 12)*

POWER LEVEL: 100% (FULL)
CONVENTIONAL OVEN TEMPERATURE: 200°C (400°F)
MARK 6

450g (1lb) wholewheat flour
1 × 5ml tsp (1tsp) salt
1 × 5ml tsp (1tsp) ground cinnamon
½ × 5ml tsp (½tsp) grated nutmeg
1 × 5ml tsp (1tsp) mixed spice
50g (2oz) light brown sugar
75g (3oz) currants
25g (1oz) chopped peel
25g (1oz) fresh yeast
15g (½oz) light brown sugar
225ml (8fl oz) milk and water, mixed
1 egg, beaten
2 × 15ml tbsp (2tbsp) oil
25g (1oz) margarine
75g (3oz) wholewheat flour
6 × 15ml tbsp (6tbsp) water
honey for glaze

1 Place the 450g (1lb) flour, salt, spices, 50g (2oz) sugar, currants and peel in a large bowl and mix well together.
2 Mix the yeast with the 15g (½oz) sugar. Heat the milk and water for 45 sec or until tepid, and cream the yeast with a little of the liquid.
3 Stir the egg, oil, yeast liquid, remaining milk and water into the dry ingredients. Mix well to give a workable dough. Turn onto a floured board and knead until smooth.
4 Place the dough in a large bowl, cover and heat for 15 sec, then leave for 10–15 min. Repeat 4–5 times or until the dough is well risen.
5 Knock the dough back on a lightly floured board, divide into 12 pieces and shape into buns. Place the buns on two greased baking sheets.
6 Cover the baking sheets with clingfilm and leave in a warm place for 30–40 min until well risen.
7 Prepare the paste for the crosses by blending together the 25g (1oz) margarine, 75g (3oz) flour and the 6 × 15ml tbsp (6tbsp) water. Place the mixture into a piping bag fitted with a plain nozzle.
8 When the buns are risen, pipe a cross onto each, then bake in the preheated oven for 20–25 min. As soon as the buns are cooked, brush each with honey to give a glaze. Cool on a rack or eat warm.

Garlic bread

POWER LEVEL: 100% (FULL)

1 short, crusty french stick
150g (5oz) butter, softened
3–4 cloves garlic, crushed or finely chopped, or 1–1½ × 5ml tsp (1–1½tsp) garlic powder

1 Cut the loaf, not quite through, into slices 2.5cm (1in) thick.
2 Cream the butter and beat in the garlic.
3 Spread a large knob of butter between the slices.
4 Protect the thin ends of the loaf with small, smooth pieces of aluminium foil.
5 Place on kitchen paper in the microwave cooker and cover with a piece of damp kitchen paper.
6 Cook for 1½ min or until the butter has just melted and bread is warmed through.

Herb bread
Follow the ingredients and method for garlic bread substituting 1 × 15ml tbsp (1tbsp) finely chopped fresh mixed herbs or 2 × 5ml tsp (2tsp) dried mixed herbs for the garlic.

Index